ONCE THEY WERE

ANGELS

D1008837

Robert Goldman

Foreword by **Nolan Ryan**

SP

SPORTS PUBLISHING L.L.C.

SportsPublishingLLC.com

Publishers: Peter L. Bannon and Joseph J. Bannon Sr.
Senior managing editor: Susan M. Moyer
Acquisitions editor: Scott Musgrave
Developmental editor: Doug Hoepker
Art director: K. Jeffrey Higgerson
Cover/dust jacket design: Heidi Norsen
Interior layout: Dustin J. Hubbart
Imaging: Dustin J. Hubbart, Kenneth J. O'Brien, Heidi Norsen
Photo editor: Erin Linden-Levy

Printed in the United States of America

Sports Publishing L.L.C.
804 North Neil Street
Champaign, IL 61820

Phone: 1-877-424-2665
Fax: 217-363-2073
www.SportsPublishingLLC.com

Library of Congress Cataloging-in-Publication Data

Goldman, Rob.
  Once they were Angels / Robert Goldman ; foreword by Nolan Ryan.
    p. cm.
  Includes index.
  ISBN 1-58261-163-7 (hardcover : alk. paper)
  1. California Angels (Baseball team)—History. I. Title.

GV875.A6G65 2006
796.357'640979494--dc22
                              2006000454

This book is dedicated to the memory of
Jack and Jackie Goldman.

CONTENTS

FOREWORD

By Nolan Ryan

$\mathcal{M}$ost baseball writers record their stories from the press box. Mine, of course, came from the pitcher's mound. They are two very diverse vantage points, and sometimes after reading a story about a game I pitched, I end up wondering if the writer and I were even in the same stadium. A third perspective is often a good and necessary thing.

I'm pleased that after all these years the story of the Angels is finally being told. I always felt it would be an interesting tale. I just didn't realize how interesting until I read Rob Goldman's *Once They Were Angels*. What makes this book unique and so worthwhile is the amount of new material gleaned from hundreds of hours of interviews with players and others who were on the inside.

I've known Rob since 1974, when he worked for the Angels as our batboy. He's friends with many of the players in this book and was present on the field or in the clubhouse for many of the club's most significant games. Who better to write the Angels' story? Rob lived it first-hand.

By choosing to build the Angels' story around 10 individual players to represent the team's history, the book allows the reader to focus on people and personalities rather than just history and events. This approach is successful because it takes the reader into the players' worlds, sometimes even into their heads, and allows for a much fuller perspective.

Today the Angels are a championship-caliber organization, but it wasn't always so. In the early days a wild bunch of mavericks ruled the roost. It's fun to read about the misadventures of Bo Belinsky and Dean Chance, and the team's miraculous finish in 1962.

The Angels have had their share of bad luck over the years. I was there in the 1970s when the growing pains were part of our daily struggle. At times it was frustrating, but toward the end of my stay we were finally able to put together a winner. It was particularly satisfying to recall through Don Baylor's reminiscences how we got Gene Autry his first divisional championship back in 1979. Don carried the team on his back that season, and it was his fierce desire to win that helped make that championship possible.

I learned a few things about my peers from this book. I wish I'd known, for instance, that the reason Rod Carew began experimenting with his batting stance was that he couldn't get around on my fastball. I'd have come up with something new to keep him from winning six batting titles after he made his adjustments. Needless to say, Rod was a tough out no matter how he stood at the plate.

It was nice to see that Reggie Jackson remembers the two times I challenged him with nothing but fastballs. My recollection is that he struck out the first time and hit an easy fly ball the time after that. Reggie claims he struck out the first time but hit a vicious line drive to left the second time. I guess one of us has a bad memory.

Although I went on to pitch many more games after my stay in Anaheim, a part of me never left the Angels. I learned more about pitching and fundamentals while with the Angels and Tom Morgan than anywhere else. The lessons I learned there enabled me to further develop as a pitcher after I moved on. I am forever grateful for my experience there.

Of course my friendship with Gene Autry remains one of the most rewarding in my 27 years in the game. Few clubs that I can think of went through tremendous ups and downs like the Angels. Through it all, Gene never lost his optimism or that genuine smile. He never let losses or misfortune keep him from seeing the bigger picture.

Once They Were Angels honors Gene, and in doing so also honors his players. Looking back on my career and my time with the Angels, it has always been the people that I remember the most. It's nice to see that after all these years that their stories are finally being told.

Nolan Ryan pitched for the Angels from 1972 to 1979, tossing the first four of his seven no-hitters during that period. He appears on the cover of this book.

INTRODUCTION

By Robert Goldman

The big 18-wheeler plows along Highway 77 somewhere in the Carolina rain. Behind the wheel is Leroy Stanton, a former outfielder who played for the California Angels from 1972 to 1976. The back of his International truck is fully loaded with parts to be assembled into grandfather clocks—all bound for a factory in Charlotte, North Carolina.

As his CB radio crackles, Stanton palms the microphone and gives his introduction: "'Hit Man' here, what's your 20?" Stanton's CB handle is—fittingly for a player who once hit 27 home runs in a season—"the Hit Man." He came over to the Angels in a 1971 trade with the Mets that netted Gene Autry a big fish—Nolan Ryan. Stanton went on to play with the Mariners and later worked for the Toronto Blue Jays as a minor-league hitting instructor. Although his hair is just about gone, Stanton's infectious smile and hearty laugh are in full supply. He may be pushing 60, but in spirit he's closer to a 20-year-old.

"Hear from Mick lately?" I ask, referring to his former roommate, Mickey Rivers.

"I saw him in Savanna when I was working for the Jays," recalls Stanton. "I was walking into a restaurant when I heard 'Hey, Road!' Mick was at a red light and got so excited he jumped out of his car and ran over to hug me. Stopped traffic for five minutes."

"What about Frank?" I ask.

"Hardness? I haven't seen Hardness. He's still managing, though, doing a good job."

Rivers created nicknames for everyone he played with, which comes as no surprise to those who grew familiar with his engaging personality and outlandish streak. Stanton's nickname was "Road" or "Hard Brown." "Hardness," however, was bestowed upon Frank Robinson. To Stanton, Hardness was a veteran teammate. But to me, Robinson was a living legend whom I got to know from a different perspective, that of batboy, a duty I fulfilled for the Angels from 1974 to 1976. Together, Stanton and I swap stories of good old days as the cab fills with laughter and the memories come roaring back.

Today, Stanton handles radio lingo like he's been doing it all his life. He's at home with his trucking life, and it's sad in a way. Not that there's anything wrong with the life of a trucker, but I never pictured him this way. I always envision Stanton in his baseball prime, standing in the out-

Indians manager Frank Robinson and the author, as an Angels batboy, in 1975.
Courtesy of the author

field during batting practice, looking strong, sleek, and fast. But time cannot be reversed: this truck driver is now the "Hit Man."

As our conversation subsides, I doze off to sleep, the patter of the Carolina rain and the rumble of the engine serving as a hypnotic spell. My mind drifts into a netherworld of springs, pulleys, ballasts, gears, and clock hands, just like the ones Stanton is hauling in the trailer behind us. I awaken with a fresh perspective: time moves on, leaving us with only what we make—or don't make—of the past. I relate this train of thought to our previous walk down memory lane. The history of the Angels franchise is much like the clock parts Stanton is hauling today—awaiting someone to assemble it.

The Hit Man is concentrating on the road, staring it down the way he once did a pitcher. And I realize instantly what needs to be done.

"What would you think if I wrote a book?" I ask him.

"On what?" he replies.

"On the Angels, and the guys we knew."

"A whole book?" he asks.

"Yeah, about their time with the Angels. What do you think?"

"I think you should do it, man!"

I ponder such a daunting task: To tell the whole Angels story I'll need to expand beyond my immediate experiences. That means seeking out players who came before and after my time in the clubhouse. Since Hall of Fame sportswriter Ross Newhan had already written the Angels' comprehensive history in his must-read book, *Anaheim Angels: A Complete History*, I decide that my format should be more personality-driven. I should choose players who not only influenced the Angels, but who also made a significant impact on the game, as well. And I should tell the team's story from their point of view.

I began to make a mental list of players. Ten seemed like the right amount. The challenge would be to find them.

Back home in Southern California, I began my odyssey with Rod Carew, a good friend who was gung-ho from the start. One by one I track other Angels down: Jim Fregosi in a golf cart at the Angels fantasy camp; Don Baylor in the visitors' dugout at Dodger Stadium; Nolan Ryan in his office in Round Rock, Texas; Dean Chance at his farm in Wooster, Ohio; Albie Pearson on the phone from La Quinta, California; Alex Johnson in Detroit; Reggie Jackson in the visitors' clubhouse in Anaheim; and Jim Abbott in Michigan. Each interview would prove to be a unique and inspiring encounter with an extraordinary man.

To flesh out the book, I collected hundreds of hours of interviews with over 80 former players, coaches, front office personnel, clubhouse attendants, trainers, sportswriters—even wives and girlfriends. In interview after interview, I was surprised by the depth of feeling that flowed from the subjects, and by the themes each person developed. By coming to know their stories and weaving them together into the larger story of the Angels, I've gained a whole new perspective on the people and the team I thought I already knew so well. I am extremely grateful to these players for entrusting me with their stories. I tried to focus on their humanity as well as their accomplishments; after all, the good stories are always the human ones.

It's now been over three years since I rode shotgun in Leroy's International. A lot of hard mileage has gone down since then, and plenty of difficult work. As I prepare the final manuscript, my thoughts return to Mick, Hardness, and my good buddy Hit Man, pulling Father Time through the Carolina rain. I hope they're all well, rounding third and heading for home. I hope they'll feel I've helped to assemble a clock that ticks to the heartbeat of a team that I love, the Angels.

Once upon a time, the men in this book were Angels. Here begins their story.

ONCE THEY WERE ANGELS

PART ONE

1

—————————— DELIVERANCE ——————————

Scott Spiezio knew he'd hit it good. How good, he wasn't sure; but from the moment he turned on the Felix Rodriguez fastball, he felt it had a chance to go out. As he left the batter's box and headed for first base, the crowd became eerily silent. Spiezio stared at the ball he had crushed just moments before, now hanging high in the sky.

"Please, God, make the ball go out! Please!," he thought to himself.

Spiezio had tattooed the low inside fastball. He had put his absolute best swing on it. And as Rodriguez whirled around to spot his pitch sailing high above the outfield grass, Spiezio paused momentarily to revel in the moment. Had he just erased 40 years of bad breaks and bad luck for the Angels? Was the misfortune of one franchise vanquished with one swing of his bat?

At that moment, the person best equipped to answer that question was Giants right fielder Reggie Sanders. Although Sanders was well aware of the game-changing potential of the ball headed in his direction, he was unaware of the emotional baggage that came along with it. He was too focused on the present to be concerned with the ghosts of Angels past.

Although the Giants were ahead 5-0, Sanders had been around long enough to know that in the postseason, momentum can change in a flash. As he raced to the warning track, Spiezio was frozen between home and first. Just like the ball, he, too, was suspended in limbo.

"Push it out, God! Push it out!," he screamed inside his head.

No matter who or what your beliefs may reside in—God, fate, baseball superstition, or curses—it's certain that *something* had kept the Angels at bay for 40 years. *Something* had seen to it that the Angels remained a frustrated franchise, occasionally on the cusp of greatness, but never able to grasp it. So why would tonight be any different?

Something suggested that it just might. Maybe it was the electric undercurrent that charged its way through a restless crowd. Throughout this wild month of

October, the underdog Angels had accomplished amazing feats. They had outmuscled the heavily favored Yankees three games to one in the divisional series. They had outpitched the Twins with relative ease to clinch the American League pennant. Now it was Game 6 of the 2002 World Series, and the Angels were staring down defeat. Just nine outs stood between the Giants and a World Series trophy. It was time for David to pull back on his slingshot and launch a killer stone at Goliath. It was time for the mighty Giants and the magnificent Barry Bonds to fall.

The slingshot in this case was Spiezio's T141 black Louisville Slugger. Just days earlier, Spiezio had been spotted among the fake rocks beyond the centerfield fence at Edison International Field yielding another weapon: his electric guitar, which he smashed into the ground—a la The Who's Pete Townsend—during the filming of a team promotional video. Spiezio's brash style and Generation X attitude epitomized the modern player. He shared nothing in common with Donnie Moore, Gene Mauch, and the ghosts of Angels past. Those Angels were long gone. It was time to make a mark for the new Angels.

The 2002 Angels had already proven that the team had the potential to be an instrument of change. Now, Scott Spiezio was poised to be the messenger and deliver the Angels into a new era of baseball. He was used to the bright lights of the small stage as frontman of an alternative rock band, but never had Spiezio been on a stage so massive with lights beaming so bright. On this night, Spiezio would thrust himself onto center stage of the baseball universe.

Miles away from Edison International Field at his home in La Quinta, California, Albie Pearson was saying a little prayer as well. Prayer came easily to Pearson, an ordained minister since the 1970s. An original Angel, Pearson had patrolled center field for the club during its first five seasons. Now, surrounded by grandkids and bowls of fresh popcorn, Pearson felt like shouting as he watched the game on TV, but instead he repeated his quiet, fervent petition, "Please, God, make it go out!"

In Houston, Texas, where he was promoting a boxing match, the Angels' first and only Cy Young Award winner squinted at his battery-operated TV and smiled a wicked smile. Dean Chance had been writing daily reports on the World Series for the *L.A. Times* and bragging to anyone who would listen that the Angels would beat the Giants in four straight. "It's meant to happen," Chance told himself as Spiezio paused between home and first. *"Unbelievable."*

"If only Gene could see this!" thought Jim Fregosi, as he leaned toward the big-screen TV in his living room in Tarpon Springs, Florida. Gene Autry's "fair-haired boy," Fregosi had carried the franchise on his back during its first 10 seasons. In his heart he had always been an Angel. Now, he was a speechless one.

"Shouldn't have taken this long," thought a reflective Alex Johnson, watching the game in his Detroit, Michigan home. "We should've won the damned thing in

With one swing of the bat, Scott Spiezio reenergized the Angels in the 2002 World Series. Courtesy of the Angels

'70!" For Johnson, the only Angel to ever win a batting title, the moment was bittersweet. The controversial slugger-turned-mechanic still believed the 1970 Angels were the real team of destiny, not this one.

But there was nothing but joy in a hotel room in San Antonio, Texas. "It's their year!" rejoiced Nolan Ryan, watching the game on his hotel room TV. The players' collective effort had impressed Ryan, who fully understood that teamwork—more than anything else—was the trait that brought about championships.

"Yes we can! Yes we can! It's happening all over again!" Don Baylor shouted to his wife in the living room of their home in La Quinta. Baylor was referring to his 1979 MVP season, when fans chanting, "Yes We Can! Yes We Can!" helped propel the Angels to their first divisional title.

A proud Rod Carew was also watching the game on TV from his California home in Cota De Caza. Just two hours earlier he'd been at the stadium to throw out the ceremonial first pitch. He left after that to go home and look after his wife. As the Angels' hitting coach in the mid-'90s, Carew had taught many of the current Angels their batting skills.

Reggie Jackson was at the stadium entertaining friends in an upstairs suite. The former Angels superstar knew a thing or two about October magic, and what was happening out on the field looked like the genuine article to him.

"We should have taken those tickets!" Jim Abbott whispered to his wife at the Café Zulu restaurant in Laguna Beach, California. The former Angel pitching ace had declined the team's offer of tickets due to a prior commitment. Now, as he sat transfixed—like everyone else in the restaurant—by the scene on the television, a wave of regret swept over him. If the Angels pulled it out tonight, Abbott would throw out the first ball for Game 7 tomorrow, and it would take a building falling on him for him to miss that one.

Up in the stadium press box, Jackie Autry was on her feet. Only moments before, wearing her late husband's Stetson cowboy hat and waving a rally monkey, Mrs. Autry had energized the dispirited crowd. She stood in awe as Spiezio's blast hung in the darkening sky, gritted her teeth, and whispered, "C'mon, do it for Gene! Win it for the Cowboy!"

Reggie Sanders could care less about cowboys. As he retreated to the outfield wall, Spiezio's crushing blow fell from the black sky. Sanders tried to leap to the fence, but on his way up his hip inadvertently hit the foam padding lining the fence. The ball landed beyond his reach, disappearing into the second row of the right field stands. The stadium erupted in acknowledgment that *something* was indeed happening—a new chapter in Angels history was being penned on the fly as Spiezio rounded the bases and touched home plate.

Somewhere a cowboy was singing....

2

CROONING FOR
RADIO RIGHTS

"*W*in it for the Cowboy!" had been a popular catchphrase around Anaheim for several years during the 1960s but then became something of a curse. "The Cowboy" was Gene Autry, a crooner of prairie melodies and star of 1930s and '40s Hollywood Westerns who switched horses in midstream to enter the lucrative field of TV and radio. By the 1960s, Autry—recognized for his famed white cowboy hat—owned dozens of radio stations up and down the California coast. He called his radio group Golden West, and his flagship station, KMPC, carried the play-by-play for the Dodgers when they relocated to Los Angeles in 1958.

Autry was a frustrated, onetime semi-pro shortstop from Tioga, Oklahoma, who moved to the Midwest—guitar in hand—and befriended many St. Louis Cardinals, including Pepper Martin, Lon Warneke, Dizzy Dean, and Tex Carlton. After he moseyed West and started riding Hollywood's idea of the range, Autry became a fixture at Pacific Coast League ballparks. Gene loved the game of baseball, and having the Dodgers' games broadcast on his station made him feel like a part of the big leagues.

Then, in the fall of 1959, the Dodgers dropped KMPC to go to KFI. Autry couldn't have been more devastated if he'd learned that his horse Champion had come up lame. But just a year later, major league baseball decided to add several teams, and Los Angeles was deemed large enough to support two ball clubs. Stanley Spero, general manager at KMPC, decided to explore the possibility of securing the broadcast rights to the new American League franchise to cheer up his disappointed boss.

Hank Greenberg and Bill Veeck were the front men for the new L.A. franchise, and they had no problem with granting the broadcast rights to Autry. But at the 11th hour, Greenberg dropped out of the deal, and all bets were off. Just as Autry was ready to toss in his chips, out of the blue an old friend called to offer something much grander than the opportunity to broadcast baseball games on the radio.

Joe Cronin had known Autry since Gene's barnstorming rodeo days over two decades earlier. Cronin, now president of baseball's American League, wondered if Autry was ready to tame the Wild Wild West's newest franchise in L.A. Autry jumped at the opportunity. It was a perfect fit, as not only did Autry love baseball, but he also had an impeccable reputation as a businessman and a person of integrity. The Singing Cowboy really had something to sing about, and with his business associate Bob Reynolds and advisor Fred Haney in tow, he hurried to St. Louis to close the deal for 2.1 million. Within days of Cronin's phone call, Autry was owner of his own major-league baseball team.

But as all this unfolded, Walter O'Malley brooded. The president of the Los Angeles Dodgers was far from thrilled about a second franchise imposing on his territory. He liked having the Dodgers as the only game in town, and if he couldn't prevent an expansion team from setting up shop there, he made sure that nobody would profit more from the deal than himself. Autry got his team, but it would have to play in O'Malley's ballparks, with O'Malley earning all of the parking and concession proceeds over the first five years. Autry swallowed hard and signed on the dotted line.

A larger challenge loomed: building a ball club from the ground up in just three months. Autry began wisely by naming Fred Haney as his general manager. Haney gave the new franchise instant credibility, bringing 50 years of experience in baseball to the party. Haney had managed the minor-league Hollywood Stars of the Pacific Coast League and was as familiar around L.A. as the Brown Derby restaurant or the Coconut Grove. Everyone liked Fred, and he had the best double-play combo going: integrity and brains.

Haney's first move was a beaut. The new team needed a name that would connect instantly with the public, so Haney suggested "Angels," the name of a long-time Pacific Coast League team in Los Angeles. Fans remembered the old Angels with fondness, and maybe their loyalty would transfer to the new big-league Angels. The only fly in the ointment was that the rights to the name were owned by one Walter O'Malley. After acquiring the PCL Angels from William Wrigley in 1957, O'Malley had the baseball market briefly cornered in Los Angeles. The matter was settled when Autry forked over an additional 350 grand for territorial rights, at which time O'Malley threw in rights to the name.

The rosters of the two new expansion teams, the Washington Senators and the Angels, were to be filled by a draft. The existing 18 major league clubs were allowed to keep all of their A-list players, potential A-list players, valued subs, and anybody who could walk and chew gum at the same time. Everybody else was made available in the draft. Naturally, the pickings were pretty slim, but Haney's solid baseball connections again came to the rescue. One of his good friends was Buzzie Bavasi, general manager of the Dodgers, who, unlike his boss, saw no reason to make things hard for Haney just because he was working for the Angels.

A week before the draft, Bavasi gave Haney the team's scouting reports. "We had a pretty good scouting staff at the time," Bavasi says, "and I'd say 60 percent of the

Angels founding fathers (left to right): Gene Autry, Fred Haney, and Bob Reynolds.
Courtesy of the Angels

people [Haney] drafted were our recommendations, including Jim Fregosi, Dean Chance, and Bob Rodgers."

In another astute move, Haney hired former San Francisco Giants skipper Bill Rigney as the Angels' charter manager. Rigney was perfect for Los Angeles. Part showman, part strategist, "Rig" could relate to everybody, from the batboy to the superstar, and would be the perfect ringleader for the gang of misfits heading his way. Like Haney, Rigney also had friends in high places. Giants General Manager Chub Feeney had been ordered to fire Rigney in 1960, and it may have been some lingering guilt that moved Feeney to slip Rigney the Giants' scouting reports at the San Francisco Airport as the Angels manager departed for the draft in Boston.

In Haney's hotel suite, he and Rigney spread their prized scouting reports over the floor like kids opening new packs of baseball cards, and set about culling the best players from both lists. The following day in Joe Cronin's office, they formally selected, among others, Fregosi, Chance, Rodgers, and Ken McBride, who would all become franchise fixtures over the next few years. In the process, Haney and Rigney kicked the Washington Senators' butt in the first-ever expansion draft in professional sports.

According to the deal made with O'Malley, the Angels would play their inaugural season, starting just three months after the draft, in city-owned Wrigley Field in south-central Los Angeles. Then, in 1962 they would move to the brand new, spacious Dodger Stadium at Chavez Ravine for the next four years. Meanwhile, Marvin Milkes, Haney's assistant, began scouting around for a spring training facility. A few sites in Arizona were considered, but Palm Springs got the nod because it was only a two-hour drive from L.A., which meant less money and time spent on travel. For a new ball club with serious budget constraints, every penny counted.

On April 9, the Angels opened to a packed house in Baltimore. Number-one expansion draft pick Eli Grba went the distance on the mound, allowing only six hits and two runs. First baseman Ted Kluszewski slammed a first-inning homer that scored right fielder Albie Pearson for the team's first runs. Left fielder Bob Cerv homered later in that same inning, and Kluszewski hit a three-run homer in the second as the Angels cruised to a 7-2 victory over the Orioles. From that point on, Gene Autry always swore that winning that first game was his biggest thrill in baseball.

3

WRIGLEY FIELD
WEST

*W*rigley Field was once the proud jewel of the Pacific Coast League, but when the Dodgers came to Los Angeles in 1958 it was forced into early retirement when Walter O'Malley, who owned the PCL Angels, relocated the team to Spokane, Washington. But now the old ballpark was alive again with fans and excitement, if only for just one more year. Quaint and fan friendly, Wrigley was the last "neighborhood ballpark" in Southern California. A landmark with a giant, Spanish-style clock tower visible for miles around south-central L.A., Wrigley was an intimate part of its neighborhood—so much so, in fact, that the houses bordering the stadium were often the repository for home runs.

A few hours before the Angels' first home game on April 26, 1961, manager Bill Rigney and general manager Fred Haney sat in the manager's office and watched equipment man Tommy Ferguson open a box marked "McAullife." In it were hats of various colors and designs from the uniform company. Going through them, the honchos were unimpressed until "Fergie" pulled out a navy blue cap with a stylish art-deco L.A. logo in red on the front. Over the logo was a silver halo.

"What the hell," said Rigney, "why not?"

"We had the halo on the hat until Haney left," Ferguson recalls. "Autry didn't like the halo, but he never wanted to upset Fred or Bill, so he just let it ride. Haney figured the lights on the halo might sparkle or something. It was a good idea because we were in Hollywood, right?"

As the players got ready to take the field for their home opener, dignitaries and celebrities gathered around Gene Autry and Bob Reynolds, seated behind the Angels dugout. Comedian Groucho Marx chatted with *I Love Lucy* actor William Frawley, while a couple rows away American League president Joe Cronin and commissioner Ford Frick conversed with former vice president Richard Nixon.

The Angels' starting nine lined up along the third-base line for introductions, and the crowd greeted each one warmly. When first baseman Steve Bilko's name echoed through the loudspeakers, though, the crowd went wild in recognition of a conquering hero returning home. "Stout Steve"—as Bilko was known from his days atop Los Angeles baseball in the 1950s as a member of the Pacific Coast League Angels—grinned from ear to ear and doffed his cap.

After Tony Martin sang the National Anthem, attention shifted to a frail old man seated in a first-row box. With 11,931 fans watching in awe, Ty Cobb stood up and tossed out the ceremonial first pitch. It would be the "Georgia Peach's" final appearance in a big-league ballpark; three months later, he would die of cancer at age 75. Catching Cobb was former Pacific Coast League great Jigger Statz. Statz in turn tossed to Truck Hannah, another PCL great, who then fired a low strike to Angels catcher Earl Averill, who would later drive in the Angels' only two runs of the game with a home run.

The Angels lost their home opener to the Minnesota Twins, 4-2, but would go on to win 70 games that year, a record for an expansion club's first season that still stands today. Haney deserves much of the credit. As the year progressed, he kept working to find that special mix of rookies and veterans. Acting on Rigney's advice, in the second week of the season Haney made one of the team's most important acquisitions, purchasing long-ball-hitting outfielder Leon Wagner from San Francisco. Wagner had languished at the Giants' Triple-A team in Toronto, and Haney scooped him up for practically nothing. With Wagner, Albie Pearson, and Ken Hunt, the Angels now had a formidable outfield.

A few weeks later, Haney brought in first baseman Lee Thomas from the Yankees, after Mickey Mantle suggested that the rookie might make a go of it with the Angels. Thomas's impact was immediate. He platooned at first base and the outfield and quickly became one of the league's best hitters. Nicknamed "Mad Dog," Thomas possessed a legendary temper to go along with his quick bat. His exploits included breaking open a glass fire extinguisher case with his bare hands and smashing countless walls, lights, helmet racks, and other immovable objects. Batboy Scotty Keene recalls that after Thomas broke his favorite bat cleanly in two, he "took the sharp end and pounded it into the earth with the blunt end, like a train spike, the whole time yelling like a banshee!"

Unlike Thomas, Gene Autry was one cool customer. His management style was simple and straightforward. He lived by the theory that shaking a man's hand made an agreement a binding contract. In business, he earned a reputation for fairness and honesty that set Autry apart from most successful entrepreneurs. Gene believed that the buck stopped with him as owner of the team. He didn't require a crowd around to kiss up and assure him that he was always right. He surrounded himself with people he could trust, including his former head radioman and the Angels' first president, Bob Reynolds. "Reynolds can get anything done with anybody," Autry liked to say of the former All-American from Stanford.

The Singing Cowboy was a little long in the tooth for chasing desperados and shoot-'em-ups, but Autry still adhered to the "Cowboy Code" he developed in the 1940s to inspire his young fans to always do their best. Its tenets included: "[A cowboy] must never go back on his word, or a trust confided in him"; "[A cowboy] must always tell the truth"; and "[A cowboy] must be gentle with children, the elderly, and animals."

With its tall Spanish-style clocktower, Wrigley Field was visible throughout Los Angeles.

However, the "Cowboy Code" didn't have much to say on the subject of bellying up to the bar, which happened to be one of Gene's favorite pastimes. Especially when he was with baseball players. According to Ferguson, "[Autry] didn't go into a bar just to drink, he went in to talk to Enos Slaughter, Ted Kluszewski, Ted Williams, Stan Musial, or whomever it was. He'd say, 'Let's have a drink, goddammit! When you gonna buy one?' Of course, Gene would usually pick up the tab."

Just like their head man, the Angels players enjoyed their hootch.

"Back then, drinking was as much a part of the baseball culture as tobacco, greenies, chasing stewardesses, and complete games," remembers Eli Grba, a starting pitcher on the original Angels and a reformed alcoholic. "Throughout my career, everybody had beer in the clubhouse. It was nothing for us to sit for an hour or two hours after a game and have a few beers and talk about the game. Of course, there were times you couldn't wait to get out of the clubhouse because you had something on the side, someone waiting for you. That was our lives—we drank and we chased women. Most of us did, anyway."

Grba recalls one hot and smoggy Sunday afternoon at Wrigley when owner and player bonded over Budweiser. Grba was ahead of Baltimore 4-1 in the fourth, when he got a surprise visit from his manager.

"There was one out with the bases loaded, and Rigney came out to take me out of the game. Hell, I was winning 4-1!" recalls Grba. "'What are you doing?' I asked him. He said, 'Well, you look a little tired.' It was all bullshit and, needless to say, I was pissed.

"We had a little bucket with ammonia water on the bench, and when I went into the dugout I hit it and broke it into a thousand pieces. Water and all kinds of wood chips went flying up into the stands, and some of it splashed all over Autry and some VIPs in the front row. I didn't give a shit, and headed into the clubhouse and punched the walls and lockers until I cut open my hand. I was throwing one hell of a tantrum, and all of a sudden Gene Autry walks in.

"Now, I was born and raised in the Gene Autry era. Gene Autry was my favorite. I used to go see his flicks on Saturdays. I'd get 50 cents from my mom and go to the show with a couple of buddies. And so here he comes. And he sees I've cut my hand knocking the shit out of the lockers. I think he's gonna be pissed, but he's real calm, and all he says is, 'Eli, are you all right?'

"I say, 'Yeah, I'm fine, but I'm mad and I'm not very friendly right now.'

"'Well' … he says sheepishly, 'can I get you anything?'

"I say, 'Yeah, you can get me a beer.' So he goes over to the cooler, grabs a couple cold ones, sits down right next to me, and we start drinking and talking. We had about four beers together. I didn't get up to get any of 'em; he got 'em all. We just hung out there drinking together for three innings. Later I thought, 'Jeez, I was just sitting there letting Gene Autry get the beers.' All I could do was shake my head."

According to Grba, Rigney and his Hollywood flair turned off some of the older veterans, and there were always a few who tried to bring him down a notch. "Rig" was one of catcher Earl Averill's favorite targets, especially if he felt he wasn't playing enough.

"Earl Averill would drive him so goofy," says Grba. "I'll never forget one day in the old ballpark when we had the bases loaded in the eighth inning of a real close ballgame. Rig's intent, watching the game closely, and Earl goes up to him and says, 'Hey Rig, I got something to tell ya.' Rig says, 'Yeah, what?' And Earl replies, 'Did you know that there are 24 lights missing on the light pole?' I thought Rig was going to have a heart attack."

Grba adds: "Averill was relentless. Tommy Ferguson used to buy Rigney sponge cake and milk for his ulcers. He'd put it up in the clubhouse, and in between innings Earl would go in and eat it. He did it on purpose. He'd get the red ass because number one he wanted to play more. Earl was bad. He loved to antagonize."

Another classic pair of original Angels was outfielder Ken Hunt and shortstop Joe Koppe.

"Kenny had hurt his arm and he was sitting on the bench, still rehabbing," Grba recalls of his old roommate. "Suddenly Rig calls out, 'Kenny, pinch hit!'

"Their pitcher's warming up and Kenny's trying to find his helmet and he's at the on-deck circle trying on different ones to find one that that would fit. He must have tried on three or four, no luck. So finally Joe Koppe takes the bucket of ammonia water, dumps it out, and throws it out to him. 'Here, put this on!' Joe shouts at Kenny. 'This'll fit.'"

There was a lot of head-shaking going on near the end of that first season. Most sportswriters had predicted back in the spring that the Angels would win 50 games at most, and they bested that mark by 20. Almost unnoticed amid the September commotion was a group of relatively unknown draftees—including pitcher Dean Chance, shortstop Jim Fregosi, and catcher Bob "Buck" Rodgers—who had been called up from Triple-A Fort Worth. Nobody knew it then, but the Angels' future had arrived. But before the new guys could make their mark, the graybeards had one more trick up their sleeves.

October 1, 1961 was the date of the last game that would ever be played at Wrigley Field. For the Angels and Cleveland Indians, it was basically a meaningless exercise, as both teams were over 30 games out of first place. But while there was nothing at stake in terms of the standings, emotions on the Angels squad were still running high. Their first season had been hectic, with players coming and going all of the time; the players still there by season's end were woozy from the long roller-coaster ride.

Angels batboy Scotty Keene had been along for the entire ride. Making a new friend one day and seeing him traded the next had taken a toll on the 15-year-old. To Scotty, the Angels were more than just a group of ballplayers, and Wrigley Field was as big a part of his young life as Keds, Slinkys, and The Everly Brothers. He'd watched his first game at Wrigley with his dad in the late 1950s, with the original Pacific Coast League Angels on the field. He wasn't keen on saying goodbye to a place that had become a significant part of his youth. Late in the game, as he knelt near the on-deck circle, it got to him so much that Scotty did what ballplayers are never supposed to do: he started to cry. At first it was just a little, but by the Angels' half of the eighth inning, he was crying buckets.

His tears might've turned to hysterical laughter had Scotty realized what was happening on the field. Tom Satriano was the Angels' rookie third baseman, and when the Indians' Tito Francona, hitting .299 on the last day of the season, came up in the first inning, Satriano moved onto the grass in case of a bunt. Second baseman Rocky Bridges saw Satriano scoot up and ordered him to back up. "It's a left-handed batter, I gotta play the bunt," Satriano explained, and Bridges responded, "It don't matter, kid, back up." Satriano looked to manager Rigney, and was surprised when he, too, instructed him to play back. Sure enough, Francona laid a bunt down the third-base line and beat it out for a hit. Then he took a huge lead off first base, and Angels pitcher Ryne Duren easily picked him off.

The next time Francona came up, the exact same thing happened, only Francona's bunt went right to pitcher Duren. "Ryne came off the mound, picked it up, read the label for what seemed like two minutes, then threw to first base late, and Francona was safe again," recalls Satriano. "Now Francona's got two hits, and

Steve Bilko, a mainstay of Los Angeles baseball since the Fifties, gave Angels fans a player they could identify with. Courtesy of Bob Case

damned if he doesn't get picked off by Duren again. I just didn't get it. I glared at Bridges and started to say something, and he goes, 'Just shut up, rookie!'"

By the ninth inning, the Indians pretty much had the game in the bag, winning 8-4. With two outs, Rigney summoned Bilko to pinch-hit, which caused little Scotty to sob even harder. Seeing his idol—the PCL legend who had once hit 56 home runs in a single season—come to the plate for his last at-bat in the final inning of the last game that would ever be played at Wrigley Field, was too much to bear.

What happened next was like something out of a mediocre Hollywood melodrama, which makes sense because it was totally scripted. Bilko belted the first pitch he saw from Indians pitcher Jim "Mudcat" Grant over the rightfield fence for his 20th home run of the season. That halted Scotty's floodgates—at least momentarily. As the home-town hero trotted around third base, Satriano saw him mouth something to Grant that looked an awful lot like "Thank you!" That's when it all fell into place for Satriano.

"Bilko ends up hitting 20 home runs, Francona ends up hitting .300, and there's my introduction to the big leagues," Satriano says now, laughing. "Now, I'm sure none of that goes on with the game on the line, but it was like, you know, guys help-ing each other out. But it was my first year out of USC, and I just went, 'Oh my God!'"

As for Scotty Keene, he eventually stopped crying, grew up, and figured out for himself that his hero's big moment of glory wasn't a gift from the baseball gods. But it's still magic to him.

"Even though Grant grooved the pitch," he says, "Bilko still had to hit the thing. He could've easily popped it up or topped it. He still had to hit it."

For historic Wrigley Field, the magic was over. The stadium stood silent for a few more years, and then fell to the wrecking ball in 1966. Now there's a park on the spot.

They could have at least saved the clocktower…

4

ANGELTOWN

Batter up, time to play, let's go Angels all the way.
Angels fly, mighty high, in Angeltown.

—Angels theme song, 1962

On February 20, 1962, John Glenn became the first American to circle the earth in a space capsule. His feat energized Americans, providing them with a sense of purpose and optimism not felt since the conclusion of WWII. A week after Glenn's historic flight, Gene Autry led the Angels on bicycles to the ball park for the first day of spring training to celebrate the nation's newfound vitality. It wasn't as historic as Glenn's mission, but the sight was almost as eye-popping. Down Indian Avenue toward the Palm Springs Polo Grounds they went, a beaming Autry in the lead, peddling away in cowboy boots with his Stetson clamped on his head just the way he used to look astride his trusty horse Champion. Spread out behind him for a full block was the entire team.

The gung-ho publicity stunt was repeated the second day, but then residents of Palm Springs started finding abandoned bikes in strange places all over town. There were a couple at the bottom of the pool at the local hotel, and out in the desert there were bikes in ravines and under cacti.

"Bicycles were everywhere," recalls rookie catcher Buck Rodgers. "It wasn't unusual for some Palm Springs citizen to discover a bicycle in his backyard."

The '62 Angels had arrived for spring training. In a town expressly designed as a playground for grown-ups, 40 players sat on their clubhouse stools, some at rapt attention, others hungover, as Angels manager Bill Rigney addressed his troops.

"Look boys, we've had one year in this town, and I know how it is," said Rigney. "I enjoy it, too. But until we get in good shape, no drinking, and I mean NO DRINKING FOR ANYBODY, for two weeks! We're a new ball club, and for some of you this is a second chance. For some of you it's a first chance! So let's dry out and get in the best shape we've ever been in in our lives. Okay?"

Rodgers hung on every word. Later, hoping to make a good impression on his roommate, the legendary Steve Bilko, Rodgers stopped at a grocery store after practice to buy sodas and milk to bring back to their room. But when he arrived at their bungalow, there was the big man draped over his bed, surrounded by empty beer cans. "Just toss the Cokes in the bathtub, kid," Bilko mumbled. Rodgers went to the bathroom to do as instructed, and found the tub filled to the brim with more beer cans.

"That tub was never empty," Rodgers recalls. "We never took a shower or a bath in that tub all spring. The older players were always in our room—Eli Grba, Ken Hunt, Ned Garver. Some of us younger players—Jim Fregosi and Lee Thomas— we'd all hang out together. When I got back after dinner, Bilko would be in his bed snoring up a storm so bad the windows would rattle."

Eli Grba had played and drank with the Yankees for several seasons, and culture shock was the least of his problems after he arrived in sunny California.

"It was a different world," recalls Grba. "You couldn't get rid of the beer like you could in Florida. There was no humidity. You had to work 10 times harder in Palm Springs. It was a different type of training there than in Florida."

The Angels did what was required. Rigney would say of that 1962 team: "They were crazy, they were chasers, but I want to tell you something: When the bell rang, they were there to play, and they came to play every day. And there's another thing: If I ever needed to get ahold of one of them, I knew what bar they were at."

One of Rig's biggest challenges was containing hard-throwing Ryne Duren, who'd joined the Angels along with Thomas in a trade the previous year with the Yankees. Duren was almost legally blind and needed to wear huge, coke-bottle glasses on the mound. One night, Grba recalls, Duren woke up the whole team by hitting golf balls in back of his bungalow that ricocheted off pitching coach Marv Grissom's roof. "What the f--k are you doing?" yelled Grba. "Playin' golf," answered Duren, at which point a bleary-eyed Grissom emerged and yelled, "Kind of an early tee-off time, don't you think, Ryne?"

Ross Newhan, a cub reporter for the *Long Beach Telegram,* was fresh out of college when he first met Duren. Newhan remembers what happened one night when the team was in Cleveland. "There was a Polynesian Restaurant in the hotel where we stayed, and the restaurant manager called Rigney and said, 'I have one of your players walking through our ponds here in the restaurant.' Rig said, 'You don't have to tell me who it is. I'll be right down.' He knew it was Duren."

"Another time in Detroit," recalls Grba, "there was a bad fire on the third floor of the Somerset hotel, with people literally crawling on their hands and knees to get out. The alarm went off at about two or three in the morning, and the players headed down on the street.

"Now they're taking roll, and the only two missing were Bo Belinsky—no surprise there—and Ken Hunt. They had been downstairs in the Kon Tiki room drinking Mai Tais and Navy Grogs, and Kenny got snookered and went upstairs to bed. I roomed with Kenny, and there could have been a nuclear explosion in the room and he wouldn't budge. Kenny had locked the door, and Joe Koppe, who was in the next room, beat on the door until he had to go downstairs. They called the room and finally Kenny answered and they told him, 'The hotel's on fire! You got to get out of there!'

"Ken says, 'F--k it, let it burn!', hangs up the phone, and goes back to sleep."

The boozing was fun at the time, but according to Grba, it eventually got out of hand.

"For some of us it became a lifelong addiction," says Grba. "It definitely shortened my career. In 1963, I gained 18 pounds and I blamed everybody else. That's part of the alcoholism. In '61, I was well on my way to becoming an alcoholic, and I won 11 games and lost 13 that year."

Off-the-field shenanigans aside, the Angels of '62 could play some ball. That summer, they did what no one expected: They actually challenged baseball's 800-pound gorilla, the Mantle-and-Maris-led New York Yankees. New York was coming off one of the greatest seasons in baseball history, one in which they won 109 regular-season games, captured the World Series title, and witnessed Roger Maris break Babe Ruth's single-season home run record. In 1962, the Yankees' record suffered from some considerable competition from the Indians, Twins, and Angels. On July 2, the Angels were actually tied for first with the Yankees, matching the effort of the cross-town Dodgers.

Bill Rigney was a disciple of the great manager Leo "The Lip" Durocher, who had once famously proclaimed, "Nice guys finish last." In 1962, Rigs could've coined a corollary to that: "Drunk guys finish third." As the season wore on, the Angels began to falter, eventually settling a distant ten games back of the Yankees, good for third place in the American League.

On the mound that year, Dean Chance's wicked sidearm delivery terrified batters, while Bo Belinsky's screwballs baffled them. Ken McBride, Don Lee, Ted Bowsfield, and Grba rounded out the starting pitching staff, while Duren, Tom Morgan, Jack Spring, and Art Fowler were effective from the bullpen. The Angels finished tied with the Yankees for the second-best ERA in the league at a single point behind the Oriole's 3.69 mark.

At first base was Thomas, whose bite was worse than his bark. Opposing pitchers wanted the "Mad Dog" chained up. Thomas's tempestuous nature kept the Angels entertained throughout the season, and he knocked in runs like an assembly line. Soft-spoken All-Star Billy Moran, voted most valuable Angel by his teammates, was at second, and shortstop was manned by the combative Jim Fregosi and Joe Koppe. At third base was the team's lone Latino, Felix Torres, whose defensive play was so erratic that for his own protection he wore a batting helmet in the field. Rounding out the infield was the redwood-like Rodgers, who caught 155 games that season, the most ever by a rookie.

Outfielders Leon Wagner and Albie Pearson set the offensive pace, as Wagner clubbed 37 homers and Pearson scored 115 runs. The popular Wagner was a graduate of Tuskegee University in Alabama and later became addicted to opium. In the

Bill Rigney possessed Hollywood flair and baseball smarts, making him the perfect skipper for the hell-bent Angles of the early Sixties. Courtesy of Mel Bailey

late 1990s, Bob Case, the Angels' onetime clubhouse assistant, found Wagner in south-central L.A., all his possessions piled in a shopping cart next to him. "How could you have done this to yourself?" wondered Case. "I done been a superstar," replied Wagner, "now I just want to chill out." A few years later the popular "Daddy Wags" would be found dead alongside a dumpster. To the contrary, Pearson never drank, smoke, swore, or chased women. The halo on his hat was genuine. After his six seasons with the Angels, he became an ordained minister.

None of the 1962 Angels were destined for the Hall of Fame. Nevertheless, that year this diverse cast of characters who weren't given a chance came together to enjoy career years while astonishing the baseball world. "It was about camaraderie, wanting to win," says Grba. "Most of these guys were damn good ballplayers who had never gotten a chance."

In '62, they got that chance to shine and made good use of it by leading a second-year team to 86 wins. Despite their diversity, they all shared one thing in common: They respected the game, even if they didn't always respect themselves.

Ross Newhan, who has covered the Angels since their inception, adds: "The '62 Angels … were not only characters, but had character in the way they went about their game. They played hard off the field and they played hard on it."

They are the story Hollywood has yet to discover.

5

"LITTLE MAN"
ALBIE PEARSON

*A*s the Washington Senators rolled into Boston during the summer of 1958 for a series against the Red Sox, Senators outfielder Albie Pearson was mired in a bad slump. His batting average stuck around .220, and Pearson—a 24-year-old doe-eyed rookie—couldn't figure out why. Pearson had just completed his last round of batting practice and was headed to left field to shag balls when a shrill whistle coming from the direction of the third-base dugout stopped him in his tracks. Then came a disembodied voice: "Hey, Little Man!"

Pearson looked around, saw no one, and, figuring it was a joke, resumed his march to the outfield. Then came the whistle again and the voice, only louder this time: "Little Man! Over here!" Suddenly a tall figure in Red Sox flannels emerged from a doorway just beyond the dugout. "Get in here, Little Man," commanded a smiling Ted Williams, waving his hand at Pearson. "Come on in."

The stunned Pearson did as ordered, following Williams through the doorway that led to a private grounds crew storage area beneath the stands. At nearly 6'4" tall, Williams towered over the 5'5" Pearson. "Having trouble?" Williams asked. Pearson told him about his batting slump, and how he had exhausted all the means he could think of to break out of it. Williams looked at Pearson square in the eyes and grinned.

"You originally signed with the Red Sox because of me, didn't you?" asked Williams.

"Yes sir," replied Pearson. "When I was growing up I never got to see you play, but we listened to your games on the radio."

Williams's grin grew wider. "Little Man, there is only one Ted Williams, and you're not him."

"Yes, sir."

"But you know what?" asked Williams. "I've watched you since you joined the Senators in spring training. You get the bat on the ball as good as anybody. You can hit."

The problem, Williams went on to explain, was that Pearson was "trying to kill the ball" with every swing. "Your shoulder's flying open and your hands are slow because you're looking fastball every time, and they're throwing you everything else but, right?"

When Pearson agreed, Williams gave him some homework.

"Today when you're batting I want you to spit on every fastball you see. You hear me? Spit on it! Keep your front shoulder in and look for the change, curveball, and slider. Don't even swing at a fastball!"

Fastballs were Pearson's bread and butter, but Pearson wasn't about to disagree with the greatest hitter of all time. As he nodded and began to stammer his thanks, Williams muttered, "Forget it," and disappeared down a hallway.

In the game that followed, Pearson let the fastballs go by and swung at everything else. The slump ended that day, as he collected three base hits and scored four runs for the Senators. As Pearson jogged out to centerfield in the ninth inning, he passed Williams, heading back to the Sox dugout.

"Thataway, Little Man!" said Williams softly. "Good job!"

Giving batting lessons to players on opposing teams didn't exactly endear Williams to his teammates, but like everyone else he was drawn to the very likable Pearson. He respected his tenacity and drive, and marveled at how Pearson could hit and throw like someone a foot taller and 50 pounds heavier. People everywhere naturally gravitated toward Pearson. His innate kindness, hustle, and ability put everyone—mothers, children, future Hall of Famers—in his corner.

For many fans, diminutive Albie Pearson will always be the most enduringly popular Angel. The first legitimate star on the inaugural Angel team, Pearson ranks right up there with Nolan Ryan and Jim Fregosi as an all-time club favorite. Despite his slight stature in person, his disarming smile and consummate hustle helped build the fan base that laid the foundation for the future of the franchise. Ironically, "Little Man," as Pearson was known around the league, almost saw his career end shortly after it began.

Named 1958's Rookie of the Year with the Washington Senators, Pearson was traded to Baltimore the following year. But then disaster struck when a congenital back condition flared up, forcing him to the sidelines. Actually it was a miracle that he even made it to the big leagues in the first place. As a baby, Pearson suffered from spina bifida, a spinal defect that can result in nerve damage and paralysis. Through sheer force of will he made his way through the ranks with an incomplete spine.

Named after Albie Booth, an All-America football player from Yale, Pearson grew up in El Monte, California, where his father ran a small grocery store. After World War II, the big chain stores started gobbling up the mom and pops, and Pearson's dad went on to clerk and sell cars.

Unlike some of his teammates, Albie Pearson, photographed here in Chavez Ravine in 1963, truly acted the part of an Angel. Courtesy of the Angels

"My daddy was one of the most courageous men I've ever known and was a tremendous athlete," Pearson fondly recalls. "He was 5'4", and he just had tremendous grit. He could run and throw, and his athletic prowess was as good or better then mine. My grandfather was a professional fighter with over a hundred professional fights. When I was 12 years old I was only 64 pounds and 4' 4". I had [athletic] ability, but [due to my size I didn't think I could become an athlete in anything] except maybe professional fighting, where you have weight classes. I had no chance."

Nevertheless, Pearson lettered in football and track, and was all-league first team as a pitcher and outfielder. But while scouts found him supremely talented, they were reluctant to sign him because of his size. "When I finally signed my contract, I asked if I could get a bonus. And they looked at me and they said, 'Albie, if we gave you a bonus we'd get fired. We'll send you to San Jose and give you $225 a month.' I said, 'I have no baseball shoes, they're worn out from last year.' So I got two pairs of baseball shoes for my bonus because I didn't have any shoes, and they bought me a suitcase because I didn't have a suitcase."

It was a remarkable turnaround for young boy with an imperfect spine. But eventually making the major leagues was only the start; once there, Pearson had to persevere.

"I ruptured my spine and Baltimore sent me down to the minor leagues," Pearson relates. "I didn't play for three months—it was a real killer because I could hardly walk. They finally let me go because my back was bad."

Baseball may have given up on him, but Pearson didn't give up on himself. In the winter of 1960, he sent a letter off to new Angels general manager Fred Haney, hoping to appeal to his reputation as a fair and savvy baseball executive. It was short and to the point:

Mr. Haney:

I'm Albie Pearson. I was "Rookie of the Year" in the American League. I've been sent down to Rochester, but I want you to know my back is well and I can play. I want to come home and play in Los Angeles where I was born and raised. Please consider this letter as you make your draft.

Sincerely,
Albie Pearson

Haney did consider Pearson's letter, and with the final of his 28 draft selections, he chose Pearson. During spring training in 1961, Pearson rehabilitated his back and was on the field for opening day. From that point on, he wore his trademark No. 28 jersey.

The original '61 Angels were considered by many to be a second-rate team that had no business playing major league baseball. Baseball writers tried hard to outdo one another, coming up with clever phrases, puns, and witticisms to mock them. "One of the worst teams ever assembled," wrote Jimmy Cannon of the *New York Post* in the spring of 1961. Dodger fans largely regarded them with indifference and curiosity. But the general negativity did not infect the team, and Pearson recalls that it was only a matter of time before the players began to gel and start believing in themselves.

"We beat the Dodgers in a spring training game, 6-5, after being behind 5-2," Pearson recalls. "I know it was just an exhibition game, but it put it into the hearts of those guys right there that the Dodgers were not going to be the only team in town."

The acquisition of Leon Wagner in April, along with Ryne Duren and Lee Thomas in May, made the Angels a legitimate contender. One of the hardest throwers in the game, Duren was also known as a two-fisted drinker. Thomas, aptly nicknamed "Mad Dog" because of his fiery temper, played first and contributed 24 homers. Wagner, or "Cheeky" or "Daddy Wags" as he was known to his teammates, slammed 28 dingers in '61.

"Cheeky was about 205 pounds and about 6'1", and could really crush the ball," says Pearson. "He never did an exercise in his life, but he looked like an

Adonis. He could flat run on the field and ran wild off it as well. We never saw him much. He was a handsome guy, and I think he had some Indian blood because his cheekbones were huge. That's why we called him Cheeky."

With Pearson in right, Wagner in left, and the talented Ken Hunt playing center, the Angels boasted a fearsome outfield. Fans gravitated most to the likeable Pearson, whose wide smile, aggressive play, and fielding skill made him the first Angel player with a real following.

"I was popular mainly because of my lack of size," Pearson admits. "I never heard a boo in my life. I was the hero for the guy who never made it. They always saw me as the underdog because I was competing at the highest level, against guys a foot taller. I got many, many, many letters saying, 'I got a kid and he's little or he's small,' or, 'I go to work and I got this boss that bugs me, but when I go and we watch the game we see you and we want you to know we love you and we're for you.' I would go to Detroit and the fans would come in early, bring their six-packs [of beer], and they'd be yelling and booing everybody that would come in the ball-park. I would take my batting practice and go out in center field and they'd say, 'Hey, Little Man! We're against everybody but you! We hope that Detroit hammers your team, but we're for you!'"

Pearson's example on the field inspired little men everywhere to rise up against their tormentors. Once, after his three-run homer off of Whitey Ford helped the Angels topple the Bunyanesque Yankees, Pearson received a most memorable letter from a fan:

Dear Albie,
I'm 5'3" and weigh 130 lbs. and when you hit that home run off Whitey Ford and beat the Yankees I went home and told off my angry old wife…

Possessing a tremendous release, Pearson had a gun for an arm and could throw with anybody in the American League. His outstanding hand-eye coordination and quick bat gave him surprising power for a little man. But his lack of size meant he had to do things differently.

"I had to think way ahead. I had to be very sensitive in deciding how to play hitters," Pearson says. "I would watch them and study their strengths and weakness. With Mickey Mantle, I could tell in batting practice by the way he held his hands if he was hurting physically or if he had too much to drink the previous night. If he was tired he would lower his hands and have trouble handling the ball. So during the game I might move on him. Play a couple of steps the opposite way."

Haney was an astute baseball man, and it wasn't only Pearson's intelligence or persistence that attracted Haney to his future star. One of the reasons he signed Pearson was name recognition. When Albie came to the Angels he joined popular veterans Steve Bilko and Ted Kluszewski—also names fans could identify with from each player's former days in the Pacific Coast League. As a minor leaguer for the PCL's San Francisco Seals, Albie played two seasons against Bilko. In 1956 and

'57, Pearson watched Bilko slug 55 and 56 homers and collect two MVP awards as well. Bilko was a natural choice to join the Angels in Wrigley for one final season in front of fans who already knew him and appreciated his play. Like Pearson, Bilko was selected in the minor league draft. Unfortunately, he never did attain numbers in the majors like he put up in the minors.

"Bilko could not handle big league stuff under his hands," says Pearson. "He could handle any ball as long as he could get his arms extended. But he was slow turning on an inside pitch, and big league pitchers picked up on that. The difference between a major league pitcher in comparison to the minor leagues is that they can throw the ball pretty much where they want to, and they kept everything inside to Steve. He just couldn't get around on the fastball."

In 1961, Pearson roomed with Kluszewski, who less than a decade earlier was one of baseball's most feared hitters. In 1954, "Big Klu" slammed 49 homers with Cincinnati and was runner-up for the league's MVP. In four seasons from 1953-1956, Kluszewski hammered 171 home runs. But by the time he signed with the Angels, the 36-year-old first baseman's best years were behind him. He still had a presence on the diamond that few could match and was a respected person in the clubhouse. As roommates, he and Pearson were definitely baseball's Odd Couple. Klu dwarfed Albie and had a good 100 pounds on him. Pearson drank milk, while Klu guzzled Rob Roys. But people close to them say that's what made their relationship unique.

"I beat up myself a lot, there was always so much pressure because of my size," Pearson says. "I don't care where I was playing, they were looking for somebody that was big and strong and could hit with power. One night against the Orioles, I got an opportunity to win the game. I got a fat pitch to hit but I popped it up in the infield. I came back to the bench and I was absolutely irate. When Ted and I got back to our room I was still mad."

So mad that he kicked over a wastebasket, spilling its contents on the floor. "Is that 'cause you popped up?" Klu asked. When Pearson affirmed that it was, the big man instructed him to go stand in front of the mirror and give himself a good stare down. Pearson resisted, but Kluszewski insisted and finally Pearson complied. As Pearson stood before the mirror, Klu said, "Now ask yourself, did you do your best?"

"Okay, now let's go out and eat," Kluszewski said with a smile. Then, in a less friendly tone, he added: "And by the way, if you keep kicking this wastebasket and acting this way, I'm going to shove these beds together and you'll sleep in a drawer. You understand?"

Pearson played right field in 1961 and hit .288, then moved to center in '62 and remained there until his retirement four years later. Manager Bill Rigney felt that with his speed Pearson could cover a lot of ground. He also proved invaluable as a leadoff batter, constantly hitting around .300. Catcher Buck Rodgers played with him for six seasons and saw firsthand Albie's value to the team.

"Albie was a good addition to that ball club," Rodgers remembers. "We didn't have anybody that could do the things he could. He was a one-of-a-kind guy on our

Original Angels Albie Pearson, in cart, and Ted Kluszewski in Palm Springs for spring training in 1961.

team. If he got hurt we didn't have anybody that could do the on-base stuff, the running stuff, and still play defense. He could still play pretty good center field."

In 1961, infielder Tom Satriano was an impressionable rookie fresh off of the USC campus when he first met Pearson. He was instantly impressed with Pearson, both as a ballplayer and as a role model.

"He was a super nice guy, very religious, he never said, 'damn' or 'hell' or anything like that," Satriano says. "It was always, 'Drat it!' or something like that. He was a real competitor and an ideal leadoff man because he had such a good eye at the plate and offered such a small target. He was just nice to be around. Nobody ever argued with Albie about anything."

If Little Man had a fault, it was that he occasionally let his size affect his outlook, almost to the point where it became a complex. Pitcher Eli Grba offered an interesting perspective on his friend and teammate.

"I liked Albie, but at times he had a chip on his shoulder about being small," Grba admits. "It was not an evident chip or a nasty chip. Never throwing brick bats at you because you were a big guy, nothing like that. But he wanted to be bigger than he was. And believe me, pound for pound, he was as strong as Klu."

Grba recalled one day when Pearson was at a restaurant with his wife, and a patron insulted him. Pearson tried to take the high road and ignore the man, but he kept badgering Albie in front of his better half. Finally, Pearson blew his top. "From what I understand, he beat the crap out of him," Grba laughs. "He was a tough cookie—you better believe it. But he had a big man's mentality as far as hitting was concerned and could pull anybody."

According to Grba, Pearson's insecurity about his stature was never far from the surface. "One game, Albie threw to the wrong base and the ball bounced in the dugout and we got beat," Grba recalls. "And instead of saying, 'I made a mistake,' Albie was making excuses left and right. Finally I said, 'Albie, just admit you're wrong and say that you made a wrong throw.' We got into a heated conversation and he said that if he were as big as I was he would hit 40 home runs. I said, 'Albie, if you were as big as me, you wouldn't be in the big leagues.' End of conversation."

In one way, though, Pearson stood head and shoulders above most of his teammates, if not most big league ballplayers in general. A devout Christian, as a youngster he heard a call that he has followed through his entire life. But Pearson has never copped a holier-than-thou attitude, which came in handy with his rambunctious teammates on the Angels. "I loved my teammates and they respected me, all but a couple," Pearson says. "I knew they were party animals, but I just could not and would not be their judge and jury. There's something in me that just says, sure, they're men, sure, they're doing their thing, but what makes me any different or better than them?"

It wasn't just talk, as Pearson's teammates discovered when they set out one day to find out if he walked the walk. It was an off day in Cleveland, and about a half-dozen Angels, led by Wagner, followed Albie around to see what secret pleasures he participated in off the field. "I was pretty much a loner," Pearson says. "I went out to eat, did some window shopping and went to a movie, got home early and went to sleep. Cheeky liked to talk about this before he passed away: 'We tried to get the goods on Little Man, but we couldn't. No way.'"

Wagner was another great asset to the team both at the plate and on the field. Wagner was one of three African-Americans on the roster at the time. But race was never an issue in the locker room or on the field, Pearson says. "I say with real conviction there really wasn't any racism. In fact, there was real camaraderie. We weren't politically correct back then. We would say, 'You got the biggest black butt I ever saw!' and just laugh. Wagner would walk in and say, 'Hey, you damn honkies! What's going on? Let's go play.' Daddy Wags was never disrespected or looked down upon in any way. We rallied around him and said, 'Hey man, you got to swing the bat for us.' We needed him bad, because he was our stick."

Pearson played five more seasons for the Angels, contributing with his bat, glove, and even his spirituality. But his greatest contribution was in those early days when the Angels were still trying to find their legs. Pearson was a rock, and his teammates rallied around his solid leadership. In 1962, when the Angels shocked the baseball world and ended up in third place, Pearson was as responsible as anyone for getting them as far as they did.

"It was one of the wildest teams ever, but we could flat-out play," he says. "We won over 30 games by one run in the ninth. We had a bunch of guys from everywhere, but we gelled."

In '63, Pearson finished fourth in the American League in hitting with a career-high .304 mark. In doing so, he became the first Angel player to hit .300; it would be another seven years until a second Angel player, Alex Johnson, would top the .300 mark in 1970. By the mid-'60s, Pearson's back problems flared up anew. In the spring of 1966, the discs in his spine had deteriorated so badly that he couldn't walk. Pearson sensed the end was near, but being the fighter that he was, he battled against the inevitable.

"I hurt myself sliding in spring training," Pearson recalls. "My leg atrophied two and a half inches, and I was in a wheelchair and in traction on and off for 36 days. I saw Opening Day that year from a hospital bed. My discs were so ruptured I literally could not move."

He spent the first half of the '66 season on the disabled list, trying to work and will himself into playing shape. When July rolled around, the Angels wanted him back in uniform, ready or not. Realizing it was his last chance, Pearson took the field. In reality, he was a mess. His body weight had drastically dropped, and the once lightning-quick Little Man could barely run the bases. "I was on so much codeine and pills that I couldn't see straight," he recalled.

In what would be his last game, Pearson was called out of the dugout by Bill Rigney to pinch hit. "When I came out of the dugout, the whole stadium stood up and gave me a standing ovation," Pearson says. "I strolled up to the plate, and when I got to the batter's circle umpire Jim Honochick said, 'Albie, welcome back, man. We're glad you're here.' I said thanks and stepped in the box, but the stadium hadn't settled down yet. Jim put out his hand to the pitcher and said, 'We'll wait.' Russ Nixon was catching, and he threw some dirt on my foot. I turned around and he said, 'Little Man, welcome back. Good luck.'"

As 40,000-plus fans stood and cheered for him, Pearson reveled in the moment and dug in at the plate, determined to make it worth their while. Trouble was, Pearson hadn't seen a pitch since September of the previous year, and he was staring down Red Sox ace pitcher Jim Lonborg. Pearson was in so much pain he could hardly concentrate; his right leg was so atrophied it dragged behind him.

Pearson figured Lonborg's first pitch would be fast and hard, and he was right. "It looked like an aspirin to me," he recalls. "Here I'd been playing 14 years, and now I'm looking at a ball I could barely see. It looked like a pea."

The pitch blew by Pearson for a strike. The second one came just as hard, but was high. With the count 1-1, Longborg's next pitch was right in Pearson's wheelhouse. Two or three years earlier, he'd have sent it screaming into the outfield. But now his once-crisp reflexes were so shot that the ball hit the end of the bat handle and limped toward the third base line. Pearson was thrown out at first by at least 30 feet. Then to make matters even worse, Pearson fell over the base.

"I tripped over it like a little leaguer and fell flat on my face in front of that big afternoon crowd," he recalls with lingering disgust. "And I'm lying on my face and trainer Freddie Frederico came out to get me because I could hardly move. I'm lying on the ground and that voice inside me said, 'That's all, son. That's all.'"

That was all for Little Man, as far as his baseball career was concerned. But Albie Pearson was far from done inspiring and leading others by example. And he had Marilyn Monroe, of all people, to thank for it.

In the spring of 1962, it had fallen to him to escort the movie siren when Monroe walked to home plate to accept a charitable donation before a game in Chavez Ravine. At their introduction, the actress's obvious sadness and the look of palpable desperation in her eyes struck Pearson. Touched and alarmed, Pearson was about to offer a word of encouragement and comfort, but then, given their surroundings, instead just gathered his glove and ran out to his spot in center field. It was Monroe's last public appearance.

"I felt the Lord had wanted me to say something to her that day," Pearson recounts almost four decades later. "I had been allowed to speak to her, but didn't."

When he heard of her suicide just months later, he was tortured. He knew he was not responsible, of course, but Pearson was haunted by what he considered a missed opportunity. "I might have been one of the last to help," he says, "and it was too late."

Pearson often prayed deep into the night and promised to dedicate his life to helping others stay off Monroe's self-destructive path. He didn't know how he would do it but knew the answer would finally come to him. It did in 1966, when he was forced to retire from baseball. "Open your house to youth," an inner voice told him. And so Pearson did.

His home in Riverside, California, became a refuge for abused and molested children. Pearson soon established a foundation to raise money to build a group home where all were welcome. From 1966 to 1972, Pearson built a youth foundation from the ground up, and shared the Gospel with wayward youth.

"I was ordained in the ministry in 1972, which launched me into a place of pioneering churches," Pearson says. "I've been a missionary with the gospel in Russia, Spain, Italy, and South America. I have organized a non-profit church corporation that has allowed us to build churches to support and send missionaries throughout the world, to feed and administer to poor people and to establish the Gospel wherever. I have also raised up more than 160 ministers that we ordained and placed throughout the world."

Pearson also established the Father's Heart Ranch for neglected and abused kids in Desert Hot Springs, California. Residents range in age from six to 12, and have been abused, neglected, molested, or abandoned. "They come out of terrible, terrible situations, and we gather them and love them," Pearson says.

Now 71, Pearson resides in La Quinta, California, where he and his wife, Helen, are entertained by their four children and grandkids. He keeps in touch with several of his old teammates, but until recently rarely watched the Angels in person. "In 2002, I went to my first World Series game. And I'm sitting there in the diamond boxes with my Helen," Pearson says. "I'm looking at the field I played on, now from a spectator point of view. And a World Series, at that! I was part of this and this is part of me. For 14 years I got to do this as a player, and now, it's your turn. Go Angels!"

The experience rekindled his pride in being one of the original Angels, an integral part of a long and storied legacy. It's an idea that new owner Arte Moreno confirmed.

"When Arte Moreno bought the team, he invited some of us oldtimers in and treated us to dinner," says Pearson. "He said, 'You guys laid in this place a history, a tradition and a foundation that we don't want to ever lose again. I want you, although you're not on the field anymore, to be a part of this.' What a thing for Arte to say, and he was humble when he said it."

Previous owners had not been as welcoming to the oldtimers, Pearson says. "You know, I'm not against Disney and all the gang. But they didn't realize baseball is more than just a business. It's also about memories and loyalty and fraternity that's very, very strong. It's being respectful to one another. Whether you've been out 30 years or are playing right now, it doesn't matter. You can't compare it to college or any thing else for that matter. Gene Autry represented that loyalty as much as anybody."

That reminded Little Man of his last encounter with the singing cowboy who'd brought American League baseball to Los Angeles. "I had played in an oldtimer's game, and when it was over I went upstairs. Gene could hardly see anymore, but he was looking down on the field and was keeping score. He had a monitor there on his left, the same kind used by radio people to help him follow the game," recalls Pearson. "I came up behind him, grabbing him around the neck in the back and said, "Uncle Gene, Jesus loves you." He turned around with the biggest smile and said, 'Albie! You still preachin'?' I said, 'Yeah, I'm still preaching!' Then I said, 'Guess what?' He said, 'What?' I said, 'God still loves you and always will.' He looked at me with a tear in his eye and said, 'Thank you,' and then he went back to the monitor. I gave him a hug and that was it."

6

— Delightful Rogue —

BO BELINSKY

*T*he town car glistened as it coasted down from the Sunset Boulevard entrance and made the sweeping turn into the Dodger Stadium parking lot. To Dean Chance, riding inside, the scene was eerily familiar. The gentle rolling hills and palm trees, the massive decks and pair of scoreboards, the 76 gas station in the parking lot near the 110-freeway exit—everything was pretty much the same in 2001 as he remembered in 1962. As the car came off the hill and the full expanse of the ballpark emerged, Chance became reflective. It was here that he had captivated thousands of fans with his blazing fastball and wicked slider. It was here that he first felt the thrill of success. Now older and wiser, he couldn't believe how the years had flown by.

Not that his time since then had been wasted. Quite the contrary: Chance had done quite well for himself since he left baseball. Over the years he had been a carnival operator, a poster salesman, and a commissioner for the International Boxing Association. He had fooled a lot of people with that slow midwestern drawl, but Dean was anything but slow, and he sure as hell was no yokel. He possessed a deadly combination of natural intelligence and street smarts; he was a wicked poker player who could charm women like a Frenchman. As a boxing promoter, he had sparred with the best. Bob Arum and Don King appreciated Chance's promoting abilities. He'd lived a big life and experienced a lot, but he knew without thinking twice he'd trade it all just to stand on that mound again and face down Mickey Mantle one more time.

"Boys, we park out in left field like we always did," Chance said. "We'll go in through the old players' entrance."

As the car pulled up behind the bleachers, former Angels clubhouse assistant Bob Case appeared outside the stadium to greet Chance. Dean befriended Bob in 1962, and the two have remained close ever since. But today isn't a joyful reunion. They're here to honor an old friend who recently passed away: Chance's former teammate, Bo Belinsky.

Chance led the men through the players' entrance alongside the left field bullpen. As he made his way down the concrete runway the musty smell of the cold gray corridors was somehow reassuring, and the sensation of entering a big league ballpark excited him again. Heading toward the elevator to the Stadium Club, they passed a door that seemed vaguely familiar. Curious, Chance peered in and what he saw hit him like a line drive up the middle: It was the old Angels locker room. Chance gasped in amazement. Nothing had changed. Freddie Frederico's training room, Bill Rigney's office, the showers and sinks, everything was still in place. Chance made his way over to his old locker and touched the ancient wood sidings and metal hooks. "Unbelievable," he thought to himself, "they're exactly the same."

When he walked over to Bo's stall, Chance imagined his flamboyant teammate standing there, his long, lean frame wrapped in a towel, sarcastically giving the business to a beat reporter across the room. Then Chance's thoughts went to the night of Belinksy's legendary no-hitter, and how that one game had changed so many lives, his included.

Chance continued down the rows of lockers naming each player as if he were still there. Steve Bilko, Albie Pearson, Joe Koppe, Buck Rodgers, Jim Fregosi. ... Finally Case reminded his friend that the service was to begin shortly, and if they didn't want to be late they better get going. As the party made its way to the elevator, Chance thought again about his old friend. "God, Bo! If only you were still here to see this."

Angel publicist Irv Kaze knew it was Bo the moment he laid eyes on him—the swagger, the shades, and that slicked-back hair. Bo was easy to spot in a crowd, even at Los Angeles International Airport. It was Belinsky. Had to be. His reputation preceded him. For an entire month, the rookie pitcher had driven management crazy with his outrageous demands, including a holdout for $2,000 more than the standard $6,500 contract for rookies. Hard to believe it, but $2,000 was a lot of money in 1962.

At last Bo had arrived. Kaze didn't budge from the terminal window, fearing that if he took his eyes off Bo, he just may lose him. He watched as Belinsky disembarked from the plane like a crown prince, and once he was safely inside the gate, the publicist approached him.

"I'm Kaze, welcome to California," he said with his friendliest smile.

"Christ, I was expecting Autry," replied Bo.

And with that, the Belinsky era had arrived.

Kaze drove Belinsky to the Angels camp in Palm Springs where a press conference awaited him at the posh Desert Inn. The place was decked out like a Hollywood premier: caterers, bartenders served mixed drinks and hors d'oeuvres.

No expense was spared for Bo's arrival. After all, the Angels hadn't had many reasons to hold a press conference during their first season. Belinsky's arrival was a major event for local sports scribes, who correctly anticipated that Belinsky's audacious behavior and sophomoric antics would keep them entertained for years to come.

Writers peppered the pitcher with questions. "How good a pool player are you?" asked one. "How many women have you had?" wondered another. Bo fielded them all like a true pro, charming everyone with his wit, giving them what they wanted to hear, always with a twinkle in his eye.

"Before I even put on a big league uniform, I was already the biggest story in the south land," Belinsky would recall later. "I stepped off the airplane into a poolside press conference. ... All the writers in L.A. had heard about this character, 'Bo Belinsky,' so I went along with it. It was something!"

For reporters covering the Angels, Belinsky's arrival was a breath of fresh air. To be a member of the Los Angeles press corps in 1962 competing against the Dodgers and their reporters was a job few wanted. A writer covering the Dodgers in the early '60s could expect preferential treatment. The club catered to the press in hopes the Dodgers would be written about in a good light. Reporters covering the Angels, on the other hand, were lucky to get a cold sandwich and stale chips in the pressroom. The Angels beat reporters were dying for headlines they could blare at the public, and, with the 25-year-old Bo, they hit the jackpot. For a month preceding his arrival, there had been stories about this pool-hustling womanizer from Trenton, New Jersey. "Million-dollar arm, ten-cent head," someone said of him. True or not, the press just ate it up.

The homecoming for Bo continued a few more days, but then Angels general manager Fred Haney got down to business. "Sign now, or we send you home," was his right-between-the-eyes message for Belinsky.

"They wanted to send me back to New Jersey and for me to pay the plane fare," Bo recalled later. "They were making it very difficult for me. Under adverse conditions, I signed for the $7,500 instead of the $8,500 I wanted, with the stipulation I could renegotiate later if I made the club."

Belinsky's pitching that spring was, for the most part, ineffective. By the end of March, Haney even tried to sell him back to the Baltimore Orioles for half of the $25,000 the Angels had originally paid for him in the draft. Baltimore nixed the idea, and the Angels were stuck with the lefty.

Gene Autry had been watching all of this unfold from the sidelines. As a former entertainer, Autry knew box office when he saw it. He had a hunch this young man with the attitude and roguish charm had star power, and Autry realized with the team moving into O'Malley's brand new Chavez Ravine, a strong drawing card could help the team rake in big profits. He urged Haney to stick with Belinsky a while longer. Haney agreed, with gritted teeth.

Manager Bill Rigney disapproved of Belinsky on different grounds. Rig enjoyed being the center of attention himself. He liked to position himself on the top step of the dugout, where with his Hollywood shades and erect posture, he resembled General Douglas MacArthur surveying the troops. Rigney also felt that Bo was distracting the team with his daily exploits in the bars and clubs and shifting the focus away from Rigney's two pet rookie projects, Jim Fregosi and Buck Rodgers. Rig wanted Bo shipped back to the minors. He felt that with Ken McBride, Eli Grba, Ted Bowsfield, and Dean Chance, his starting staff was complete. With Ryne Duren, Art Fowler, Tom Morgan, and Jack Spring in the bullpen, there was simply no place for Bo.

But Haney reluctantly convinced him to keep the New Jersey native a little longer, at least until the 28-player cut-off date in late April. So, by the skin of his teeth, Belinsky remained on the roster. He took up residence in the dugout tunnel, where the only workout he received was flicking away the cigarettes he smoked down.

On April 18, Bowsfield came up with a sore arm, forcing Rig to give Bo his first assignment against the Kansas City Athletics. The skipper must've been taking elocution lessons from Haney, because his message was as subtle as a hooker's perfume: "Win or you're gone." For Bo, the stakes had never been higher. To relax himself before his big debut, he picked up a "broadie" on the Sunset Strip and stayed with her until four o'clock in the morning. Then he went to the ballpark for the game.

If Bo was nervous, he certainly didn't show it. He won 3-2, with a little help from Fowler, who pitched the game's final three innings for the save. In his next start a week later, Belinsky beat the Cleveland Indians, pitching a complete game in the process. He followed that outing up by defeating the Indians a second time. Belinsky was off to a 3-0 start, and the press was going nuts. "Rookie of the Year" blared one headline. "Angels to Win Pennant" declared another. Suddenly the girls got prettier, their legs longer. As Bo partied hard while the press feasted on his every action on and off the field, Kaze and Autry beamed from afar. The Angels were legitimate media darlings. For all that, nobody could've predicted what would come next.

On the night of May 4, in what had become his pregame ritual, Bo picked up a dark-haired beauty on the strip. They danced to Mexican music for a few hours, went to her pad, and after just a few hours of sleep, Bo left for the park. That night at Chavez Ravine with the brunette's perfume still lingering on his skin, Belinsky pitched the first major league no-hitter on the West Coast. Bo shut down the Orioles, striking out nine and walking four, as his offense scored two runs for him. The City of Angels went ballistic.

"What made the no-hitter so unusual," remembers his catcher that night, Rodgers, "was that he didn't have all his pitches working. He didn't get his screwball over the plate until the fifth inning. But he was so overpowering. He'd go 2-0, get behind, and challenge them: fly ball to center field. Challenge them: pop-up second base. Even the last pitch of the game, Dave Nicholson hit a 3-1 fastball and popped up to third base. So right down to the end, Bo was behind in the count,

For three seasons this latter-day Butch and Sundance—Dean Chance, left, and Bo Belinksy—ruled L.A. Courtesy of the Angels

and he just challenged them. The hitters were always ahead 2-0. We had to say, all right the first guy is going to have to hit the ball out or whatever, and that is why it was such a powerful no-hitter. He was that good, at least that night."

More than 30 years afterward, Belinsky recalled the evening as "my happiest moment. From the time of the no-hitter, I was a star in Hollywood. Millions of dollars could not buy that experience." Bo became an overnight sensation, the talk of the baseball world. He was no longer just a local story—he now belonged to the nation at large. Baseball fans everywhere were intrigued by this delightful rogue in white flannels who, notwithstanding his devilish behavior off the field, wore a halo on his cap. "Where he's from?" the public asked. "How did this obscure minor leaguer who quoted Shakespeare and read *Mad* magazine achieve such astounding success in such a short amount of time?"

More than 45 years later, people are still asking.

For all of his flamboyancy during his playing days, later in life Belinsky became quite media shy. He refused requests to be interviewed, and preferred to remain out of the limelight. In a rare and unpublished 1994 interview with Alana Case, wife of former Angels clubhouse assistant Bob Case, Belinsky reflected back on his life, career, and the carefree attitude that made him a household name:

I had a dream. I always wanted to go to the Naval or Merchant Marine Academy or Westmont. Of course it was an impossibility, not having the education or the money for college. But I always felt if I had the opportunity, that type of training and discipline would fit right in with my personality. Unfortunately, I never had the opportunity, so I went the other way with professional sports.

I was what they called "jam in the middle of the toast," a sort of displaced human being. My father was Polish-German-Catholic. My mother was a Russian-German-Jew. From the get-go I didn't know where I belonged. If I tried to hang around with the Jews, I was a gentile. If I tried to hang around with the gentiles, I was a dirty Jew. So I never really felt I belonged anywhere. My family was never really close with the neighborhood and we didn't have many friends. As a result, I became a self-defensive child. I had no real values except survival values, so I learned tactics. In Trenton there was nobody to protect you, and it wasn't unusual for older kids to beat up on you. My only self-defense was that I had a good arm, and up to 30 feet I was accurate with rocks to cut anyone down. It was a David-and-Goliath kind of training field. I learned how to pitch by throwing rocks and boulders.

As I got older, I realized I had to get out of Trenton, which to me is still the toilet of the East Coast. They have a big bridge that goes across the Delaware River starting in Trenton saying, "Trenton makes, the world takes," and I remember I used to look at that bridge and say, "World, please take me." I was going to find a way to get out. Baseball was one of them, but I had other avenues. As a young kid I learned how to gamble and play pool. I could shoot pool as a professional—I was that good.

I didn't have any heroes or role models. For some of the boxers who were fighting in those days—guys like Joe Louis—it didn't make any difference if they were white, black, or green, as long as they were successful. My biggest influence was fear. The emotion fear [drove me]: fear of being locked in; fear of being battered; fear of being sent away for life; fear of seeing some of the people I was hanging with there at an early age, being sent away, or dying on the streets.

I never played little league, high school, or legion ball. I signed a contract when I was 18, playing in the city recreation league. Pittsburgh had a birddog scout who saw my arm and offered me $185 a month to travel 1,500 miles to play in Georgia somewhere. I laughed at him. Told him it was a ridiculous offer. At the time I was making more money playing pool. I told him to forget it, but then something happened and I had to get out of town fast, so I called the guy up and I said, "I'll sign for the $185."

I was probably the only professional rookie that ever showed up in camp with a pair of spikes and a pool cue. I didn't even have a glove. There were all these Pennsylvania hucksters, these rookie phenoms from high school with their $4,000 bonuses, and they all got train tickets down. Me? They gave me a bus ticket. They all had new gloves, shirts, and spikes, and I came in with my pool cue. I needed it to make a living. It was still a matter of survival with me and I did whatever it took to get by. A couple times I had to disappear two or three days to hustle in Jacksonville, Florida.

I [brought] streetwise tactics into professional ball, and the poor manager couldn't fig-ure me out. He said, "I have never seen a ballplayer show up with a pool cue and disap-pear for two days to go hustle. You got a lot of nerve to even tell me you do something like this." And I told him, "I'm not going to argue, but this is how I'm going to have to survive playing baseball." I was honest—$185 a month, paying rent and eating, you're not going to survive too long.

I lasted two months. He called me in and said, "You know, seriously, you don't belong in professional ball." I said, "You may be right!" and I went back to New Jersey. Fortunately, someone saw me from another 'D' Independent team and they sent me a con-tract and signed me for a little bit more money. The next year I went to Pensacola, Florida. It was there I really kicked off my career and started to get a feel for what pro-fessional sports were.

I spent six years in the minor leagues. When the expansion teams came in 1961-'62, the Angels drafted me off of the Baltimore Rochester roster for $25,000. I was in South America at the time; had hired myself out to play winter league baseball there and had a great year. I felt I was really coming into my own.

In 1962, it was said that Hollywood and the Sunset Strip were the "Last Frontier of Glamour." Fur coats, suits and ties, and evening dresses were the norm, and the trendy nightclubs along the mile-long section of Sunset Boulevard were magnets for the high and mighty. It was the era of the big blonde, the big band, and the big Cadillac convertible. Songs like Bobby Darin's "Mack the Knife" drift-ed out from swank clubs like the Peppermint Twist, the Whiskey, Ciro's, or PJ's, where limos lined up to drop off their affluent clients. The Strip was also a hang-out for Hollywood columnists, whose clout could make or break a rising star or starlet with just a mere mention in one of their columns.

Sixty-year-old syndicated columnist Walter Winchell was the King of the gos-sipmongers and wielded his power with the authority usually reserved for heads of state. Following Belinsky's sparkling no-hitter, Winchell contacted Bo's new agent, Paul Caruso, who introduced the two men. Winchell and Belinsky became drinking buddies and fast friends. Soon Winchell began writing regularly about the playboy Angel in his column. Top Hollywood agents seeking media exposure for their clients eagerly pushed their starlets on Winchell in hopes of having them linked with Bo. The list of hangers-on was impressive and long and included Juliet Prowse, Connie Stevens, Ursula Andress, and Ann Margret.

It was heady stuff for a 24-year-old palooka from Jersey who only a few years earlier scraped out a living in pool halls. But Bo adapted quickly. After all, he had been chasing "broadies" all his life; now they were just a little glossier is all. Charm, hustle, and savvy had gotten him through some tough times back east. Though Bo was young, he was experienced enough to handle anything La-La land threw at him.

What he needed was someone to hang with, a partner in crime. Bo gravitated to a fellow rookie pitcher named Dean Chance. Although the two were complete opposites, somehow they hit it off. Soon Chance began accompanying Bo to the bars and restaurants up and down the Sunset Strip, taking it all in with wide-eyed wonder.

Chance and Belinsky were an unlikely pair, to say the least. Dean was a farm boy from a small town in Ohio, whose drawl was thicker than the cream that came from the family cow. Bo was East Coast to the tenth degree. "They were like Frick and Frack," said clubhouse man Bob Case. "But Bo was kind of a loner, and the only guy he really trusted was Dean."

After his no-hitter, Belinsky moved into a penthouse suite off the Sunset Strip, close to all the action, and the all-night partying quickly took a toll on the playboy pitcher. It couldn't have happened at a worse time for the team. Despite the odds stacked against them, the Angels were in the thick of the pennant race. The gang of cast-offs led by Leon Wagner, Pearson, Thomas, and rookies Fregosi and Rodgers were in contention. With their pitching staff of McBride, Grba, Belinsky, and Chance, along with 39-year-old reliever Art Fowler and Jack Spring, the Angels were firing on all cylinders. But then their rookie ace went into overdrive.

From May 21 to August 11, Belinsky lost five games against just two wins. He was the subject of some poor luck, pitching well enough to win a few of those games and even seeing his team no-hit in one of his losses. However, those close to him recognized that his off-the-field behavior was beginning to impact his on-the-field performance. Belinsky's inconsistency on the mound continued down the stretch. He won his final start of the season—thanks to three and two-thirds innings of scoreless relief from Chance—to nearly even his record at 10-11. But considering the hot start, Bo's finish was a downer despite a 3.56 ERA and a team-best 145 strikeouts.

Bo's new starting lineup away from Chavez Ravine included sex siren Jane Mansfield, Queen Soroya of Iran, and actress Tina Louise of *Gilligan's Island* fame. A column in the *Herald Examiner* called "The Steam Room" by Bud Furillo chronicled Bo's everyday exploits, which weren't exactly G-rated. The Angels reluctantly went along with Belinsky's published exploits because of his popularity. In a town ruled by publicity and hype, Bo was the gold standard.

"The Angels needed a star, so they created Bo," says Case. "Here was a flamboyant guy who dressed flashy, wore suede shoes and a trench coat with slicked back hair. His shirts and underwear were all monogrammed with [his initials], "BB." He was suave, had women all over him. He had something about him that just made them melt. They were around by the hundreds, phone calls all night long. In those days all you knew about players was from the box scores. Well with Bo, you knew everything about him because they were writing about him every day."

In Los Angeles, Bo rivaled crosstown ace Sandy Koufax in terms of popularity and press coverage. Stadium crowds were no longer sparse for Angels games. When the Yankees came to town, crowds of up to 50,000 a night gathered. A three-game series in June against the Yankees attracted a record 146,623 people. Some say excessive partying was one reason the Yankees found it difficult to beat the Angels at Chavez Ravine in 1962, although they took the season series five games to four.

"It was a social event when the Yankees would come to town," recalls Chance. "Johnny Grant used to throw them parties out at his home. I mean everybody came. Angie Dickinson. Every starlet. It was the place to be seen."

Chance may have been Belinsky's sidekick in '62, but he held up better than Bo down the stretch. After bouncing from the rotation to the bullpen and back to the rotation in late July, Chance went 7-4 over the final two months of the season to improve his record to 14-10. Among his accomplishments that year was a one-hitter, an 11-inning shutout, eight saves, and a 2.96 ERA. He played no small part in the Angels' newfound success.

From May 18 to June 30, the Angels were the hottest team in baseball, playing .600 ball and winning 27 games. On June 30, after winning their first game ever in Yankee Stadium, they jumped to second place in the standings. Chance got the save—his third in five games—for Bowsfield.

"HEAVEN CAN WAIT, ANGELS IN FIRST ON THE FOURTH," screamed the sports page headline in the *Los Angeles Times* on July 5. Fresh off a three-game sweep of Washington, the Angels led the division. More than 3,000 fans greeted them at the airport when they returned home.

On July 21, McBride won his 10th straight, beating the Indians 4-0. Ten days later, Leon Wagner was named outstanding player in the second All-Star Game after hitting a homer and making a game-saving catch in left field. The offense was firing on all cylinders, too. Fregosi, Pearson, and second baseman Billy Moran were setting the table for Wagner, who was protected by Lee and George Thomas, Rodgers, and third baseman Felix Torres.

On August 1 the misfits from La-La Land were still rolling along, only four and one-half games out, when out of nowhere came a devastating one-two punch. Two days later, McBride broke a rib, sidelining him for the rest of the year. Three days after that, ace reliever Art Fowler, who at the age of 39 was having a sensational year, was struck in the eye by a line drive in batting practice. Rumor had it that instead of paying attention to the action on the field, he was spying some girl in the stands. "King Arthur" permanently lost the use of the eye. That, combined with the loss of McBride, put a severe crimp in the Angels' chances to finish first.

But they weren't flat-lining. On August 11, Bo got his first win in nearly two months, shutting out the Twins 3-0. When Don Lee shut out the White Sox 4-0 on August 26, the Angels were in third place, only three games off the pace. That set the stage for a Labor Day doubleheader at Yankee Stadium in front of 55,000 people. The Angels dropped the first game as Belinsky got shelled. In the nightcap, they were down 5-0 heading into the eighth when Pearson rallied the troops with a two-run, two-out homer. The Angels scored four more in the ninth to squeak by, 6-5.

They returned home on September 12 still only four games out of first. But with just 16 games remaining, they had their work cut out for them. Back in Belinskyland, storm clouds were gathering. One night, Belinsky, Chance, and a young female were returning home from a party. Belinsky and the woman got into an argument, the car hit a lamppost, and her head cracked the windshield. The incident made a big splash in all the papers, although no charges were filed. But the publicity didn't fare well with the Angels front office. Haney was just about at wit's end with Bo. It was one thing to quietly suffer his quirky behavior and eccentricities when he was winning, but that hadn't been happening lately, and the suits decided it was time for Bo to go.

In a late-July deal, the Angels acquired Dan Osinski, a hard-throwing righty from Kansas City for "a player to be named later." Osinski would prove to be a real asset in the bullpen down the stretch, but yet another wild hair in the clubhouse. As for the "player to be named later," that was Belinsky, as Bo learned a couple of weeks later from Kansas City Athletics manager Hank Bauer when the Angels were in K.C. Not surprisingly, Bo was angry. He had no intention of leaving Los Angeles and instinctively knew that if news of the trade leaked out, it would most likely be negated. Seeking maximum coverage, Bo chose a weekend series in New York—the epicenter of the media—to announce that his head was on the chopping block. "If traded," he declared, "I'm not going."

Haney and Rigney were naturally incensed. They knew the deal was no longer viable and they would have to keep Belinsky. Bo's lawyers appealed to the commissioner's office, but Ford Frick, not wanting to deal with it, let the clubs settle it themselves. Eventually, Ted Bowsfield became "the player to be named later," and Bo remained an Angel—albeit the biggest traitor, as far as management was concerned, since Lucifer.

The addition of Osinski wasn't enough for the Angels to overcome the loss of Fowler and McBride, and on September 12 they began a six-game losing streak that knocked them out of the race once and for all. The Yankees were again destined to be American League champs, while the Angels finished in third, 10 games behind the Yanks. Still, the third-place finish was an incredible accomplishment for the sophomore team that had been expected to finish no better then seventh. Rigney was named Manager of the Year and Haney the league's top executive. All in all, 1962 was an amazing feat that rivals 2002 as the team's greatest season.

Unfortunately, there was a big valley ahead. Over the next seven years, the Angels would never finish higher than fifth.

The end-of-the-season skid wasn't a total loss for the team's Bad Boy, Bo. Along the way his pal Winchell introduced Bo to Mamie Van Doren, another Hollywood blond bombshell. At first meeting, Van Doren wasn't too impressed with Belinsky. However, there was enough of a spark to eventually start a fire.

"He vibrated sex," Van Doren says of that first encounter. "I think it was more a lust than anything else, because it certainly wasn't his bank account. There was something about him—he was just different."

Belinsky contacted Van Doren again during spring training in Palm Springs in 1963. This time they clicked. The two stayed at the Riviera. Chance joined in the fun and the three of them cruised around in Bo's red Cadillac, taking in the beauty of the desert and getting their kicks.

Cruising the scene in Palm Springs was certainly more exciting than the Angels' 1963 season—a year of floundering that saw the Angels regress back to 70 wins and finish in ninth place. Bo's record, 2-9, was almost as abysmal as his ERA, 5.75, and management blamed it all on his now-torrid relationship with Van Doren. The Angels front office made no secret of its unhappiness about the situation, but Bo had no intention of appeasing them. Despite thousands of dollars in fines issued by the team, nothing could keep him from the nightlife and Mamie—or from being frank with the press.

"I like to play, on and off the field," Bo said with pride. "I mean, [it] don't make me a bad guy. I used to date some very pretty gals. It's just I never realized what curfew was. I didn't understand that. I used to say at the beginning of the year when I signed my contract, 'Why don't you just take $1,500 out up front? Because I'll miss at least three curfews, I'll tell you that right now.'"

In an effort to rein him in, the brass split Bo and Chance up and started rooming Belinsky with the wholesome Albie Pearson. Haney figured Pearson's squeaky-clean example would inspire the fallen Angel to walk the path of righteousness. Almost 40 years later, Pearson is still trying to get over the shock.

"Nobody, I mean nobody, did it like Bo!" Pearson recalls. "I remember one day in the room in Palm Springs he had this woman on the phone. He said, 'What did you say? I didn't hear you,' and he handed me the phone real quick. The voice on the other end said, 'Bo, would you marry me? Let's be together the rest of our lives.' It was either Mamie or Tina Louise, one of the two."

According to Little Man, Belinsky needed a social secretary, not a roommate. "I couldn't tell you how many women were lined up. I mean beautiful women who'd come down from Hollywood. I tell you, it was something. One day we were in the room and there's a knock on the door. He said, 'Roomie, can you get the door?' and he went into the bathroom. I opened it and there's a pretty young woman standing there. I said, 'Hi, Bo's not available. Can I take your number or tell him where you'll be?' She said, 'I didn't come for Bo, I came for you!' I was flabbergasted. I said, 'You've got the wrong guy.' I kind of stammered, 'I got a great wife. I got children, really I'm not...' Let me tell you, I was a mess. I let her out and Bo opened the bathroom door and he was laughing up a storm. He said, 'Roomie, you passed the test, man!' I shouted, 'You rat! You set me up!' He replied, 'Yeah, you don't mind, do ya?' I asked how much he paid for her and he said, 'Oh, I gave her fifty.'

"I roomed with his suitcase for three months. Technically, I was his roommate, but I never saw him."

Mamie Van Doren and Bo Belinsky at the Peppermint Twist in 1963. AP/WWP

Finally, Pearson confronted Bo about his lifestyle—not out of pique or an excess of missionary zeal, but rather sincere concern. What Belinsky told him astounded Pearson.

"My goal," Belinsky stated, "is to live fast, die young, and leave a good-looking corpse."

"What then?" the stunned Pearson asked.

Belinsky looked at him soberly and said, "Little Man, I'm not against you nor religion, and you know that I'm for you, but that's not my thing. God's not my thing."

Pearson said, "That's cool. I'm not pushing anything. I just wanted to know what you got going after you leave the good-looking corpse?"

Pearson felt genuine friendship toward Belinsky, but as the 1963 season progressed, he was getting less and less sleep on account of Belinsky's nocturnal activities. Pearson informed Haney and Rigney that it would probably be best if he had a different roommate. Haney obliged and soon Bo was back with Chance. "People used to ask why I roomed them together," Rigney once said, "and I told them it was because I didn't want to screw up two rooms."

During their time together, Pearson saw a different side of Belinsky that was often overshadowed by Bo's illustrious image. He learned that behind the bravado and inflated ego lurked a kind and generous human being.

"Down in Bo's heart, he wanted to please people," Pearson says. "It was almost as if with this girl thing he was really attempting to fill a void, trying to capture a purpose and identity. Boy, because of his looks and charm, this is where he had that vibe. But as far as a person, I liked him. Was his the same lifestyle as mine? Totally the antithesis of it. But I saw in his heart during our time together a man just wanting to do good. He did everything with a wink."

To his teammates, Belinsky was rarely a problem. He never flaunted his celebrity status. In fact, sometimes it offered a pleasant diversion from routine. Players would often look forward to coming home after a long road trip to see what long-legged beauties would be waiting for him at the airport. Often when the team arrived home after a late-night flight, Bo would have someone else grab his bags and leave with some babe to a standing ovation from his bleary-eyed teammates.

Tom Satriano remembers, "Bo had the respect of everybody because he never bitched if you made an error or did something wrong. If he lost a game he'd never point a finger at anybody."

Some of the older players found it difficult to relate to Bo's lifestyle, though. Veterans like Eli Grba liked Belinsky personally, but didn't really understand him.

"He was from a different planet," says Grba. "He was the first one I ever saw bring a hair dryer into the locker room. I said, 'What is this? Is this guy a fag? What the hell! Get out of here!' You didn't do that in those days. He sat in front of the mirror and all that kind of stuff, and not only that, but when he got home from a road trip there was Mamie Van Doren waiting for him. It was nuts."

Bo's involvement with the sultry sex kitten widened the media spotlight on him, for sure. Both the Hollywood press and the sports pages followed their every move. It was not your typical storybook romance, however.

"I loved Mamie. She was very beautiful, but the train could never meet at the station," Bo said. "She was an actress, I was a ballplayer, and I think it was a matter of trust. I still wasn't ready."

To Van Doren, Bo was a mixed bag of emotions and contradictions.

"I was nuts about Bo," says Van Doren more than four decades after their intense relationship. "I mean I was really crazy about him. He added another dimension to my life. It was like I'd known him all my life. But I also found him to be never satisfied. He was always in want of money. He liked to gamble. He was always wanting something he didn't have. I don't think he had very much when he was in Trenton, and he was always letting me know there was no money in that family. He told me how he left school when he was 14 and he said some really bad things happened to him. I think that sort of stayed with him; he was really, really scared.

"When other girls came around, he was very cool. They liked him more than he liked them, and he didn't have to try and get a girl. And the girls he wanted always had money. He thought that money was the most important thing—more so than sex."

In addition to his mental health, Van Doren was also concerned for Belinsky's physical well being. His incessant smoking and drug taking were constant concerns for her.

"He didn't take care of his body; he drank too much and he smoked like a chimney," recalls Van Doren. "I never allowed him to smoke in the bedroom. I always made him go outside and he didn't like that. We had so many differences. I don't drink, don't smoke, and don't do drugs. I didn't recognize the fact that he was on drugs. I would sit at the ballpark and watch when he was pitching and he'd go back in the dugout. I'd see a red flame light up in the tunnel and I knew he was sucking on a cigarette. He was smoking a cigarette when he needed all that energy."

In 1963, President John F. Kennedy's New Frontier was in full swing, in the ring-a-ding, Rat Pack sense of the word. Bo jumped in with both feet when he began keeping company with one of JFK's tootsies: Judith Campbell Exner, to be exact, courtesan of presidents and mobsters and, apparently, an expert on fine jewelry. It was Exner who picked out the engagement ring Belinsky bought for Mamie Van Doren.

"We became engaged on April 1, 1963, and I thought he was pulling an April Fool's joke on me, but he really wasn't," Van Doren says. "He brought me a ring but he also brought President Kennedy's girlfriend, Judy Exner, along when we bought it. He had her pick out *my* ring! We were at the jewelry shop over on Beverly Drive in Beverly Hills and she picked out a real nice ring. I said, 'What is going on with you? This is incredible! To have some girl pick out my ring?' He said, 'This is where Kennedy picks out all of his jewelry for Judy.' I said, 'That's nice.'"

Not long after that bizarre episode, Belinsky was in bed with Van Doren at his Hollywood digs when the phone rang. It was Exner. "Jack wants to meet Mamie," she told Bo. The news hit Belinsky like a right cross. Van Doren explains: "This was shortly after Marilyn had just died, and so he was raising hell about it."

The Mamie-Bo love match was tempestuous from the start and was dealt a death blow soon after the phone call. Van Doren felt that despite Bo's astounding successes with the opposite sex, he would never truly be comfortable with any mate in the long term. "Bo had no respect for women—none whatsoever," she insists. "He really didn't like them."

Bo was drawn to women with money, but according to Van Doren, once he won them over, he thought them to be spoiled and resented them. She also believes his ego made him extremely jealous. She recalled that when she started dating New York Jets quarterback Joe Namath, Bo went "ballistic" even though he had broken up with her, had her followed, and made harassing phone calls.

For his part, Belinsky admitted that he always had problems relating to women beyond a certain point, but knew how to show proper respect. "You got your dingbats, and they were fun, too," Belinsky said. "But I always knew when I was in the presence of a real woman. I had that ability. And yes, I respected 'em."

When it was all said and done he and Mamie remained friends, and Van Doren is glad they never took the big plunge. "When I look back, I'm just glad I didn't marry him," she says. "I was feeling different then. I probably would have married him, but it probably would not have lasted."

When the 1963 baseball season got underway, Bo got off to a horrendous start. By the end of May Belinsky's record stood at 1-7, and Haney had no choice but to send him down to their Triple-A affiliate in Hawaii. Belinsky initially balked, but once he arrived in Hawaii and saw all it had to offer in terms of native beauty, he thought he had died and gone to heaven. The island paradise and the tropical ladies rejuvenated his arm and his psyche. Bo even took up surfing.

On the diamond, he went 4-1 in Triple-A, and the Angels called him back up in mid-August. Belinsky had grown so fond of Hawaii that he seriously considered staying put, but Hollywood wasn't exactly chopped liver, either. He returned to L.A. in August to a hero's welcome—and picked up right where he left off, driving management crazy with his antics and erratic pitching.

Bo's road trips were legendary at this time. Chance recalls a night in Boston when the team's hotel caught fire.

"It was the Somerset hotel in Boston," Chance recalls. "It's 4:00 a.m. and I get a call from Bud Furillo of the *Herald Examiner*: 'Dean, there's a fire!' I say, 'Bud, you're drunk. Let me sleep.' Now the operator calls and says, 'Don't get excited. Just get up. Don't dress. Don't get anything. Just come down to the lobby.' So I go down to the lobby and there's Buddy Blattner, our radio guy, in his pajamas. Little Freddie Frederico comes up to me yelling, 'Where's Bo? Where's Bo?' I say, 'Shut up, Freddie! He's not in yet.' And then up comes a cab and Bo gets out—caught cold turkey just coming in."

One of Bo's own favorite stories involves Gene Autry. "We were catching the plane to New York City, and Gene Autry decided to take the trip along with Fred Haney," recalled Belinsky. "I had a friend who was a Duchess, and she was going to pick up Dean and me in her limo at four o'clock in the morning at the airport at JFK. We wound up landing in Newark, and I told Dean we're not going to get picked up by the Duchess. At the same time, Autry and Haney had a limousine waiting for them at JFK, and here we pull into Newark and here's this white limousine pulled up right there at the airplane. Autry figures it's his and everyone is patting him on the back saying, 'How did you do this? How did you let them know that we were going to be here?' He was a big hero. Well, they walked out to the limousine and got straight-armed by the chauffeur, who told him, 'This is Bo Belinsky's and Dean Chance's.'

"The Duchess had figured it out and she had the limousine waiting there for us. I mean, I could see this guy pushing Gene back and his cowboy hat flying off. Autry thought he was kidding him, so he sneaked around to the other side of the car and opened the door and the Duchess's two poodles came out, 'ARF! ARF! ARF!' and attacked him. His hat went blowing off again and I said to Dean, 'This may be the last year with the Angels with me and you.' I don't think they appreciated that too much."

But it was a scrap Belinsky got into with a Los Angeles newsman that finally got him the boot in 1964. Among the beat writers who followed the Angels was Braven Dyer, 60-year-old sports editor for the *Los Angeles Times*. Like most card-carrying members of the Fourth Estate, Dyer liked his booze. The team was in Washington when one night Dyer, angry at Bo for not giving him equal treatment, got sauced and called Belinsky up and challenged him to a fight. Belinsky told him to go to bed and sober up, but instead the enraged newsman came pounding on his hotel room door at 2 a.m. Chance was in the bathtub at the time, and heard Bo go to the door and say, "What are you doing, Braven?"

Cursing mad and snarling, Dyer repeated his challenge, and Belinsky responded by throwing the glass of water he'd been drinking into Dyer's face. Chance heard the sounds of scuffling and hurried from the bathroom to investigate. He found Dyer unconscious on the floor with blood seeping out of one ear. Chance thought he was dead.

"Christ, call Freddie Frederico!" he told Belinsky.

It turns out Dyer wasn't dead, and he came around when the trainer administered smelling salts. Then Frederico took the old man to the hospital to be checked out.

Belinsky claimed Dyer swung at him first, but Dyer insisted that Bo started it by hitting him with the water glass. Chance, the only "ear witness," still sides with Belinsky. "You don't go to a guy's room and challenge him," he said. "Let's just be grateful Braven didn't get hurt."

Trouble was, Dyer was tight with Fred Haney, and the Angels general manager sided with him. The incident provided the excuse Haney needed to get rid of Belinsky. First the team suspended him without pay. Then they shipped him back to their Triple-A affiliate in Hawaii. Belinsky's lawyers claimed that he was being treated unfairly and appealed to the commissioner's office for a ruling. Ford Frick said it was a club matter, and given that leeway, the Angels dealt Belinsky to Philadelphia when the season ended.

Ironically, Belinsky was pitching as well as ever up to the altercation with Dyer. Although his record at the time was 9-8, with more run-scoring from his teammates he could have easily posted double-digit wins. His ERA at the time of his banishment to the minors was 2.86. Chance, still bitter over the whole affair, believes Haney used the incident to get rid of Bo. "They rammed it right to Bo," Chance says. "If they tried that today, they'd be sued."

Bob Case agreed. "The Angels used him like a pawn. They created Bo like they did in the old studio system. They made him into a star and then they dumped him. Bo Belinsky put the Angels on the map—not Fregosi or Chance. ... Bo got the Angels equal media attention and bigger headlines than the Dodgers, and once they were done with him, they tossed him in the streets."

Belinsky played for Gene Mauch's Philadelphia Phillies for two seasons, and then was drafted by the Houston Astros in the 1966 Rule V Draft. Unwilling to put in the necessary time and effort, Bo never recaptured the magic of his early days and was out of baseball by 1970. There was simply no more gas in his tank. His lifetime record was an unimpressive 28-51, but nobody in the history of baseball got more mileage out of 28 wins.

His knockout of sportswriter Braven Dyer in 1964 officially ended Bo's three-year reign with the Angels.
AP/WWP

After his career was over, Bo returned to Hawaii, where he met and married Jo Collins, a former Playboy Playmate of the Year. They had a daughter, but within two years they divorced, after Collins alleged infidelity. Two more failed marriages followed—first to heiress Jeanie Weyerhaeuser, who Bo met after saving her life in the Hawaiian surf. That union brought forth twin daughters before its demise. Belinsky's third marriage also ended badly, and Bo was forced to leave the Islands with almost nothing in his pockets.

His financial woes and marital failures brought on despondency. Belinsky ended up living in Malibu, California, where the drug and alcohol use that had started as his pitching career tailed off began to accelerate.

"I got involved in the '60s with the uppers, the amphetamines," Bo recalled later. "They had some real good stuff back in those days. Legal prescription. And I got hooked on them a little bit. Toward the end of my career, I started having aches and pains and that set me up for drinking. I became a full-grown alcoholic and became unsafe to myself and the people around me. I went off for six years like that, and I just wanted to die.

"I got to be a very sick and dangerous guy. People just started fleeing from me. There were some real horror stories. Two years after I was in the major leagues, I was underneath a bridge with a brown bag wrapped around a bottle of musca-doo-dle (cheap wine), saying it can't get any worse. We're talking about things that I've done that were just unreal."

Bob Case maintains that the drinking and drugs were never a problem until Bo got out of baseball. "He was like a lot of athletes when they get out of the limelight. All of a sudden, there's no one around. Nobody's giving you free dinners to come to their restaurant or this and that, and it's a culture shock for any athlete, especially a guy like Bo."

Van Doren recalls a poignant but disturbing meeting the two had around that time. Bo had scheduled a press conference at the Biltmore Hotel in downtown Los Angeles to announce the release of a new autobiography he had written. For whatever reason, he wanted Mamie there to share in the moment. She initially declined but the old Belinsky charm got the best of her, and she reconsidered. Van Doren showed up dressed to the nines and even brought along a special gift.

When they were dating, Bo had presented Mamie his 14-karat gold necklace that he was wearing when he pitched his no-hitter. It had been purchased in Venezuela in 1960 while he was playing winter league baseball. He told Mamie, "I want you to have this." Mamie declined, but Bo persisted. "No," he said, "I want you to wear it. It will bring you luck. It brought me luck, and I want you to have good luck, too."

Van Doren wrapped it in a box and placed it in her purse. When she saw him at the hotel, Mamie presented it to him. "He got really choked up," Van Doren fondly remembers. "I think Bo was really moved."

Once the press conference ended, Bo insisted that they get in his limo and head out to the Villa Capri and to all the old haunts they used to frequent together. Van Doren told him too much time had passed, knowing it would never be the same.

"It was so sad," she recalls. "I knew he was being self-destructive. The whole time he had a drink in his hand. Everywhere! Walking down the street, at the café, everywhere! I said, 'Jesus, Bo, you're drinking way too much!' He just ignored me."

Bo finally hit rock bottom in the early 1980s. With the help of his friends, he began down the path to recovery. He joined Alcoholics Anonymous, and Chance found him work in Las Vegas at a car dealership. Through friends like Pearson, Bo got deeper into religion. Cleansed of his demons, he remained sober and never looked back.

"There was probably no human power on this earth that could have saved me," Bo said in 1994 in his interview with Alana Case. "I now associate myself with people that stay sober, and they're my true friends. I have a little more value and look at things a little differently. I'm not talking about perfection, but I have a lot better attitude than what I used to have. There is talk about doing a motion picture on my life, and we'll see what happens regarding that. But for now, it's just one day at a time and taking life on life's terms. It's going to be all right."

There were more trials to come, however. A lifelong smoker, Belinsky developed symptoms of chronic lung disease as his heart began to act up. He developed diabetes, and in 1996, he was diagnosed with bladder cancer. Bo lost weight and his once-handsome face became deeply lined and old. The combined pain from his ailments was so excruciating that one night he attempted suicide by stabbing himself in the stomach. A quick response by friends and medics saved his life. It was only through their support and proper medical care that Bo pulled through. Pearson was among those who helped turn things around yet again.

"I visited him in the hospital," recalls Pearson. "We prayed together after his suicide attempt, and he opened up his heart to the Messiah in a powerful change."

By now Bo was a devout Christian, believing that God must have kept him around for a reason. Though his later years were still filled with physical pain, he courageously fought on. Keeping a low profile, Bo continued to sell cars and appear at an occasional card show or old-timers game. He dedicated the final few years of his life to speaking to youth about alcohol and drug abuse.

"The drugs handicapped him, but he came back strong," says Bob Case. "He was accepted in Vegas and helped people in outreach, visiting cancer patients. Although he had his demons, Bo, at the core, was a good and generous person. His friends were loyal. Most of them believe during his final years he found the peace that for the most part had eluded him all his life."

In his interview with Alana Case, Belinsky reflected on life, baseball, and his legacy: "At times my life was like a blur. It was really tough to focus. Today I probably would have gotten a little more serious with my career with the money they were putting out. I probably would have liked to have been born a little later. But then again, the '60s were such a fantastic time to be a star. In those times you could go out and still have a little bit of fun."

Today Belinsky remains a mythical and popular figure in Angel lore, the rare individual who eclipsed baseball's boundaries and became a cultural icon. To most, Bo's name will always be synonymous with "playboy" and "rogue." In his later years it sometimes frustrated Belinsky that his reformation was never as newsworthy as his swashbuckling adventures, but in the end that wasn't what really mattered.

"A lot of people never let me forget my youth," Belinsky reflected. "They write articles in magazines about my wild days in the '60s and '70s. Do you want to find out what I'm doing today? No, not really. 'We want to remember you when you were wild in your good old days.' I can understand, this is the press and these are people who remember Bo like he used to be, and that's okay just as long as I know where I'm at with myself.

"The funny thing is that after all these years, the name Bo Belinsky is still alive. I only won 28 major league baseball games and you mention Bo Belinsky to a lot of people, they still remember the name. You have to win 300 games or hit .300 ten seasons in a row to earn that kind of recognition. I find that quite flattering, so somewhere along the line I must have done something right, and I kind of have fun with that.

"My theory when I was young was 'Live fast, die young, and leave a good-looking corpse.' And I'm still living."

On November 23, 2001, Bob Case was at his home when he received a phone message from Bo wishing him and his wife Alana a happy Thanksgiving. Bo also wanted to remind them that he planned to visit Los Angeles to talk to some producers about a possible film version of his life. He told Case he wanted to stay close by so they could spend some time together. But just a few hours later came another call, this time from a mutual friend in Las Vegas informing Case that Belinsky had just been found dead of an apparent heart attack in his apartment. Bo was 64 years old.

Six days later at Chavez Ravine, a memorial service of sorts was held for the fallen Angel in the Stadium Club. Flowers surrounded an oversized photo of Belinsky in his playing days. One by one, old friends and teammates stood beside the photograph and reflected on his life. There were a few funny stories to share, but mostly they talked about Bo's good nature and generosity.

Chance recalled how Belinsky had saved his first victory in 1962. Case spoke of Bo's soft spot for regular people. When Case was a 17-year-old clubhouse attendant, Bo was one of the first to take a sincere interest in him, and had made it a point to make him part of the team.

Former Angels beat writer Jack Disney reminisced about the night Bo invited him to Scandia's Restaurant and brought him a very special present. "I get there and in came Bo, and he had my birthday present on his arm. She was beautiful! Stayed with me for three days."

Bud Tucker, another beat writer, said Bo gave him his greatest interview. "Two o'clock in the morning the phone rings, and it's Bo. 'Listen, come up to my room, I got an exclusive for you.' I go up to the room and there's Mamie Van Doren. Bo says, 'Bud, Mamie and me are getting married.' ... What a great interview! I stayed there for two hours. Of course, Mamie was totally nude."

Former major leaguers Darrell Evans, Jay Johnstone, and ex-Trenton resident Al Downing also paid their respects. Evans said as a kid he was a big fan of Bo's, and that he was the first player he knew who really showed a human side.

Naturally, Albie Pearson spoke about how Bo had made peace with himself and God. He was particularly touched because when Bo died, lying next to him on his bed was an open Bible.

Altogether, there were about 200 people in attendance. Irv Kaze, who'd greeted Bo at the airport that long-ago day in 1962, and Scotty Keene, the first Angel batboy, were there. So were former teammates Buck Rodgers, Tom Satriano, Ed Kirkpatrick, Clyde Wright, and George Witt. Tim Mead, director of public relations, represented the current Angels. Reporters Ross Newhan, Bud Furillo, and others were there from the old guard.

As the service dwindled down, a former Belinsky flame approached Chance and Case to say hello. Time had not handled her gently, and they were taken aback by her aged appearance. When she left, Case noticed yet another former Belinsky squeeze sitting at a nearby table. Case asked if they should go over and say hello. Chance mulled it over for a moment, then looked at the smiling photo of Bo and sighed.

"No, Bob," he said in that slow, mid-western drawl. "Let's just remember 'em like they were."

7

THE DEAN
HAS ARRIVED
DEAN CHANCE

*A*s he peered out toward the pitcher's mound on a sunny July day in 1964, Mickey Mantle was a bundle of nerves. Hours earlier, he had rehearsed this moment in his head; then he even talked about it during batting practice.

Albie Pearson overheard Mantle talking to Roger Maris behind the batting cage: "When Chance pitches, I want to go hide."

The former home run king shook his head in morose commiseration, for Maris was apprehensive himself about going up against Dean Chance. In three years, Maris hadn't hit a single home run against the Angels' pitching ace. But the M&M boys weren't the only Yankees with that problem. It seemed the entire team couldn't hit Chance.

Against the Yankees in 1964, Chance was a pitcher possessed, allowing only 14 hits in 50 innings against the defending American League champs. Of his five starts against the boys from the Bronx, he had thrown four complete games. Ironically, in the only game he didn't finish—which was also the one game the Angels didn't win—Chance threw 14 innings, outlasting Yankees hurler Jim Bouton, who lasted just 13 frames. Over those 14 innings, Chance allowed just three hits, struck out 12, and walked only two batters. He was relieved in the top of the 15th—the game still scoreless—and the Angels pen promptly allowed two Yankees to score. Fifty innings pitched against New York: one run allowed.

Mantle dug his spikes into the box, attempting as best he could to concentrate. If push came to shove, he could always try to bunt for a hit. He had successfully done that a couple times against Chance; trouble was, the present situation didn't warrant a bunt.

The count was 1-1, but Mantle never really saw the two previous pitches. Chance's release point was hidden in a tangle of flying fingers and gesticulating movements. A precursor to the Hideo Nomo and Luis Tiant school of pitching—

where a pitcher's "wind up" is taken to the absolute extreme—Chance's unortho-dox style showed his back to the hitter first, then hid the ball so it was impossible to pick up. To top it off, he glared at the batter menacingly, almost as if he were an assassin on strict orders. His was the kind of half-crazed, half-in-control look the hangman gives his victim a second before the chute is pulled. And that's what Mantle saw when he looked at Dean Chance on the mound—nothing but a six-foot-four tower of holy terror.

Mantle turned to catcher Buck Rodgers and shrugged his shoulders. "This is a waste of time, Buck. I got no chance."

Rodgers couldn't help but chuckle to himself. There wasn't a hitter in the whole league who didn't feel the same way. In '64, no one could hit Chance. Rodgers set up inside and called for the curveball. Chance went into his delivery. It was all arms and legs, and Mantle missed the release point entirely and whiffed over the ball by a half-foot for his second strike. Mantle plaintively stared over at the dugout at his teammates, almost pleading for someone to help him. In the on-deck circle, Tom Tresh turned away. He had no answers.

Mantle regrouped. "Concentrate!" he told himself. "Get your head in the game!" Rodgers called for the fastball outside. Mantle picked it up about a third of the way in. The pitch was sinking, clearly a ball. Mantle swung anyway, dipping his shoul-der and swinging recklessly, with all of his might.

Forty years later, Rodgers recalled the moment. "[The pitch] was about six inches off the ground, and he golfed it over the fence like a seven iron. That's the only pitch Mantle could hit off Chance. If he had got it up another foot, he would have blown it right by him."

Rounding first base, Mantle knew he was the luckiest son of a bitch in Chavez Ravine. His megawatt smile lit up the stadium. As he jogged past second, Mantle glanced over at Chance, who was glaring at the Mick like he had just caught him key-ing Bo Belinsky's candy-apple red Cadillac in the parking lot. Mantle's smile melted away, and that familiar fear bubbled back up. He almost felt like apologizing.

Chance covered his face with his glove and let loose a primeval scream from the depths of his soul. Mantle hurried along. He knew he had cheated the hangman. For now, anyway.

It was the only run that Chance would allow against the Yankees that season.

Dean Chance will be forever linked with Bo Belinsky. Although this latter-day Butch and Sundance make for nostalgic and entertaining discussion, it overshad-ows Chance's place among baseball's elite pitchers in the mid-1960s. Teammates and opponents alike agree that Chance was one of the most intimidating and over-powering pitchers in baseball. Facing the big righthander in the batter's box was the baseball equivalent of receiving a root canal.

In 1964 alone, Chance put together one of the most incredible seasons in recent history. More than four decades later, the numbers are still astounding. In a league-best 278 1/3 innings, he allowed just 194 hits while striking out 207 batters. More impressive was his miniscule, Major League-leading 1.65 ERA, which was nine one-hundredths of a point better than Sandy Koufax's mark the same year. In posting 20 wins, Chance tossed 15 complete games and 11 shutouts. Incredibly, he gave up only seven home runs the entire season, an average of one every 40 innings.

Phil Pepe of the *New York World Telegram and Sun* summed up Dean's domination best when he wrote, "It's Chance, not CBS, who owns the Yankees. Lock, stock and barrel." Pearson, who played behind Chance in centerfield, never saw anything quite like it: "When Dean pitched, the Yankees became a bunch of guys in pantyhose. ... They had no chance."

"It wasn't enough to just be loose [against the Yankees]. You had to psyche up," Chance recalls. "Shit, they were the Yankees! You could never let up against those guys. Maris never got a home run off me, and I didn't have any trouble with Mantle. I just tried to overpower him."

"'Amazing,' is how I'd describe him," says Rodgers of his battery mate, Chance. "I never saw a pitcher so overpowering. The greatest hitters in baseball—Killebrew, Maris, and Mantle—would just shake their heads in disbelief. Some were visibly scared—he was that overpowering."

First baseman Lee Thomas agreed. "I know Bob Gibson and Sandy Koufax had some great years, but that one season was probably as good as anybody ever had."

For Chance, the '64 season began inauspiciously. A blister on the right index finger of his throwing hand limited him to bullpen duty. By the All-Star break, he had only five wins and four saves. But his first half wasn't without its thrilling moments, such as his 14 innings of shutout ball on June 6 against the Yankees. Chance considers that marathon the greatest game he ever pitched. It impressed manager Al Lopez enough to have Chance start on the mound in that year's All-Star game at Shea Stadium.

It was his first time performing on a national stage, and the hard-throwing Midwesterner didn't disappoint. In front of more than 50,000 people and a nationally televised audience, Chance threw three innings of shutout ball. "I struck out Roberto Clemente on a hanging slider," Chance recalls. "His eyes lit up like a light bulb and he [swung out of his shoes], but he missed it. In three innings they got no runs, just one infield hit and one other."

With the painful blister fully healed, Chance went on a tear in the second half of the season, winning 15 of his last 20 games and posting eight shutouts. His 20th win on September 25 was his sixth 1-0 decision of the season, tying him with Walter Johnson, Joe Bush, and Carl Hubbell for the most 1-0 wins in one season. His 20 victories represented nearly a quarter of all the Angels' 82 wins that season. And at age 23, Chance became the youngest pitcher ever to win the prestigious Cy Young Award.

Chance says that a number of things came together for him in '64, and that his teammates deserve equal credit for his numbers. "I got the breaks, every good thing that could happen, happened for me," recalls Chance. "Instead of getting beat 1-0, I would get the win 1-0. Instead of going through for a hit, a ball would go for a double play. Bobby Knoop had a tremendous year behind me at second and made a lot of great plays."

Chance also credits cavernous Chavez Ravine and the cool night air for keeping the ball in the park. "I only gave up seven home runs that year. That's the biggest feat, I think."

Born Wilmer Dean Chance on June 1, 1941, in Wooster, Ohio, Chance was about as far removed from America's national pastime as one could get. He was using his right arm to milk cows long before he learned how to throw a baseball with it. The backbreaking chores he performed every day on his father's farm instilled in Chance the work ethic he used to blaze a path to sports stardom. Chance's hero as a youngster was another rural farm boy who made a name for himself while pitching for the Cleveland Indians—Hall of Fame pitcher Bob Feller. It didn't take long for Chance to follow in Feller's footsteps.

At Wayne County Northwestern High, Chance was all-state in both basketball and baseball, but it was on the diamond where he really shined. In three years at Northwestern, Chance compiled a mind-boggling 51-1 record, with 18 no-hitters. In his senior year, Dean averaged 14 strikeouts a game and marched his team to the state championship. Twelve of the 16 major league clubs offered Chance a contract, and he also attracted more than 100 college scholarship offers in basketball.

Chance's competitive nature was nurtured by a local nemesis who, like Chance, went on to national prominence in sports. Future Indiana University head basketball coach Bobby Knight lived nearby, and the two faced off numerous times on the court and ballfield. "When we were growing up, the two of us played baseball and basketball against each other," Chance recalls, "and the lesson we learned was that it meant something to win. In our day, winning was everything. If you lost, you felt like crying."

Chance signed with the Baltimore Orioles for a $30,000 bonus, and was playing at the Class B level when Angels general manager Fred Haney selected the 20-year-old in the 1960 expansion draft. "I always felt I had a beaut," Haney later said about Chance. After being drafted by the Angels, Chance began the season with their AAA affiliate in Dallas-Fort Worth, where he quickly learned the finer points of pitching.

In 1962, skipper Bill Rigney brought him to spring training, where Chance earned a spot in the bullpen to start the season. Impressed with his winning attitude and how he overpowered the opposition, Rigney soon moved him into the starting rotation. Chance didn't disappoint: He went on to win 14 games, save eight others, and post a 2.96 ERA. For his efforts, he was voted the league's best rookie pitcher.

The following year, Chance and the Angels struggled due to anemic hitting. "I figured I was a cinch to win 20 that year. Hell, I damn near lost 20," Chance recalls.

Dean Chance's '64 season—in which he posted a 1.65 ERA—is considered one of the most dominating performances in modern times.
Courtesy of Mel Bailey

"I lost 18 that year, and in those games we only scored 21 runs. I got shut out 11 times! They never even scored a run for me."

However, according to Chance, the Angels' struggles at the plate actually made him a better pitcher. Pitching without the comfort of a big lead forced him to focus. "If you have a big lead, you don't work as hard," he says. "Of my 33 career shutouts, 13 were 1-0 [decisions], because I was bearing down all the time."

In 1964, with the emergence of shortstop Jim Fregosi, the Angels fared better. He and rookie Bobby Knoop gave the Angels a solid middle infield. Buck Rodgers, who in '62 set a record for most games caught by a rookie catcher with 155, blossomed into a solid handler of pitchers and provided the team some needed stability behind the plate. The Angels finished with a respectful 82-80 record and a fifth-place finish behind the Yankees, who narrowly edged the White Sox and the Orioles to capture their fifth straight pennant and 14th over the previous 16 years.

Chance's exploits on the mound in '64 drew inevitable comparisons to Sandy Koufax, who ruled the Southern California market in the early Sixties. The Angels believed they had someone in Chance who compared to the great lefty, and played it to the hilt. The L.A. press tried to turn the two into rivals, but Chance says any comparison of him to the Dodger great is ridiculous. "He was so much better than me, it was unreal. As far as pitching goes, there was no one even close to Sandy Koufax. ... He was just unhittable. He's the best ever—trust me," relates Chance.

Chance's unorthodox delivery actually was more like that of the Dodgers' other great hurler, Don Drysdale, than that of Koufax. During his windup, Dean would turn his back to the batter, then rear back with a wicked, fully extended motion. Chance maintains that the stress on his arm may have cost him a few years, but he has no regrets. "My delivery was a lot like Drysdale or Ewell Blackwell. We came from the side, which helped us; but it's also very, very hard on you."

Asked if Rigney overthrew him, Chance's answer is forthright. "Rig gave me the ball, and he had confidence in me. I'd pitch relief or start, it didn't matter. Nowadays, if they get a great arm, they want to preserve it. Back when I played, I didn't think about it. I just wanted the ball."

Along with his uncanny delivery, Chance's icy demeanor allowed him to unhinge the hitters' psyche. "Everybody was afraid of me. I don't see too well out of my left eye, and I had to fight to have control all the time. I was aware of what I was doing to these guys, and I used it to my advantage. My ball would sink when I threw it across the seams. It would really ride."

His combative nature combined with his hatred of losing made for a volatile personality. Eli Grba claims that Chance despised losing so much that he still broods over losses 40 years after the fact. "In early 1962, he came in as a reliever and blew a game for me that he's never let me forget," says Grba. "A few years go by, and the first thing out of his mouth is, 'You know Grubsi...' I tell him, 'Dean, don't talk about that game. It's ancient history.' He says, 'Yeah, but I had that son of a bitch, and he hit it to right field when I should have had him.' I say, 'Who cares? That's a hundred years ago.' ... He can't let it go. When he reminded me that he had 18 complete games one year, I almost fainted. He had hellacious stuff."

First baseman Lee Thomas echoes Grba's sentiments. "He would have cut your heart out if he could have got you out. He was mean, knew what he wanted to do, and he did it. He had a violent wind-up. After he threw the ball, he came across his body like a whip. He threw so hard I thought his arm was going to fall off. He had a heavy sinking fastball that just ate you up. Right-handed hitters were petrified of him."

Albie Pearson adds: "He was wild and mean, and it didn't matter if you were Mickey Mantle, Bill Skowron, or anybody else. You'd better be loose because Dean would knock your head off as soon as look at you. ...Nobody wanted to get near him. Outwardly they would never let it show. They are big leaguers, they all come out there with hoopla and say, 'Let's go for it, let's beat 'em today.' But down in their heart of hearts they're saying, 'You know what? I don't want to be here right now. I don't like this guy.' They would hit him on occasion, but in those few years with the Angels, 1962-'66, I can't remember anyone that [earned] any more respect on that mound than Dean Chance. He was one of the best pitchers I've ever seen in a short period of time."

Chance's free spirit and competitive nature could infuriate his teammates. Tom Satriano recalls one game where Dean's actions came back to hurt him: "I was catching for Dean on the mound in Detroit, and Norm Cash was up. I put down a curveball and Dean shakes me off. I signal for a fastball and he shakes me off. Then I put down the curveball and again he shakes me off. What's crazy is he only had two pitches! Finally, he throws a fastball, and Cash hits it over the moon and we lose the game. Next day in the paper, the big headline reads: 'CATCHER CALLS THE WRONG PITCH.' You should have heard Fregosi. I mean, you talk about standing up for somebody! He was right there behind me. He said to Chance, 'You stupid shit! You could have shaken your head one more time. Hell, you shook it enough! Don't blame Satriano! He didn't throw the pitch, you threw the pitch!' That was Dean..."

Satriano caught for both Chance and Belinsky, and claims they were polar opposites when it came to temperament and demeanor on the mound. "Bo didn't flaunt his off-the-field escapades at all. Not so with Dean. He was more verbose about it," says Satriano. "Bo was a team player, a player's player. Dean was more for Dean. But Dean just had amazing ability, while Bo had talent but tended to take it easy. I figured they traded Dean because he wasn't a team type of player."

Lee Thomas played two seasons with Chance and remembers him as a mixed bag—an intimidator one minute and a free spirit the next. In Palm Springs, he generally presented his kinder, gentler side. "Every spring training Dean brought his home-made ice cream-making machine and made ice cream for all of us," recalls Thomas. "Dean was a fun-loving guy and kind of goofy. I'd call him a flake, but a kind-hearted one."

Despite Chance's best efforts, the Angels' woes continued. In 1965, their hitting was once again dismal. The team went 75-87 for the season and finished in seventh place. The only bright spots were the continued excellence of Fregosi, then coming into his own as a perennial All-Star, and Knoop, who continued his brilliant glove work in the field. Chance was still a respectable 15-10, with a 3.15 ERA.

As the Angels kept losing, the crowds diminished. There were times when weeknight crowds at Chavez Ravine were less than 3,000 people. Chance was growing tired of pitching his guts out only to lose by a run. One afternoon he was so disgusted after a loss to the Yankees that he blew out of the clubhouse. It wasn't until he was on the freeway that he realized he had forgotten something back at the ballpark.

"I had a no-hitter going into the eighth inning," recalls Chance. "Bobby Richardson was the hitter; two outs, runners on second and third. I shook Rodgers off twice. I wanted to throw a slider, and the little shit Richardson hit a little dinky line drive on the chalk line for a double. I lose the no-hitter and the game, 2-1. I was so damned mad I left early, got in the car, and headed for home. I drove for a while before I realized I had left my wife and son at the ballpark."

Autry had decided in 1963 that there was no way he would renew the club's option to play at Chavez Ravine. He had studied possible sites, with Long Beach and Anaheim most often mentioned as the Angels' likely new home. Long Beach was considered the front runner until city officials insisted that the team be called the Long Beach Angels. Autry knew that mouthful would be a publicist's nightmare, and with the quiet support of Mayor Rex Coons he began to lean toward Anaheim. Orange County was one of the fastest growing counties in the United States and had huge potential. Only 45 minutes from downtown Los Angeles, Autry felt Anaheim would be perfectly suited for major league baseball. Long-term growth forecasts were favorable, and its proximity to Los Angeles guaranteed a huge fan base. On March 10, 1964, the Angels and the City of Anaheim unofficially joined forces. A few weeks later, county supervisors voted to finance the stadium and formalized the deal.

In August of '64, Chance and an Angels photographer drifted down to the proposed site in Anaheim to take a few publicity photos. Gazing at the endless rows of alfalfa and citrus trees, it was hard for the pitcher to visualize a world-class ballpark there. The site was tranquil and rural, with tall eucalyptus trees acting as windbreaks and an occasional horse prancing into view. To the ace pitcher, it was more like Ohio, and certainly a far cry from Chavez Ravine.

On August 31, wearing hard hats and holding shovels whose handles were made out of baseball bats, Autry, Anaheim mayor Frank Paulson, and developer Del Webb broke ground for the new park. Autry was beaming his best singing cowboy smile, as this marked his first step toward true independence. The deal included a 35-year lease and called for the team to be renamed the California Angels. Since Anaheim Stadium would be municipally owned, it would serve as a multipurpose facility— something that would eventually come back to haunt the team.

Right after the ceremony, a platoon of earthmovers began leveling the vegetation, and within weeks the outline of the stadium and its giant parking lot took form. Webb, who had backed Autry at the 1960 winter meetings when the deal for the team was approved, received his just reward. Not only was he commissioned to build the new $24 million structure, he was also hired to construct the new Anaheim Convention Center across from Disneyland about a mile away.

The stadium was finished in two years, and when it opened in the spring of 1966, it was considered one of the finest facilities in baseball. Unlike Dodger Stadium, the seats were close to the action. Fan friendly and safe, it was a comfortable place to watch a game. On days when the smog was sparse, magnificent vistas of the Saddleback Mountains were visible beyond the outfield. A giant A-shaped scoreboard was placed in left field and the looming structure soon became a landmark. Players and fans alike loved "The Big A," considered the stadium's focal point.

On April 9, 1966, Chance became the first Angels pitcher to take the mound at the team's new home. "I threw the first pitch ever in Anaheim Stadium," recalls Chance. "We played the Giants in an exhibition game. Hal Lanier was the hitter. Emmett Ashford was the umpire, and he gave it the big strike. Before the game, Walt Disney put on a big show. It was a tremendous day."

Ten days later, the White Sox spoiled the real home opener by beating the Angels 3-1. Angels regular-season leftfielder Rick Reichardt—who had already made history months earlier when he signed with the Angels for an unprecedented $200,000 bonus—hit the first home run in Anaheim Stadium. He was the last of the big "bonus babies," as one year later baseball instituted the amateur draft.

Chance played out the year at the new ballpark, but to him it wasn't the same as Chavez Ravine. Anaheim held none of the glory that Los Angeles did, especially now that Belinsky's time with the team was history. Chance went 12-17 in 1966, posting a solid 3.08 ERA in a team-best 259 2/3 innings, but weak hitting yet again made for a long season. The team finished sixth, two games under .500. But on the bright side, attendance jumped from 500,000 the year before to the magical one-million mark. Autry had been correct: Orange County was indeed hungry for baseball.

With the Angels desperate for hitting, Chance became expendable. In December, Haney dealt him to the Minnesota Twins for outfielder Jimmie Hall, first baseman Don Mincher, and relief pitcher Pete Cimino. Chance thought going to the Twins was a blessing in disguise. He desperately wanted to play for a winner, and with sluggers like Bob Allison, Harmon Killebrew, Tony Oliva, and a sensational rookie named Rod Carew, the Twins promised to be a contender. Asked about the trade almost four decades later, Chance replies, "Hell, I was happy! I hated to lose. I only won 12 games in '66, and [the Angels] couldn't score any runs."

With the departure of Chance, the Belinsky era officially ended. And with Pearson retiring, the only players left from 1961 were Rodgers, Fregosi, Satriano, and pitcher Fred Newman. The times were indeed a-changin'.

The trade was in fact a shot in the arm for Chance, still a relative young pup at 26 years old. He was simply spectacular in 1967, going 20-14 with a 2.73 ERA. He tossed his first no-hitter that season to boot. Chance was named the American League Comeback Player of the Year.

The Angels were competitive as well—coming in fifth, only eight games off the pace—to break their string of losing seasons. And again the team drew well over a million fans out to the park. Mincher provided some much-needed pop in the middle of the order, hitting 25 home runs and driving in 76 runs, both team highs.

The Twins were among four teams in a race for the pennant. On the last day of the season, Chance had a shot at helping the Twins snatch the flag. Minnesota was tied for first with Boston, and the winner was going to the playoffs. However, making his third start in 12 days, Chance and the Twins were defeated, 5-3. The Twins' defeat, combined with the Angels' win over Detroit in the second game of a doubleheader that day, enabled Boston to win the pennant by one game.

Chance was named *The Sporting News* American League right-handed pitcher of the decade for the Sixties. Brace Photo

Anaheim was chosen to host the 1967 All-Star game, and Chance, making his second appearance in the mid-summer classic, got the call to start. The game was the longest in All-Star history—lasting 15 innings—and was finally won by the National League on a dramatic home run by Cincinnati's Tony Perez.

Chance played two more seasons in Minnesota, but the wear and tear on his arm from pitching so many innings with his unorthodox delivery took a toll. He posted a 16-16 record in 1968 with a fine 2.53 ERA, but then struggled to remain healthy in 1969 as the Twins won the AL West. After brief stints with the Indians and Mets in 1970, he closed out his 11-year career with the Detroit Tigers in 1971.

Compared to other pitchers of his stature, Chance's career was short but memorable. In an era loaded with great right-handers like Juan Marichal, Bob Gibson, Drysdale, and Gaylord Perry, Chance more than held his own. *The Sporting News* agreed, naming him the top AL right-handed pitcher of the Sixties. Years later, his '64 season still remains a high-water mark. He and Bartolo Colon are the only

Angels to ever win a Cy Young Award. Along with Nolan Ryan, Chance is considered the greatest pitcher in Angels history.

Chance was only 30 years old when he retired, but today he considers himself lucky to have lasted as long as he did. "I guess we should all have taken better care of ourselves," says Chance. "But when I look back, I feel I'm just luckier than the devil to get my required 10 years in the big leagues and get the maximum on the pension."

Following his baseball career, Chance ran carnivals and state fairs until embarking on a career as a boxing manager. He managed anvil-fisted heavyweight contender Earnie Shavers before he lost him to a slick-talking newcomer in the boxing world named Don King. A couple decades later, Chance became president of a boxing sanctioning body called the International Boxing Association (IBA), a position he holds today.

As IBA president, Chance has worked closely with and against some of the biggest names in boxing, including King and Bob Arum. "They're very shrewd businessmen," Chance says of the two promotional icons. "If you'd play them in cards, they'd want you to play with their deck and their rules. So that's why I hardly do anything with either of them. As long as you don't deal with 'em, you get along great with 'em."

Chance enjoys the fight game and has been involved with several notable promotions, including what Chance considers his crowning achievement: the 2001 Oscar De La Hoya vs. Shane Mosley championship bout. When he isn't busy promoting fights across the globe, Chance operates the family farm in Ohio. Chance and his 81-year-old mother, known as "Mama" Chance, still live on the family farm in Wooster. Somehow, he also makes time for his true passion, professional gin. On the card circuit, he is considered a world-class player.

But for all his post-baseball accomplishments, Chance will forever be linked to the Angels and his former sidekick, Bo Belinsky.

Noted Bob Case, "Throughout Bo's trials and tribulations, Chance always stood by him. They talked to each other daily and would have died for each other. ... After baseball, Dean negotiated all of Bo's deals, and when Bo got sick it was Dean who took care of Bo until his death."

Chance valued his friendship with Belinsky and treasures the memories of their time together far more than his pitching accomplishments. "The last time I saw Bo we had a big party at our place out in Las Vegas for him. God, he didn't look well. I don't know if it was the cancer or them unfiltered cigarettes. ... But Bo really did have some good friends who really cared for him, and they all showed up in Las Vegas. The whole town adopted Bo. ... He's buried in Vegas in a beautiful cemetery. And he went out on the high side. He turned to religion."

And now, as he enters his sixth decade on earth, Chance has opened himself up to God as well. "Everybody, by the time they're 50, they're selfish as hell," states

Chance. "Everybody thinks only of himself or herself. Then, when they hit 60, they want to turn to religion and want to forgive everybody. They want to go to heaven, and that's the stage I'm in."

Chance looks back on his baseball days with genuine pride. He has been offered thousands for his Cy Young trophy but claims he doesn't need the money. A shrewd investor, Chance has done all right for himself.

"The smartest thing I ever did was buy real estate," says Chance. "Hell, I lost my ass in boxing in the beginning, then I had a friend of mine who had a big poster company where I worked for a while. I was in carnival amusements for a while and had trucks and units playing all over Canada and the United States. I did that for 17 years, and that is really work. But I always kept all my land.

"I've got great memories from baseball and from my carnival days. From the boxing I made a lot of friends. Hell, you never know who you're going to run into. A few years ago I was at Vegas at a fight and this old guy come up to me. 'Dean, you remember me?' Christ, it was [former *L.A. Times* sportswriter] Jim Murray, the greatest writer ever, more talent then anyone. But I'm at the stage now where I'm too old to make new friends. I just do the best [I can] to keep the ones I have."

When Belinsky died, it was Chance who arranged the memorial service at Dodger Stadium. He also handled arrangements for his burial in Las Vegas. For the last three decades of Belinsky's life, Chance continuously watched out for his friend and made sure Bo never fell too hard. Every time Chance got an offer to appear at an autograph show, his acceptance came with one condition: "I don't do a card show unless Bo Belinsky comes, too." Chance never told anyone, but he always passed his portion of the take on to Bo.

He figures that Bo would have done the same for him. Chance recalls the night they were heading home from the Coconut Grove when Belinsky and his date got into a fight and she ended up screaming loud enough for somebody to call the cops. Chance was married at the time, and before the Beverly Hills men in blue arrived on the scene, Bo insisted that he take off so that he wouldn't share the headline in newspapers or the wrath of the Angels management.

"Just before the cops showed up, I ran off and hid in the bushes and my name never showed up in the police reports," Chance said. "We had a couple broads with us in the car; my wife never found out because Bo covered my ass.

"Now *that's* a true friend!"

More than anything, it's the friendships—the unique characters fused together to make a team—that best characterize the early Angels teams. They weren't the best performers in Angels history, but some four-plus decades later, it's certain that they were among the most memorable.

PART TWO

8

TRUEST ANGEL

JIM FREGOSI

*H*e seems to be everywhere, shouting encouragement and overseeing the four-diamond baseball complex with the quiet authority of a respected general. "Skeeter! What's the score on field four?" he shouts. "Hud! Make sure everyone hits!" His tone is firm but light, and conveys the sense of a man totally at ease and in his element.

It's been 44 years since No. 11, Jim Fregosi, donned his first Angels jersey. It's been 26 years since he managed the club to its first divisional championship, and 12 years since his Phillies lost Game 7 of the 1993 World Series. Currently he's in charge of a fantasy baseball camp, where adults go to get a taste for life as big leaguers. It doesn't matter to him that none of the 50 or so players he's in charge of are major leaguers. To him they're ballplayers, not just fantasy campers. "They're taking it serious," Fregosi says, "and dammit, so will I!"

Known around the fantasy camp as "The Commissioner," Fregosi, who serves as a special assignment scout for the Atlanta Braves during the season, is both commandant and counselor at the same time. His "field officers" include ex-Angels Bobby Knoop, Clyde Wright, Buck Rodgers, Roger Repoz, and Rex Hudler, all of whom report to him. The mood of the camp is positive, with lots of jocular humor. On the surface, it appears as if the steely seriousness and occasional arrogance that have been Fregosi's calling cards are missing in action.

Fregosi is engaged in a friendly conversation with Brian Downing, a Fregosi favorite when he managed the Angels in the late Seventies. Fregosi was in the middle of an interview with a young writer when Downing arrived at camp. When Fregosi saw his former star, he bolted from the cart in mid-sentence, leaving the poor writer holding his microphone in the wind. As the two converse about old times, Fregosi intermittently shouts an order or word of encouragement to a fantasy camper. After several minutes, the conversation subsides and Downing goes over to say hello to Bobby Grich, who is watching the action over on field two.

Fregosi is momentarily alone, and the young writer, hoping to complete the interview, makes his move. "Hey, Jim! When do you want to finish? Is now a good time?"

Fregosi turns like a lion on a deer and fixes the writer with a glare that could freeze a polar bear. He blares in a voice that has the same effect as a Dean Chance fastball to the ribs: "What? You think I got all day? You don't have enough? You're not gonna stir up a lot of shit are you?" The embarrassed writer briefly considers driving away to search for the nearest cliff to jump off of, but then bravely presses on. "Just a few more minutes, Jim. You're important to the book." A few painful seconds pass, and Fregosi relents. After straightening his cap he thrusts his thumbs back in his waistband and marches back to the golf cart.

Seated again, he throws on his sunglasses and sits back behind the wheel like nothing has happened. "What," asks the writer gingerly, "was your biggest thrill?" Fregosi sighs, leans back in the seat and gets a faraway look in his eyes. "When we won our first divisional championship in '79. I'll never forget Gene's eyes when I saw him after the game. ..."

"Yes We Can! Yes We Can! Yes We Can!" The cheer from the stands shook Anaheim stadium to its foundation.

Jim Fregosi looked on in awe at the scene unfolding before him. The California Angels were one out away from their first divisional championship, and the crowd was going ballistic, anxiously creeping closer to the rails in anticipation of charging the field after the final out. Fregosi's thoughts drifted back to countless Angels who had preceded him. He realized that this moment was not just special for him, but for many others as well.

As their manager in 1979, he had taken the Angels further than the franchise had ever gone before. Now, on September 25, 1979, the Angels were about to realize an accomplishment 19 seasons in the making. When the Kansas City Royals' Darrell Porter hit a slow roller to Rod Carew at first to end the game, the crowd erupted from the stands. Fregosi was swept along with them to the pile of celebrating players and coaches forming on the first base side of the infield.

As the players fled to the safety of the clubhouse, Fregosi spotted Gene Autry and his special guest, former President Richard Nixon, waiting at the doorway to congratulate him. The two embraced and Fregosi beamed with pride as Autry made the congratulatory rounds around the clubhouse. When shortstop Jimmy Anderson poured a beer over Nixon's head, Fregosi didn't know who looked more shocked, Nixon or the Secret Service man assigned to protect the ex-Commander-in-Chief.

"To see Gene Autry's face after winning, and to finally get the black cloud out from over our organization, was a special moment," says Fregosi years later about that magical night. "Gene was just so excited. It was the first time he ever won anything in all the years he had the ballclub. For him to finally win was a special moment for him and for all the people who had been with that organization since the beginning."

The celebration eventually subsided and Fregosi finally got a moment alone with Autry. As he hung his champagne-soaked jersey over his chair, he thought of some of the others with whom he would have loved to have shared this moment: guys like Fred Haney, Tommy Ferguson, Bob Reynolds, Lee Thomas, Bobby Knoop, and Buck Rodgers. Fregosi smiled and shook his head. Then he grabbed a beer and made a quiet toast to those who came before.

The skinny kid at shortstop gives a defiant look over toward the fungo circle. His intense glare is partially hidden by the sweat-stained cap that covers his neat crewcut. Coach Joe Gordon slaps a sharp grounder to the kid's right. With the grace of a seasoned veteran, the kid glides over to it with ease. Scooping up the ball in one fluid motion, he locks in on his target, sets himself, and fires. The ball sails five feet over the outstretched first baseman's reach. "Heads up!" someone shouts as the ball careens off the top of the dugout rail and ricochets back on the field, scattering players and barely missing the trainer.

Gordon turns to the young shortstop, shouting, "Over the top! Over the top!" Then, shaking his head, Gordon announces to manager Bill Rigney, standing behind the batting cage: "The kid's gonna kill all our season ticket holders!"

This is what spring training is all about: a chance for rookies to prove their mettle, to show off their talent, to fight for a roster spot. On the expansion Angels in 1962, spring training took on a whole new meaning, though; without the benefit of an established roster or a lineage of veterans, the possibilities were limitless for a young kid with talent.

Wearing a pair of baggy flannel pants that appear two sizes too big for his frame, the kid wipes the sweat off his brow and opens his mouth, as if about to say something. But instead he keeps his mouth shut and readies himself in a crouch, awaiting the next ball off Gordon's fungo.

Joe Gordon chuckles. He has seen a lot in his 40-plus years in the game, having come up to the majors with the Yankees in 1938—just in time to watch Lou Gehrig's career end and Joe DiMaggio's career begin. A former MVP and veteran of 11 World Series, Gordon knows a real ballplayer when he sees one, and he knows this kid Fregosi is a keeper. He also knows the best athletes usually end up in center field.

"He's a natural, Rig!" shouts Gordon. "Got centerfielder written all over him, I don't know why the hell we have him at short. He runs like a gazelle! He should be in the outfield."

Leaning on the batting cage, Rigney impassively glances over at short before speaking: "My mind's made up, Joe. Besides, I got Pearson in center. I don't need another outfielder. I need infielders. Let's see if the kid can handle short. At least give him a shot."

Gordon shakes his head, and glances over at Fregosi. "The kid can't weigh more than one-fifty." Preparing to hit another grounder, Gordon smiles once more. "C'mon kid! You're okay! Over the top now, over the top."

Fregosi eventually got his throws down and became the starting shortstop on the '62 Angels. For the next nine years, the Angels never had to question who was playing shortstop. Fregosi dominated not only the position but the franchise as well. A six-time All-Star, he became the Angels' first proven leader, and as the team went through its growing pains, Fregosi was synonymous with the Angels and vice-versa. Journalist Ross Newhan said it best: "He, along with [Dean] Chance, gave the Angels an identity and national presence in the days when the team sorely lacked one."

"I can still remember him coming up from Dallas-Fort Worth," recalls pitcher Eli Grba. "He was trying to put on an air that said, 'I can play here,' but inside he was just as scared as the rest of us. I saw ability, but I saw something else that really set him apart. I saw a fire in his belly."

According to Grba, that fire—sometimes uncontrollable—was what set Fregosi apart. In the late Sixties, Rod Carew, then with the Twins, slid into second trying to break up a double play and in the process inadvertently cut open the leg of Fregosi's pal, second baseman Bobby Knoop, with his spikes. "A hundred dollars to anyone who takes Carew out," an incensed Fregosi announced to his teammates.

Of course, no one took it seriously, but the incident is still telling. To Fregosi, baseball was a war, an eye-for-an-eye proposition. Even years later when he managed Carew, Fregosi still held a grudge over what happened to Knoop. "We never really got along," acknowledges Carew. "I don't think he ever really forgot."

Born James Louis Fregosi in San Francisco on May 4, 1942, this future firebrand was first exposed to baseball by his sports-minded father, whose grocery store sponsored a local baseball team. "My father was a great athlete who had to go to work and never had the opportunity to play sports," Fregosi says. "He used to tell everybody, 'I want this kid to work in the store, and he wants to go play ball all the time.'

"My role models were the typical West Coast stars of the day, but my dad probably had the biggest impact. I was a big fan of the [Pacific] Coast League at that time, and of course Joe DiMaggio was always a big hero; but it was my dad, a gifted athlete himself, who instilled in me the gifts and the work ethic to be competitive. That's where I got it from."

Fregosi likes to tell about what happened at his dad's wake, when "an old Italian guy from South San Francisco walked in the funeral home, came down the aisle, and leaned over and kissed my dad on the forehead in the coffin. Then this old guy came over, looked at me and said, 'You couldn't have made a pimple on

In the Angels' early years, it was Jim Fregosi who led the team both on and off the field. Brace Photo

your father's ass as a ballplayer!' Then he walked down the aisle and out of the place without another word."

Outside opinions aside, Jimmy excelled in several sports as a youth, and by his freshman year of high school was primed to become one of the Bay area's premier athletes. "Some really fantastic athletes through the years have gone to Sierra High School in San Mateo," he recounts. "John Robinson, Lynn Swann, Barry Bonds, and Tom Brady. I mean, you're talking about some great competitors. I was fortunate enough to have had the opportunity to play four sports: basketball, football, baseball, and track. I had numerous scholarship offers in football, and several scouts were interested in me for baseball. Back then, if you signed a pro contract you couldn't play any other sports, that was it. If I had one thing that I would probably change it's that I would go to college and get a college education; but I had an opportunity to sign with the Boston Red Sox and I took it."

San Francisco Giants GM Chub Feeney heard about Fregosi and informed his friend Bill Rigney prior to the expansion draft in 1960 about this "can't-miss kid" from South San Francisco. Haney nabbed him in the draft and assigned the youngster to Dallas-Ft. Worth, where, along with Buck Rodgers and Dean Chance, Fregosi was fast-tracked for the big club. Chance remembers Fregosi's big break.

"Fregosi, Rodgers, Bob Sprout, Chuck Tanner, and I got called up after the '61 season was over in Dallas," says Chance. "In '62 we all went to spring training and

Fregosi's arm was kind of erratic, so they decided to send him back to Triple-A for more seasoning. Meanwhile, we had a series with the Yankees, and Joe Koppe slid into home plate. Yogi Berra's shin guards hit Koppe right in the nuts, and the poor bastsard could hardly walk. He had to walk bowlegged. So they called Fregosi up, and he was our shortstop from then on."

Fregosi hit .291 in 58 games in 1962 and .287 the following year. But his greatest contribution didn't show up in the statistics. Prior to 1963, the Angels had no single player the team could really rally around. Pearson and Wagner were leaders, sure, but they lacked the kind of charisma and take-charge attitude that the young shortstop possessed in spades. Like moths drawn to light, players—particularly the younger ones—gravitated toward this charismatic, productive infielder.

"We were both scared rookies when I first met Fregosi in '61," recalls Tom Satriano. "I didn't see him again until 1963, and I couldn't believe the transition. He had become the backbone of the team. If there were any problems, Jimmy was the guy who would handle them. He would help guys who were in slumps, and if you weren't hustling, you had to deal with him. If we'd see a hole in the defense or pick up the pitcher's signs, Jimmy would gather everybody around and say, 'C'mon gang! The catcher's tipping off the signs! If anybody gets on second base, here's what you do.' … Whenever he ran, he'd always take the extra base. If he was in a slump, he'd run even harder, which in turn made us play harder."

Fregosi—whom Lee Thomas says "played like a kamikaze"—says he was merely filling a leadership void. "When you have a little success as a player like I did, your confidence level changes, and you begin to see what a team needs," says Fregosi. "The difference was I took such great pride in the organization that I wanted to do something to make it successful. I knew I had to take some leadership role because of the fact that there weren't any other players there who could do the job. I was an original Angel, and I was one of the first young players to really play well enough to have some leadership ability on the club. You lead by example, and I always played hard. The team saw I cared more about winning than about the individuality of the game, and players will generally gravitate toward that kind of player."

Albie Pearson agrees: "He and Dean Chance were the ones that we built upon. When the chips were down and we needed a clutch play in the field, Jimmy would come up with it. Jimmy had ability, and his teammates loved him."

Fregosi became the face of the young Angels, and because of his attributes a bond emerged between him and the team manager and owner. Autry and Rigney looked to him like a son, and Fregosi responded accordingly. He and Buck Rodgers dissected Rigney's every move and absorbed him like a sponge. It is no coincidence that both would later become successful managers in their own right.

"Rigney would go out of his way to take Jimmy and me off to the side to explain why he did things," Rodgers recalls. "He said, 'Listen to me, because someday you guys are going to manage.' We're just 25, 26 years old, and he's telling us we were going to be managers some day. I said, 'Well, boy, I hope you're right.'"

Fregosi recalls his Angels experience fondly. "Bill Rigney taught us how the game operates, but he also taught us a love of the game that never left. We grew up in that organization, and a lot of us stayed in the game for a long, long time, and that was because we appreciated the lifestyle and what the game gave to us. It was such a great atmosphere. Everybody who ever played in the Angels organization had a special feeling for it. Everybody was treated great there. When they moved to Anaheim, Buck Rodgers, Bobby Knoop, and I used to sell season tickets during the offseason, and we went to numerous events to represent the ball club. The end result was something that was put together as a family."

In the early 1960s, camaraderie amongst teammates was much more valued than it is today, and it wasn't unusual for players to have a few beers after the game and discuss baseball deep into the night. Fregosi joined a group of like-minded players that included Rodgers, Lee Thomas, and Knoop. They became inseparable, and came to be known not only for their hard style of play, but for their legendary off-the-field antics, as well.

Knoop was a particular favorite of Fregosi. He joined the team in 1964, and immediately hit it off with Fregosi. "Friendship is when two guys can sit in a room and not feel compelled to say anything for three or four hours," Knoop says. "[Jim and I] were very much different, but great friends nonetheless."

Brought from the Milwaukee organization by farm director Roland Hemond in 1963, Knoop possessed defensive skills that were second to none. After struggling to start the 1964 season, Knoop came around eventually, earning his keep with his glove work. He and Fregosi began turning double plays with remarkable consistency. From 1964-'68, they led the league in double plays. A three-time Gold Glover, Knoop encouraged Fregosi to rise to a higher level.

"Knoop was a prince of a gentleman, absolutely admired by everybody," recalls Satriano, a fellow infielder. "He was very intelligent and an absolute magician at second base. He had at least one or two phenomenal plays every game. It was remarkable how many times he did it."

Rodgers was another integral part of the Angels as the Sixties progressed. He came in through the expansion draft and became the starting catcher in 1962, a role he would hold for several more seasons.

"He would play hurt more than anybody I know," Satriano says of Rodgers. "His hands were a real mess. His fingers went in all different directions. He used a glove that had a little pocket, and since he caught everything with two hands they were constantly being hit. They were splintered and split and looked like they came out of a meat grinder. I remember one time seeing him coming out of the trainers' room and he could hardly hold his hand. With this concerned look on his face, Rigney said, 'Buck, can you make it?' And Buck answered, 'Sure, Rig, I can play.' He never bitched once.

"The three of them—Knoop, Fregosi, and Rodgers—were inseparable. Those three guys were the backbone, the team leaders. Nobody said a bad word about any of them."

Gene Autry, center, stands with two of his favorites: Jim Fregosi, left, and Bobby Knoop, right. Courtesy of the Angels

Traveling secretary Tom Ferguson says that Fregosi was invaluable off the field as well. In the summer of '66 the Angels landed in Chicago in the middle of a heat wave. Upon boarding their bus the team realized that there was neither a driver nor air conditioning, and with the temperature busting across the century mark, Ferguson knew he had to find the driver fast before all hell broke loose. Figuring there are only two places the driver could be—getting a cup of coffee or in the men's room—Fergie took off in a frantic search.

"I'm charging through the United terminal going from bathroom to bathroom shouting, 'Hey bussie! Angel bus driver! Are you in here?'" recalls Ferguson.

He eventually located the driver and escorted him back to the bus, but before entering the bus he paused just outside to tie his shoelace.

"No one could see us," recalls Ferguson, "and I hear Fregosi in the back [of the bus] say, 'Sit the hell down, Reichardt! Fergie's looking for the driver right now! I'll let you know what he wants us to do.'

"I wondered what the hell that was all about, and when I asked him later, Jimmy said, 'The S.O.B. Reichardt wanted to get a cab and go in alone. I told him to sit the hell down.' Jimmy knew if Reichardt left the bus, everyone else would have followed.

I would have had 20 guys all wanting cabs and expecting the club to pay their fare. Management would have been all over me! We were on a budget, for Chrissakes!"

"From that day forward, I knew I would have no problems with anybody 'cause I had Jimmy behind me. He had a quiet authority. If you had a problem in the clubhouse in those days you talked it over with Jimmy and he'd get it straightened out."

Fregosi had things straightened out on the field, too—at least for himself. From 1964-'70, Fregosi was the premier shortstop in the American League. At 6'2", 190 pounds, he had surprising speed and agility. While he wasn't a basestealer, he was one of the fastest in baseball going from first to third. He consistently hit around .270 and even picked up a Gold Glove in 1967.

"When I first came to the big leagues, I had a reputation as a good fielder who couldn't hit," he says. "But as I got a little bit older and stronger and became familiar with the pitchers, I became a very good offensive player. There weren't many shortstops back then who hit second and third in the lineup who were counted on to drive in runs and help win games offensively."

Fregosi was aggressive off the field as well. His philosophy was firmly rooted in the early Sixties Angels tradition of hard play and hard partying, and it seemed that as Fregosi's batting average grew, so did his penchant for the nightlife.

"When I came up," recalls Albie Pearson, "Fregosi looked to me with respect and as a mentor. But as he got further into his career and became a very successful player, I believe our perspective on things outside the ballpark changed and didn't make us as close as some of the other players. Jim played hard. He was a leader and he was a wild hair, yet when I say that I don't mean it in a negative way. He just lived and played hard, and that's the way he is."

Eli Grba believes Fregosi's off-the-field antics were an offshoot of his enormous energy and confidence. "No doubt about it, he had a swagger about him," says Grba. "He could be classy and charming, and with his Italian good looks he became a target for the ladies. … He had to wait a couple years to catch up with the rest of the club as we had a few years on him. But when he caught up he surpassed us by leaps and bounds. He was too handsome, in fact, and if you were trying to hustle a broad in a bar and Jim would come in, you'd take a hike, because the gal would focus on Fregosi."

Some found Fregosi's boundless self-confidence offensive, but for the most part players appreciated him.

"He could be arrogant and cocky, but not to the point where he was irascible," says Grba. But to play in the big leagues at 19 or 20 like he did, you had to have some pizzazz! As his career progressed, he became a student of hitting, and after a while his winning [ways] overtook a lot of his shortcomings."

In 1967, Fregosi hit .290 and helped lead the Angels during one of the closest pennant races in history. Into August, the Angels were in the thick of things. Heading into a key seven-game stretch against the Twins and the Red Sox, the Angels were just one and a half games out of first place. The Angels dropped all seven games to send them spiraling backward to a six-and-a-half-game deficit in

A six-time All-Star, Fregosi had a "fire in his belly" according to teammate Eli Grba. Courtesy of the Angels

the standings. The team never fully recovered from that spell, finishing the season in fifth place, seven and a half games behind the Red Sox.

The next season, the Angels went back to being forgettable. They finished eighth, causing some disgruntled shareholders to sell their shares of the club to the Signal Corporation. The transaction left Autry and Reynolds with a controlling interest of 51 percent of the club, but the new board, intent on turning around a losing tradition, insisted on changes. In December of 1968, Autry reluctantly dismissed long-time friend Fred Haney as general manager. Haney was 70 then, and age may have been a factor in Autry's decision. But many felt Haney was part of a bigger problem that festered in the organization: a fixation on competing with the Dodgers.

The choice for new general manager, oddly enough, was a former Dodger vice president who had served as O'Malley's hatchet man during the period the Angels served as tenants in the Dodger ballpark. Dick Walsh, a former Marine, had been partly responsible for the miserable conditions the Angels endured then. Evidently, Autry and Reynolds believed his hard-nosed approach was what the team needed, and they awarded him a four-year contract.

Autry discovered too late that the decision was a poor one. Walsh lacked people skills, and his strong-arm tactics that worked with the Dodgers totally backfired with the Angels. "I think Walsh's brief tenure was something of a reign of terror," says Ross Newhan. "Players called him 'The Smiling Python.' He wrote letters to wives claiming that players were fooling around on them. Players hated him, and they were scared of what he might do. It was pretty grim."

When the club got off to an 11-28 start in 1969, Walsh fired Rigney, replacing him with his best friend, Lefty Phillips. "He miscast [Phillips] as the manager when Lefty should have been his front office advisor on player personnel and acquisitions," says Newhan. "Lefty was a great scout, and people respected his baseball knowledge and ability, but he didn't have the magnetism or the personality to lead a team on the field. Their relationship eventually imploded."

Walsh showed Rigney the door on the heels of an 0-10 road trip. Walsh's reasoning was that the club needed a change, but many felt that Walsh just wanted his own man, Phillips, at the helm. Rigney was promptly hired by Minnesota, and he didn't disappoint. The Twins won the division the next two years, and had a hand in knocking the Angels out of the pennant race in 1970.

Fregosi saw the direction the club was going and instinctively knew it was wrong, but as a player he didn't feel it was his place to discuss it. "We kept bringing people from the Dodger organization into the Angels, and it never solved any problems," relates Fregosi. "It's easy to look back and second-guess now, but we couldn't compete with the Dodgers. They were the first club out here and very successful. As an expansion club it was almost impossible to compete with them. We felt we had to do some things to get the recognition that we were a good baseball team in our own right, rather then playing in competition with the Dodgers. We needed to build our own tradition. Moving to Anaheim helped a little bit, and so did winning our first divisional championship in 1979. We built on that by winning again in the Eighties, and the end result was that the Angels now have won a world championship and that gives them the background and tradition to build from there."

But that championship was still some years down the road in 1969. In the meantime, mismanagement dominated the Angels' executive landscape. Newhan saw it all first-hand and believes the problems were twofold.

"A couple of things occurred early on that hurt the franchise for many years," says Newhan. "One was that Autry and his initial group of investors took out some of their money instead of leaving it alone or putting more in and taking advantage the wealth of free agent talent that flourished in Southern California. Also, the success of 1962 hurt to an extent in the context they thought they were a little better than they were, and they didn't make moves that they should have made.

"The Angels missed a golden opportunity to build the team during the seven or eight years before the free agent draft. They could have swept Southern California, and being a young team had several opportunities for young players. When you look back on that era, nobody came out of it. Tom Satriano came out of USC, and for several years that was it. I think there was not enough money put in that direction. I fault Fred a little because there wasn't a commitment to scouting and finances for new players. Roland Hemond had to go to Haney in tears and beg for money to sign Rick Reichardt. I think Fred Haney had a lot of his cronies on the scouting staff, guys who didn't have the energy and foresight. I have great appreciation for Fred's career, but I think that was a mistake.

The second problem was that the Dodgers' slew of pennants and world championships intimidated the Angels to the point where important executive decisions were often influenced because of them. Newhan seconds Fregosi's notion that the Angels suffered from an inferiority complex where the big, bad Dodgers were concerned. "No matter what they did, the Angels were always in the Dodgers' shadow. Always," states Newhan. "The Dodgers were the established team in L.A. They were the ones the fans and all the press were interested in, and rightfully so 'cause they had been there since '58 and had earned a following. The Angels never really had the respect from the fans or the press. The Angels were always on the second or third page, while the Dodgers were always on the front page. It was tough. I don't think we ever got equal billing at all until the World Series."

"Redheaded stepchildren, that's what we were," agrees Knoop. "We were second-class citizens when we were in L.A. Obviously the Dodgers owned L.A., and we were tenants. And that's the way tenants are treated. That didn't change until we moved to Anaheim, got a new park, and began to get our own identity."

According to Buzzie Bavasi, who was general manager of the Dodgers at the time, it was owner Walter O'Malley who was responsible for the difficulties.

"Walter didn't want the Angels at all. When they played in Dodger Stadium the rent was terrible, so high that Walter had to at least be semi-guilty. Gene Autry got no money for concessions or parking, and he had to pay for the clean-up. I don't know how Gene did it. It was unbelievable. The Angels were only drawing 900,000 [fans a season] and we were drawing two million, but Autry was still paying half of it. And you know why he finally moved? The Dodgers charged him $350 dollars for washing the windows in his office, and they had no windows! The office was underneath the stands, and O'Malley charged him $350 anyway. So Gene finally said, 'The hell with you!' That was absolutely the turning point.

"... The people on the baseball end of the operation liked the Angels, but Walter didn't. I think Gene's favorite speech at luncheons went, 'There was nothing Walter wouldn't do for me and there's nothing I wouldn't do for Walter.' And that's exactly what they did for each other—nothing! They were different characters. Gene was a baseball fan—he just loved the game. Walter was just the opposite. Walter was in for just one reason—financial."

Bavasi, too, believes that Autry was chasing phantoms trying to compete with the Dodgers. The Angels' real competition, he says, never even threw a baseball.

"It wasn't the Dodgers, it was Vin Scully! Scully was the most valuable man the Dodgers had. Because that's where the money was—in radio and television. I've always maintained this, even when I was there. They always thought the Dodgers were their competition. They were wrong. It was Scully."

Haney and Rigney were among the first of the old guard to go in 1969, but not the last. Also dismissed was fan favorite and four-time Angels "Owner Award" winner Bobby Knoop. The Gold Glover was traded to the Chicago White Sox in mid-May for second baseman Sandy Alomar and reliever Bob Priddy. Although Alomar proved to be an asset down the road, the loss of Knoop left longtime Angels fans feeling empty. The old guard was leaving fast, and Fregosi seemed to be the only survivor.

The Angels played .500 ball from June through September in 1969 and ended up in third despite just 71 wins. During the 1969 offseason, the facelift continued, most notably with the acquisition of a moody, hard-hitting outfielder from the Cincinnati Reds named Alex Johnson. Johnson suffered psychological problems and was a train wreck waiting to happen; but for the time being, the Angels had their first star hitter since Leon Wagner.

Led by Johnson and Fregosi, and with a group of young pitchers that included Andy Messersmith, Clyde Wright, and Rudy May, the Angels had their best season in three years. They were competitive right up to the end and finished third in the AL West with 86 wins. Fregosi had another solid year at short, hitting 22 home runs and driving in 82 runs—both career highs—and was again selected to represent the Angels in the All-Star game.

The following offseason, Walsh acquired hard-hitting outfielder Tony Conigliaro from Boston to bat behind Johnson. Tony C. was an East Coast version of Fregosi, with his Italian good looks and charisma. He entered the league in 1964 as a rising star, and promptly smacked 84 home runs over his first three seasons. But just as he was really coming into his own it all but ended, and it was the Angels who were culpable. In a mid-summer game at Fenway Park in 1967, Angels starter Jack Hamilton drilled Tony C. in the face, almost killing him. It was one of the most publicized beanballs in baseball history. Hamilton was accused of throwing a spitball, but Angels catcher Buck Rodgers still feels it was one that just got away.

"Tony would crowd the plate so much that his head was actually in the strike zone," says Rodgers. "And when Hamilton threw the pitch, Tony just kind of flinched and it hit him in the face. Instead of trying to get out of the way, he just froze. I don't think you can blame Hamilton. ... The ball sailed, but it wasn't a spitball."

Conigliaro's damaged eye never completely healed, and the emotional and psychological baggage he carried from the incident ground him down in 1967, leading later that season to a bizarre 5 a.m. press conference at which Conigliaro tearfully announced his retirement. After taking 1968 off, he returned to the Sox in '69, and posted career highs in 1970 in home runs (36) and RBI (116). After the 1970 season ended, the Angels made their move to land Tony C.

Early in '71, the club seemed to be stronger, ready to make noise in the American League West. Fregosi felt that with the addition of Conigliaro and Johnson, the Angels had the best hitting team in their short history. But that season turned out to be the stormiest in Angels history. On the surface, Alex Johnson came across as a steely, reserved player. But behind that facade was a disturbed young man ready to explode. When he finally blew, the repercussions would be felt by the entire club.

Throughout his tenure with the Angels, Fregosi never hesitated to confront a player or manager if it was for the betterment of the team. A prime example occurred during a losing streak in 1971 when a rookie outfielder named Mickey Rivers was having trouble breaking into the starting lineup.

"Jimmy wanted to win, and when I got there the team wasn't winning a lot," Rivers recalls. "So one day he told Lefty Phillips, 'Hey, let the kids play! We aren't winning and maybe we can turn this around!' So Lefty put me in and I got two hits that day and three the next. The following day he took me out."

An incensed Fregosi confronted Phillips, demanding to know why Rivers had been benched. Says Rivers: "Lefty just stared at him, but he kept me in. Jimmy sacrificed a lot on his part for me. He's the one who really got me the chance to play. He talked to the manager and told him to 'Let the guys play!' and that's how a lot of the young guys got into games."

By 1971 Fregosi's tenure as an Angel was coming to a close. The guy who had carried the team on his back for 10 seasons would have to endure one more, and it wasn't easy. By the end of the season, Johnson, Phillips, and Walsh were gone. The new general manager, Harry Dalton, was eager to exorcise the team of all its ghosts, including Fregosi. That winter he unloaded the shortstop for an inconsistent right-handed speedballer from the Mets named Nolan Ryan.

But by that time, Fregosi had already made his mark on the Angels franchise. With his spirit and desire, plus a lot of stubborn arrogance, Fregosi helped establish Angels baseball in Southern California. Without his presence on the team, it's hard to say how the Angels would have fared as the shine of a new franchise wore off. Gene Autry never forgot his contributions and loyalty and promised himself when the time was right he would bring Fregosi back to Anaheim.

True to his word, Autry hired Fregosi in 1978 to replace Dave Garcia as manager. It wasn't sentiment that guided the decision. The fit was as natural as a Fregosi-Knoop double play. Fregosi piloted the Angels to a second-place finish in '78, and to their first divisional championship a year later.

When he approached Autry in the clubhouse following that 1979 championship game, Fregosi was struck by the old cowboy's demeanor.

"I'll never forget Gene's eyes when I saw him after the game," Fregosi says. "It was as if a black cloud had been lifted from his head forever."

9

DEFIANT ANGEL

ALEX JOHNSON

*L*ike repetitive rifle shots, the sound of the bat striking the ball reverberates off the nearby building, alerting all within earshot that something serious is going down in the batting cage.

Crank, swish, smash.

Crank, swish, smash.

Peering into the cage one expects carnage, but instead one finds a black man in white flannels hitting baseballs with staggering verve and force. Alex Johnson turns with such violent precision on the ball that it seems to deaden on contact before it smashes into the cage's nylon netting. Kids along the edge of the cage squirm, not sure if the net will contain the comets screaming their way.

Johnson's stoic, menacing gaze is unsettling to say the least. But he counters that with an occasional smile that is almost childlike. It leaves one to wonder if Johnson would rather hug you or kill you. Then there is his nickname, "Black Bull," an appropriate moniker for a player who is strong, surly, and defiant.

The pitching machine—or "Iron Mike," as it is called—is Johnson's most frequent companion. Its metal arm slings ball after ball at game speed, serving as a self-sufficient avenue to success in the real batter's box. Most good hitters spend a fair share of time staring down a pitching machine; Alex Johnson lives 60 feet from one.

Crank, swish, smash.

Crank, swish, smash.

Just when you think that Johnson—or the machine—may need a rest, he does the unthinkable: he creeps up on the machine. Then you fully grasp the strength, timing, agility, and quickness that Johnson displays as he smacks pitch after pitch. Johnson, whose forearms resemble bridge cables, continues to move forward as he hits, until he is almost halfway between the implacable machine and home plate. It's an awesome display of bat-speed, concentration, reflex, and most of all, defiance.

The batting cage can't contain his defiance, which makes him a great batter. Like a Lakota warrior, his existence has been built around warfare. His Louisville Slugger is his war club, his means of survival, and his life's work; it's an expression of self, his manhood. Best not mess with a warrior's weapon, or so goes the legend. *Herald Examiner* reporter Dick Miller tried once, and Johnson retaliated by putting coffee grinds in the scribe's typewriter. Who's to say that warriors don't have a sense of humor?

This, of course, is only his exterior. This "hit man" is both physical and cerebral. But no one really knows the real Alex Johnson. How could they? At this point in his life, he doesn't even know himself.

Suddenly something happens so unexpected you need to blink for comprehension. Like Sonny Liston singing Christmas carols, it just doesn't take. During a lull in Johnson's massacre of baseballs, one of the kids works up the nerve to ask for an autograph. Without smiling, Johnson walks over with the same purpose and conviction he displayed in the cage, takes the boy's scrap of paper, and writes legibly and deliberately: A-l-e-x J-o-h-n-s-o-n. The script is slightly tilted forward, crisp and legible. Like his hitting, he takes pride in his cursive.

Just like that, this big bad wolf has morphed into a Pied Piper of sorts. More kids emboldened by the first brave lad cluster around and begin to thrust their bits of paper toward Johnson. There is a conviction in their body language that says this is not just a regular player. Sincere love and adoration widens their eyes as if they have some secret connection to this hero that grownups could only dream about.

As the mob of kids grows, one smallish tyke in front is being crushed by the onslaught. The growing pack is oblivious. The tyke's air is squeezed from him but he defiantly holds on, extending his paper as far as his small arm can take it. It seems to him his idol's signature is worth dying for.

Alex observes the child and as he reaches for his scrap barks with authority, "Move back." Like obedient toy soldiers, the kids obey. Once assured the child is out of harm's way, Johnson continues signing, and the gasping boy celebrates by running everywhere to show everyone his prize.

For the next half-hour, Johnson signs his autograph for adoring fans. Sweat drips from his chin onto the scraps of paper in his hands. But the kids don't seem to mind. To them, it is the sweat of gods, and only makes their paper scraps even more precious. When all are satisfied, he heads back into the cage, into his own private sanctuary, the place "where coaches fear to tread." He pours a fresh bag of balls into Iron Mike, takes his stance, and attacks.

Crank, swish, smash.
Crank, swish, smash.
Crank, swish, smash.

The snowstorm was so fierce it shut down Detroit. Downed power lines and ice forced drivers to abandon their cars on the freeways. For the newest Angel, Alex Johnson, it meant he was going to be late for spring training, and as he waited out the storm in a diner, he wondered if the storm was an omen of the season ahead. Would his first season with the Angels be this bleak?

A few days later, the skies cleared and Johnson resumed his drive to California and his new team. As his car crossed the Michigan line into Indiana, his mind raced back to other teams, other storms. To Philly where it all began, and Gene Mauch, who called him the fastest runner he had ever seen going from second to home. Johnson chuckled to himself recalling when Richie Allen had called him "the baddest of the bad... even badder than myself." He also remembered Allen telling him that his bad rap was his own doing: calling everyone "dickhead" scared the front-office guys to death.

Allen also liked to talk about the day when a stadium employee's car broke down on the expressway, and how Johnson jumped in his own car and helped him out. "He came back an hour later," Richie said in wonderment, "grease up to his elbows. Now, is this man a mental case, or is this a man I want as my friend? Just leave him alone and let him play baseball!"

"That would have been nice," thought Johnson. In St. Louis, the managers thought they knew more about hitting than he did. Skipper Red Schoendienst tried to change his approach at the plate, and when Johnson refused, they traded him to the Cincinnati Reds. In Cincy, manager Sparky Anderson didn't seem to care for Johnson, thinking he was lazy. Despite two productive seasons, he was dealt again—this time to the Angels. Maybe Anaheim would be different.

When the sun rose the next day he was in Utah. The flatness of the terrain reminded him of Detroit and the dusty sandlots he played on as a teen with Willie Horton and Bill Freehan. They both played for the hometown Tigers and had won a championship in 1968. Johnson was still searching for his.

As Johnson neared Las Vegas, thoughts of home rushed to him. He thought of how proud his dad was of him and his brother Ron, who had rushed for 1,000 yards for the New York Giants the previous year, and of how well they got along. As he crossed the California border the desert reminded him of the Roadrunner cartoons he watched as a kid. His dad had kept switching the channel to the baseball "Game of the Week." Johnson didn't like that at first, but soon he warmed to his dad's appreciation of the national pastime.

He thought of Arkansas, Indianapolis, and Detroit, how his family had struggled at each place with segregation, stares, and disappointments. It was hard for a black man to get started, but Johnson's dad was tough. He began on the assembly line, then started his own trucking repair business. Johnson used to tell Allen, "That's where I got my big arms, from shoveling junk around at the shop."

When he finally arrived in Palm Springs, the Angels were out of town. Injured outfielder Jim Hicks was there, though, and he let Johnson know what lay in store.

"Jim Hicks didn't know me, he just knew about me and he assumed the sportswriters wouldn't like me," Johnson recalls. "He told me a few things about

Anaheim. He told me about different characters, how I was going to relate to them. And, sure enough, it all turned out to be true."

Alex Johnson is the most complex and compelling figure in Angels history. He has been labeled the following, often by the same person: brilliant, self-destructive, mentally disturbed, incredibly talented, chronically depressed, and downright surly. For all his ups and downs, Johnson became a key cog in an emotional roller-coaster ride that lasted two seasons but shook the franchise for years.

Although much has been written about Johnson, very little can be attributed to him directly, because he did not trust sportswriters and rarely granted interviews during his playing days. Of the few interviews he did acquiesce to, most degenerated into emotional, obscenity-laden diatribes. Some former teammates are also not anxious to talk about Johnson. "Blown out of proportion," says Jim Fregosi of Johnson's impact on the team. "Leave it be," advises Clyde Wright. Now, some 30 years later, others are finding it easier to talk, including Johnson himself. Possibly, time heals wounds. It speaks to the severity of the wound, however, that it took that long for sufficient healing to occur.

When Johnson hooked up with the team in the spring of 1970, he discovered a young Angels club loaded with potential. Clyde Wright was the unproven veteran of the rotation at age 29. He was complemented by a trio of youngsters—Andy Messersmith, Rudy May, and Tom Murphy—each ripe with promise. Together they formed a solid pitching staff that was bolstered in the pen by 33-year-old Eddie Fisher, rookies Dave LaRoche and Greg Garrett, and second-year closer Ken Tatum. Jim Fregosi and first baseman Jim Spencer anchored the Angels offense, and second baseman Sandy Alomar contributed speed and smarts.

The Angels remained competitive for most of the 1970 season, thanks in no small part to the offensive contributions of Johnson, who led the team with 86 RBI and a .329 batting average. They were led by manager Lefty Phillips, who had the team playing .500 ball over the final three-quarters of 1969 season after taking the reins from Bill Rigney. Overweight, with the long face of a basset hound, Phillips could chew a cigar and spit tobacco at the same time, although not artfully enough to keep from constantly streaking his chin and jersey with tobacco juice.

Phillips's timid nature and poor communication skills left him ill-equipped to handle a force like Johnson. He could not comprehend Johnson's occasional lack of "enthusiasm," and did little to solve the problem. On top of all of that, Phillips suffered from chronic asthma and other health ailments that interfered with his coaching career and ultimately ended his life at age 53.

Johnson's reputation had certainly preceded him, and almost from Day One it was rough going for the temperamental star. "I got kicked out of my first game in

Alex Johnson told Jim Fregosi in 1970: "You hit when you can. I hit when I want to." Courtesy of the Angels

the American League, and I said, 'Well, if they're gonna play that game, I'm gonna take care of some motherf---ing business out here,'" Johnson recalls. "My first job was to be a person, not a slave to somebody doing something wrong."

Even though he was a leader with a bat in his hand, Johnson was criticized for "dogging it" in the press. His reaction was to heap epithets on every sportswriter who came near him. When Ross Newhan became the beat reporter for the *Los Angeles Times* and joined the Angels midway through the 1970 season, Johnson was ready to give him a proper introduction.

"I had heard vicious things about Alex, but had made up my mind to make my own decisions about him," Newhan recalls. "I walked up to him on the field in Yankee Stadium and said, 'Hi, I'm Ross Newhan. I'm going to cover the club for the *L.A. Times* the rest of the way.' He glared at me and before turning away called out, 'You're no different than those other motherf---ers.'"

Newhan recalls another incident when he and another reporter, Dick Miller, pulled up to the team's hotel in Cleveland in a cab. "We were taking the bags out and all of a sudden we hear this guy screaming, cussing us out. We look out, and it's Alex leaning out of the hotel window just throwing invectives at us."

Johnson denies nothing, but says his outbursts were occasioned by reporters' refusal to abide by the unspoken credo of the day: "What you see here, what you hear here, stays in the clubhouse."

"I cussed them out, there's no question about that," he readily admits. "They used their jobs as opportunities for payback. There were some of them who were really genuine, who wrote the truth, but some were just inhibited by evil, who liked to write 'interesting things' to sell some papers, and they didn't give a damn about the truth."

Besides, he says, he wasn't damning anyone to hell, just doing some innocent cussing.

"You don't have to use profanity to wish evil on people," he says. "Profanity is just a word to call somebody's attention to the fact that they're doing something wrong. ... I'm ornery to the point of determination, but not evil. When I played, I was considered a mean and ornery person. 'Mean' is not necessarily a bad word. For example, if you've got a football player and he tears somebody up, you would say, 'That's a mean S.O.B.!' But if you're playing a game, it can also be construed as excellence. In that context, the word 'mean' can be another word for determined."

Whatever the rationale, nobody on the ball club dealt with the problem, because the Angels were competing for the pennant, and Johnson's bat was even scarier than his tongue. Combined with a career year from Fregosi, who hit 22 home runs and drove in 82, the Angels had a nice 1-2 punch. But pitching was the Angels' strong suit. Wright, on his way to 22 victories, threw a no-hitter in July. A native from Jefferson City, Tennessee, with a down-home Southern twang to his talk, Wright was a treat to both fans and sportswriters, in counterpoint to Johnson.

By July the Angels were serious contenders for the divisional title. Inside the clubhouse, though, they were contenders for the title of Most Dysfunctional Team. Johnson's problems with sportswriters and even teammates worsened. Two of his favorite targets were *Herald Examiner* reporter Dick Miller and infielder Chico Ruiz. Nicknamed "Hog-head," Miller had been with the team since its inception and had a reputation for aggressive reporting, which of course put him high up on Johnson's hit list.

"I'll tell you one thing about Dick Miller: God, could he lie!" Johnson says. "He could fabricate some things."

The friction between the pair reached a head when Miller, who didn't know when he was well off, hid Johnson's bats right before a game. Johnson found them, but then refused to take batting practice on the grounds that the reporter might steal something else of his. Not long after that, Johnson took some old coffee grounds and sprinkled them in Miller's typewriter. Much to Miller's chagrin, Phillips found the coffee incident humorous. Johnson recalled Lefty coming up to him and laughing; "You got that son of a bitch!" His teammates agreed. Says Wright: "Some of the shit Dick Miller wrote, he deserved to have coffee grounds poured in there."

As for Ruiz, he was actually Johnson's best friend when they played together on the Reds. Johnson had even made Ruiz godfather to his adopted daughter. But their relationship frayed in Anaheim, and they were constantly at each other's throats.

It seemed the only solace for Johnson was hitting. He spent hours with "Iron Mike," experimenting with different approaches to batting and developing several theories about the art.

"One of the reasons I liked baseball was that its creativity is unlimited. There's always a multitude of things going on there and I enjoyed that. As kids in Detroit, we used to play between two telephone poles at the field," Johnson says, "and my job was to hit straightaway between them. So consequently my power was to centerfield. What I was trying to do in the cage was to redevelop, restructure my body to pull a little better."

His teammates were awestruck by Johnson's hitting ability—and paid special attention to his habits in the batting cage. His method of creeping up on "Iron Mike" during batting practice became known throughout the league, and made opposing pitchers hesitant to throw him fastballs.

"They started throwing me curves, but I was a good breaking-ball hitter, too," Johnson says. "The key to hitting a breaking ball is attacking the ball. I had no trouble with it."

Johnson's well thought-out theories might've made for good reading on the sports pages, but that would've required him to have an obscenity-free conversation with reporters, which wasn't in the cards.

"It was difficult covering the club because you would walk into the clubhouse and here would come this stream of epithets directed at the writers," says Newhan. Even when the reporters were interviewing other players, Johnson would scream at them in the background. It finally got to the point where several reporters jointly petitioned the league office to do something about Johnson's foul mouth. The Angels issued a letter over Johnson's signature informing the press that henceforth the hitting star would not have anything to say to reporters, period.

Despite the ongoing battles off the field, the Angels were still playing well on the field as August gave way to September. Heading into play on September 1, the club was only three games behind the league-leading Minnesota Twins. Then, on September 4, the Twins visited Anaheim Stadium for a three-game series, and promptly swept the Angels. After that, recalls Johnson, the team collectively gave up.

"I was on the bus getting ready to go to the airport, and the guys were down," says Johnson. "They all had the attitude that said, 'Let's go home now, because we ain't gonna win anyway.' They carried that stigma with them the rest of the season, and we lost six more games. ... The team gave up, no question about it. I'm not knowledgeable enough to say what it was that made 'em quit on themselves, but it was obvious they lacked the substance and desire to follow through. A blind man could see it."

Quitting was not in Johnson's vocabulary. "No way in hell Alex liked to lose!" Wright says. "That was his one big quality. When he played, he played to win. If

This infield single against the White Sox on October 1, 1970, secured Johnson the only batting title in Angels history. Courtesy of the Angels

some other guys didn't play up to their capabilities, he would just stare at them and they knew exactly what he was thinking."

Even with the season lost, Johnson had one personal goal to accomplish. Never before in the club's history had an Angel won a batting title. With one game to go, Johnson trailed Boston's Carl Yastrzemski in the batting crown race by .005 percentage points. To win the title, he needed to go at least two-for-three against the White Sox, who were starting Gerry Janeski, a rookie with a 10-17 record. In his first at-bat he grounded out to first, but in his second at-bat he singled to right. When he got up again in the fifth inning he needed just one more hit to win the crown.

"I wasn't thinking about winning the batting championship at the time because Lefty had said I needed to go two-for-two or three-for-three to win it," recalls Johnson. "In my next at-bat I hit one over to Bill Melton at third that I beat out for a single, and when I got to first I heard a lot of noise and saw the scoreboard lighting up. Suddenly I saw Jay Johnstone running out of the dugout toward me. He's yelling, 'You've got to leave the game! You've got to leave the game! Lefty says you've got to leave the ball game whether you want to or not!' It totally surprised me. Then I looked at the scoreboard and my name was ahead of Yastrzemski's. So I put two and two together. Maybe I had heard Lefty wrong or something, but the next thing I knew, people were cheering and I was running into the dugout."

Much has been made in the press about how Johnson himself wanted to be taken out to ensure his coronation. But he calls that just another media lie.

"I wasn't gonna go out unless Lefty told me to come out," says Johnson. "I was willing to stay in the game whether I won the batting title or not. When he told me I had to leave, it was a total surprise, because I figured I still had to get at least another hit depending how long the game went."

The game went 13 innings, with the Angels winning in dramatic fashion, 5-4. But the real winner that day was Johnson; capturing the title would turn out to be his crowning achievement. Meanwhile, the Angels finished the season in third place with 86 wins, a distant 12 games in back of the Twins. The win total tied the franchise mark, set in 1962. It was just the fourth time in ten years that the Angels finished above .500. They wouldn't do so again for another eight seasons.

Johnson's baseball world crumbled rapidly the following year. Fined repeatedly for "loafing" in spring training, Johnson rebounded magnificently in April and was named the American League's Player of the Month. But then old demons returned, and the fines and benchings for lethargic play began piling up, just as the media began piling on.

Herald Examiner reporter Melvin Durslag wrote on June 3, 1971: "'As I see it,' says Lefty, 'Alex zones himself. He believes he has so much strength to spread over 162 games. When he hits the ball through the infield, he automatically decides how many bases this will be worth. If he judges it as a single, he won't hurry and make the big turn. If he sees a double, he will run accordingly.' The only flaw, according to Phillips, is that the play may not always go exactly the way Johnson first judges it. The outfielder, for instance, may fumble the ball, and instead of being at second, Alex is still at first."

Jim Fregosi seconds the notion that Johnson's ferocity on the field depended on the situation and who was watching.

"When we played in Detroit and his family was in the stands, he ran every ball out and played his ass off," says Fregosi. "Other times, he wouldn't even run to first base; he would take two steps out of the box and that was it. He played hard when he wanted to play hard. If he didn't feel like it or something was bothering him, he took it onto the field rather then just letting it go."

But Wright feels that Johnson's attitude was blown way out of proportion.

"If he hit the ball hard right at somebody and it was obvious it was going to be an out, sometimes he just didn't run," says Wright. "But if he hit a ball that he thought he could beat to first base, he would run the thing out. If he wanted to go catch a line drive or a fly ball, he could go get it. He convinced me he could play when he wanted to.

"I say it was 50-50. Half of it was Alex's part, the other half was the fans and some players and the writers. I wouldn't go one way or the other."

Johnson admits his actions may have influenced the team at times, but he blames unfair treatment by the press, the fans, and management—not himself.

"In essence, I'd agree that I didn't have enthusiasm, and that I let the team down," says Johnson. "I'm not gonna deny it. There were times I had the flu or genuinely saw something wrong with how the game was being played. I didn't even want to be in the game in a situation like that.

"The problem was fans would come to the game to boo me because of what they read in the newspaper. It became disheartening simply going out on the field. I was highly spiritual during the game. I rose to a different level out there. But sometimes it just wasn't there. I just couldn't rise to a different level. Sometimes I wasn't as fast as other times, and other times I didn't run with as much enthusiasm as I may have before. ... Sometimes you lose the fire."

But even if he let the Angels down, Johnson says, the team "wouldn't have won anyhow, the way it was acting. There were some games I shouldn't have really been playing. The reactions they were giving me told me I wasn't going to get a fair rap from the umpires or anyone else."

In June, Walsh tried to trade Johnson—whose production had taken a nosedive from the previous season—to the Milwaukee Brewers for Tommy Harper. Milwaukee nixed the deal at the last moment and the Angels were stuck with him. On July 5, 1971, Ron Firmite of *Sports Illustrated* wrote a cover story on Johnson titled "The Fallen Angel." The piece, which Johnson maintains "caused a lot of trouble," quoted several Angels who didn't hold anything back when it came to discussing their erratic teammate.

Pitcher Eddie Fisher said, "This man is the most unusual ballplayer I've ever run into in 14 years in the game. Every man on the team has tried to reach him. None of it has worked." Phillips echoed Fisher's frustration: "I came up in this game the hard way. I can understand if a man plays bad when he has no ability, but this fellow has great ability, super ability. ... This fellow won't even try. And that's not just bad for us, it's bad for baseball."

Asked by Firmite to respond to his teammates' assessments, Johnson suggested that the whole problem boiled down to racial prejudice against him.

"Hell yes, I'm bitter. I've been bitter since I learned I was black," he was quoted as saying. "The society into which I was born and which I grew up in and in which I play ball today is anti-black. My reaction is nothing more than a reaction to their attitude. But they [the whites] don't keep their hatreds to themselves. They go out of their way to set up barriers, to make little slights so that you're aware of their messed-up feelings."

But according to Cuban-born infielder Chico Ruiz, racism wasn't the problem at all.

"The white guys on this club may dislike you, but I'm as black as you are, and I hate you!" the *Los Angeles Times* quoted Ruiz as telling Johnson in June of that year. "I hate you so much I could kill you!"

In the Firmite piece, Tony Conigliaro may have come closest to the truth in suggesting that Johnson was suffering from a mental sickness. "He's got a problem deep inside him that he won't talk about. He's so hurt inside it's terrifying. He's a great guy off the field. On the field, there's something eating away at him."

Wright points out that for all of Johnson's tirades and verbal altercations, he never got physical with the targets of his wrath. But that doesn't mean he wasn't aggressive—nor does it mean that he would back down. Wright remembers one particular day in the locker room in Kansas City when Johnson got on him about something and Wright stood up and, brandishing his stool, challenged Johnson to fight. Whereupon Johnson picked up his own stool, broke it over his own head, and yelled at the pitcher, "That stool is not gonna save you!"

"Being a pretty smart lefthander, I took my stool and just set it back down on the floor and sat back down on it like a weak little old mouse," Wright recalls. "I knew right then I was no match for Alex Johnson."

Johnson's feud with his former best friend Ruiz came to a strange head in June. They almost came to blows one day near the batting cage, and on June 13 another strange incident occurred after Johnson was taken out of a game for a pinch-runner. He headed to the clubhouse, showered, and then left. As he entered the long tunnel under the stadium leading to the players' parking lot, he encountered Ruiz, who he said had a gun in his hand. Johnson reported it to the first policeman he saw, and the next day the media had a field day. There were subsequent reports about other players packing heat, and the Angels' clubhouse became known as the "wildest clubhouse in the West."

Today Johnson insists that his rift with Ruiz was caused, oddly enough, by Walsh. "Chico and me were good friends, and what happened was Walsh's fault. There were a few days to go before the cutoff date and Chico had just bought a home near San Diego. He wanted to stay with the team because if he got sent down to Triple A, he would lose his house.

"Walsh said the players needed more harmony on the team. So the ones who were against me were most likely to get cut. Someone had told Walsh that Chico was an instigator, and Chico thought I had said it. I told him it wasn't me, but he didn't believe me. What happened is they turned Chico against me."

In any case, with the Angels in a state of near anarchy, Walsh finally pulled the trigger, figuratively speaking. On June 25, after failing to run out a ball, Johnson was suspended without pay for "failure to hustle and improper mental attitude." The Players Association, under Marvin Miller, immediately filed a grievance demanding Johnson be reinstated but put on the disabled list with full pay. Clearly, Miller said, Johnson had emotional problems that required treatment.

But the mindset in baseball at the time was that only physical disabilities qualified for compensation. Major League Baseball feared that if Johnson's mental condition was sanctioned as a disability, other players would cite psychological problems anytime they wanted a break. On July 21, Johnson met with Miller in his New York office, and came away more convinced than ever that his client was mentally unstable.

"I'm only a layman in psychiatric terms, but it didn't require a genius to see Alex was a disturbed person," Miller says. "He didn't stop talking for hours and he had these notes on him, all kinds of pieces of paper—airline folders, scraps of paper. And these were all scribblings that he had put down on the trip to New York so that he wouldn't forget them. Well, he didn't need those notes because he just talked without even referring to them."

To everything Miller asked, Johnson's response was, "It wouldn't do any good." "He adopted that as kind of a personal turtle shell he retreated into," recalls Miller. "He was firmly convinced that no matter what he said, it would sound like an alibi, that nobody was sympathetic enough to examine it. I'm sure that racism was a good part of this. What working-class black in Detroit would not have carried this burden? But I think more specifically his baseball experiences were like that. He wasn't dealing with great liberal thinkers out there with the California Angels."

Following their meeting, Miller contacted American League President Joe Cronin and informed him that Johnson needed immediate help. He reminded Cronin that baseball had gone to bat for other players with mental illnesses, including Cleveland's Tony Horton and Boston's Jimmy Piersall, both of whom had suffered nervous breakdowns. Horton had once crawled back to the dugout screaming on his hands and knees after striking out, and Piersall had climbed up on the backstop during a game and began shouting obscenities.

Cronin argued that those cases were different from Johnson's, and Miller found himself wondering if Horton and Piersall had been given the benefit of the doubt because they were white. When Cronin went on to say that it was a mistake "excusing players like Johnson who refuse to play all out," Miller demanded to know what he meant by "players like Johnson," and the conversation was quickly terminated. "With Joe Cronin, there were overtones of racism, no question about it," Miller says.

Baseball Commissioner Bowie Kuhn subsequently removed Johnson from the suspended list and placed him on the restricted list, in preparation of suspending him indefinitely. Meanwhile, the case moved to the arbitration phase. That's when Miller met with whom he still considers "one of the most indignant men" he ever met—Dick Walsh.

"People used to ask me about him and I would ask them if they read that book about Captain Queeg. That's who he reminded me of," Miller says, adding that even the Commissioner's office found Walsh offensive. "The Fuehrer" is just one of the nicknames Miller heard applied to Walsh.

During the hearings, several witnesses were presented by Major League Baseball to testify to Johnson's flawed character. One of them was Phillips, whose catalog of sins against Johnson included his refusal to run out a ball when President Richard Nixon was in the stands for a game. Walsh called Johnson lazy and branded his demanding batting practice routine with "Iron Mike" as odd. In his excellent autobiography, *A Whole Different Ballgame*, Miller points out the contradictory nature of Johnson's remarks, stating that somebody who stood for hours hitting against a pitching machine was hardly lazy.

When the hearings moved to Detroit, Johnson and his psychiatrist, Dr. Lawrence Jackson, both testified. Johnson told how, as a youth there, he had constantly faced racial injustice, and how its ramifications affected him later on. Throughout his whole career, he said, he had been treated unfairly by baseball, and in Anaheim, Walsh had made his life especially miserable. At times he rambled, but his pain was obvious, and it was clear that Johnson was not a well man.

Dr. Jackson testified that after weeks of talking with Johnson his diagnosis was that Johnson was suffering from severe reactive depression, whose symptoms included excessive anxiety, anger, and feeling low and irritable. Johnson disagrees. "There wasn't no damn anxiety!" he says. "I was just anxious to take care of some motherf---ing business. I get over anxiety about things because I've got ambition. But I can stop it if I want to. Anxiety is ambition. Ambition is determination.

"I didn't have trouble with no damn depression out there. As far as severe reactive depression, if I've got it, I don't know about it. And if I've got it, that means I'm doing a damn good job because I'm trying like a motherf---er."

A few weeks later, arbitrator Lewis Gil informed Miller that he was ruling in favor of Johnson and removing him from the restricted list. But as a sop to the owners, he upheld the $3,750 in fines Johnson had received over the course of the season. And Gil intended to issue a statement proclaiming that it would be inadvisable for any player to cite his ruling as a basis for using emotional stress or mental illness in an effort to avoid disciplinary action.

The proposed statement appalled Miller, who told Gil that it negated the entire basic premise of the whole case—that Johnson was emotionally ill. How could Gil justify the fines, Miller asked, when the testimony of two medical experts was that Johnson was ill? But the decision and attendant statement still stood, despite Miller's outcry.

Johnson was traded to the Cleveland Indians that October for Vada Pinson. He played five more years for the Indians, Yankees, Rangers, and Tigers. Although he never regained the stroke he attained during his successful 1970 campaign with the Angels, he remained a solid outfielder and designated hitter.

Johnson's relations with members of the press mellowed considerably following his years with the Angels, but he always remained somewhat leary of them. At least one member of the press has also mellowed considerably since Johnson's days with the Angels. If, as Johnson claims, the press was responsible for his situation, Ross Newhan is surprisingly willing to accept a portion of the blame on behalf of the Fourth Estate.

"I don't recall the group that covered the Angels in those years, including myself, trying to delve into what made Alex the way he was, and that was probably a mistake on our part," says Newhan. "I don't think it was reflective of journalism, necessarily. I just think we were so fed up with Alex, the way he treated us, that who cared? I think if some of that same stuff went on today it would be dealt with quite differently."

However, Fregosi, who played alongside Johnson for the two years, says that Johnson's problems may have stemmed from a deep-rooted inferiority complex that didn't qualify as mental illness.

"When he wasn't in uniform he was one of the nicest guys you ever want to be around," recalls Fregosi. "He was a very charitable guy. He hung around with the batboys and did things locally with kids. How can you be emotionally disturbed when you're in a uniform, and off the field be a great guy? He was a pain in the ass as a player, but I don't think he was emotionally disturbed. I think that once he put that uniform on, he was a changed person. I think he had to put that face on it because of some of the insecurity he had."

Johnson's arbitration hearing was a watershed event in major sports for several reasons. Not only did the case shed light on the owners' insensitivity to mental illness. Johnson's case along with Curt Flood's landmark case in 1969, was among the first instances of a players union showing support for an African-American. Prior to that, minorities had been virtually ignored.

Marvin Miller: "I think the Alex Johnson and Curt Flood cases were an advertisement—at least the other black players in the major leagues took it as such—that this organization was not like others they had known or experienced. That a player with a legitimate problem got a hearing, and a sympathetic one, regardless of the color of his skin."

Miller is reminded of an experience he had in his first year as a union head. It involved a Puerto Rican player, Pedro Ramos. Ramos had a small problem that Miller ironed out, and to the lawyer's amazement, within six months almost every Latin player was familiar with every detail of the case. "Word of mouth was unbelievable. So a case like Johnson's, which was not trivial and had wide publicity, was almost certainly talked about," he says.

Most importantly, Miller says the treatment Johnson received helped him move on with his life. "It broke his stubborn philosophy that it doesn't do any good to complain. I saw him in spring training the following year, and he was clearly better. I'm not talking performance-wise; I think he was somewhat past his prime at that point. Morale-wise, though, you could just tell talking to him for a minute or two that he was quite a bit better."

Although adamantly shunning the mental illness defense, Johnson concedes that Miller helped him recognize some things in himself and is grateful to him.

"Marvin Miller's a brilliant man," says Johnson. "I was astonished about the type of character and the knowledge he had. He was extraordinary. Of all the people I met in the game, I put him at the top of the list. He explained some people's actions toward me that I didn't pick up. I see clearly now some of the things that happened to me."

But even with this new understanding, Johnson says that given the chance to do his career over again, he wouldn't change a thing. If anything, he'd be even more obstinate.

"I'd do the same thing, period," he says. "Matter of fact, what I would do is drop a couple more cuss words a little quicker. The thing they didn't like about it was the fact that I would not surrender. And the more I wouldn't surrender, the more they just kept coming. And that's the reason I left baseball so quickly."

Today, Johnson attends autograph shows, and when people tell him "Thanks for the memories," it makes the self-described "God-fearing and doting grandfather" wish he had given them even more to remember. But today he's more concerned about the state of America's youth than his baseball legacy.

"Children are my No. 1 pleasure in life," he relates. "I've got five grandkids and about 10 other ones who call me 'Granddaddy,' and it hurts me because this young generation is really lost. I blame the corporate people, the people who took prayer out of school. The people who decide they know more about human nature than God knows about human nature. It really hurts you to see some things out here. Depression isn't economical or mental all the time; sometimes it's spiritual, too. That's what we've got going on now, a spiritual depression."

Johnson will forever be characterized by certain memorable incidents that happened at the ball park, but possibly it is time to consider rewriting the past in favor of what we know now. Take, for example, yet another testimonial to Johnson's nature away from the field. Ed Farmer, Johnson's teammate when they played together for Cleveland in 1972, remembers that Johnson always carried a book about electronics with him. One summer in Texas, Farmer learned first-hand it was a subject that Johnson took very seriously.

Farmer and some of his teammates had borrowed the visiting clubhouse attendant's car and were about to head to the ballpark in Arlington from their hotel in Dallas when they realized the car wouldn't start. After several minutes of working on the engine in the hotel parking lot they looked up to see Johnson coming down the road. After pulling up and studying the situation, Johnson told the men he'd be right back, and several minutes later he returned wearing overalls and hauling a tool set.

"I remember thinking, 'Oh my goodness,'" says Farmer. "Alex then ordered me to 'Get in the car,' and he told me, 'When I tell you to turn on the key—turn it!' After a few minutes of tinkering with the engine he yelled, 'Turn it!' and sure enough it started right up.

"The last thing I remember him saying to us was, 'Make sure you get all the way to the ball park and don't stop! Once you stop the car won't run.' We got to the ballpark and I turned it off. But I was curious; I wanted to know if Alex really knew what he was talking about. So I turned the key again, and sure enough it was as dead as a doornail.

"Two things I learned about Alex Johnson that summer: he could hit and he definitely knew cars."

Clyde Wright agrees that it's time for everybody to remember the kinder, gentler Alex Johnson.

"Everybody made him out to be a bad person, but Alex is not a bad person," says Wright. "I've never seen him threaten a player. I've seen him holler at players and I've seen players holler at him, but nothing ever came of it. I think more people remember him for the times he didn't run out ground balls than the time he won the American League batting title, and that's not a good way to remember him. The one big thing that stands out in my mind about Alex Johnson—and nobody ever put this in the paper—is that he never left a stadium without signing every piece of paper put before him. And to me that shows you something right there."

10

TEXAS SAVIOR

NOLAN RYAN

Nolan Ryan knew the moment he dropped his arm where the ball was going. He tried to warn the batter, but once Doug Griffin froze it became a question of not whether it would hit him, but instead where and how hard. Then came the sickening thud—followed, after the game, by the gut-wrenching phone call.

"My mommy can't talk right now," said the tiny voice on the other end of the line. "She's at the hospital with my daddy."

Nolan Ryan put down the receiver and shuddered. His heart began to pound. It hadn't been on purpose, he told himself for the umpteenth time. The situation called for a sacrifice bunt, but when Griffin squared away, he threw high to force him to pop it up. In doing so, he inadvertently dropped his arm and the ball sailed in with disastrous results. Ryan walked toward home plate and what he saw made him physically ill. Griffin's eyes were rolled back up in his head and he wasn't moving. Ryan thought he had killed him.

His thoughts now turned to his own son, who was the same age as Griffin's daughter. What would Reid think if the man who put his daddy in the hospital called him on the phone? The question he asked himself later that night was different, one he had already asked thousands of times, going back to his Little League days: Could he ever truly harness his God-given talent and discipline his wild arm?

It hadn't happened with the Mets. But with the Angels, under the diligent eye of pitching coach Tom Morgan, he discovered that he had the potential to throw his fastball accurately, and with confidence. Then he mastered the curve and changeup, and together with his fastball they wreaked havoc on opposing hitters. But then came the day—April 30, 1974—that he accidentally hit Red Sox second baseman Doug Griffin's head.

As a power pitcher, throwing inside was a part of his game. Bob Gibson, Don Drysdale, Juan Marichal, and Sandy Koufax all used the inside of the plate. The difference was that they knew where their pitch was headed. Pitchers graveyards are filled with power pitchers who didn't. Guys like minor league phenom Steve Dalkowski, Sam McDowell, and Ryne Duren, to name a few. They were pitchers who threw hard but never managed any control, nor mastered themselves. Ryan thought he had proven over the last two years that he could do better. Now he had second thoughts.

By nature he was kind and nurturing. Aggression was something he had learned. By becoming physically aggressive, he grew mentally aggressive. That was his secret, his mechanism, his game face. But that game face was just a part of Ryan, not his whole. And when he looked in the mirror that night, the real Nolan Ryan found himself looking into the face of a man who nearly killed another player, a little girl's father, someone's loving husband.

Ryan was having a doozey of a mid-career crisis. He knew his very survival as a big league pitcher was at stake. He had trained and disciplined himself to not give in, to be aggressive and use the inside of the plate. He had committed to that road, and he wasn't one to retrace his steps. But the beaning gave him great pause, and for a while, Ryan stopped throwing inside.

Griffin was out for over 50 games but eventually recovered. On August 12 of that year he was the starting second baseman when the Red Sox visited Anaheim Stadium. That day's starter for the Angels: Nolan Ryan. In the second inning, Griffin struck out. But in the fifth he sought his revenge, when he singled to center and later scored. But Ryan had already turned the corner by that point. Knowing that he could not pitch effectively with a defensive mindset, he recommitted himself to pitching inside. And with great results: on that day, Ryan struck out 19 batters and pitched a complete game as the Angels won, 4-2. It was his second 19-strikeout performance of the season, with both coming against the Red Sox. The pair of dominating outings tied the Major League record for most strikeouts in a game.

The Griffin incident was a terrible setback, but it also gave a stark clarity to Ryan's thinking. He would never again give pause before pitching aggressively. The Griffin incident also reminded hitters around the league of something they already knew but tried not to dwell on: Ryan's command, or occasional lack thereof, was cause for serious concern.

Oomph! Psssst… Kaboom!

"Tighter, Nolie!" barked pitching coach Tom Morgan, making it more of a challenge than an order.

Oomph! Psssst… Kaboom!

"Better!"

Morgan knew that molding this stubborn, uncut diamond into a shiny jewel wasn't going to be easy. They had tried to fix Nolan Ryan in New York, but Gil

Nolan Ryan gave the Angels a badly needed national media presence during his eight-year stay in Anaheim. Walter Iooss Jr./Sports Illustrated

Hodges and his pitching coach Rube Walker decided to quit on him. With Tom Seaver, Jerry Koosman, and Gary Gentry on their pitching roster, the Mets figured he was easily expendable, anyway. So they traded him to the Angels for shortstop Jim Fregosi.

Morgan wasn't in such bad shape, either, with Andy Messersmith, Rudy May, and Clyde Wright anchoring his rotation. Luckily for the Angels, Morgan welcomed the challenge. But for the tall, lanky Texan wearing number 30, trying to dump a lifetime of bad habits in one month was a frustrating process. Everything Morgan taught him was new and awkward, and at first he fought it. No one had ever taught him how to properly pitch. Not like this, anyway.

"You're losing power by coming down to the side!" yelled Morgan, who for the rest of the session stood directly beside Ryan, forcing him to follow through in a straight line.

Oomph! Psssst… Kaboom!

"Feel the difference?" Morgan quipped, hoping to loosen his pupil up.

"Yep," Ryan answered through gritted teeth.

If this workout—as mentally tiring as physically challenging— wasn't enough, there was the ever-present conditioning coach, Jimmie Reese, waiting in the wings with his sawed-off fungo bat.

"C'mon, Nolie, get in the outfield," ordered the 71-year-old Reese when Morgan was finally done. Reese then proceeded to hit Ryan fungos to his right and left for an hour straight; Ryan was so tired afterward that he almost threw up.

It was Reese, Morgan, and another tutor, catcher Jeff Torborg, all spring, all the time. This was Ryan's first spring with the Angels, and they made certain it would prove to be a turning point for the young fireballer.

His relief from these excruciating workouts came in the form of Interstate 10. For after many practices, Ryan spent two hours on the road, driving back to Anaheim where his wife, Ruth, and their four-month-old son, Reid, awaited him each evening.

Cabazon, Banning, Colton. For Nolan Ryan, the towns along Interstate 10 between Palm Springs and Anaheim were becoming all too familiar. He made the trip a dozen times in a borrowed Volkswagen, and he was getting to know the highway between Palm Springs and Anaheim better than he did the interstate between his home in Alvin, Texas, and Houston.

All this because of that lousy rule! How could a team ban wives from staying with their husbands at the team hotel? The Angels were hardly promoting family values. It had been no different in Palm Springs than in Holtville. Too poor to afford a motel, the couple and their infant son roughed it out living in a tiny, borrowed trailer for a month. While he went to the field for practice, Ruth and Reid stayed back at the campsite in the 100-degree heat.

Calimesa, Redlands. Ontario. He told himself that what they were going through was only temporary, and reminded himself that no matter what hardship they might endure, anything was better than New York. Passing a power line near Beaumont, waves of static reverberated over the tiny radio. As Johnny Cash faded in and out, he turned down the volume. Ryan's mind drifted again, this time back to their little apartment in Queens and the row of tomato plants he tended to in the back. It had been his only connection to the natural world. "At least Anaheim has trees," he sighed wistfully.

He wondered how Tom Seaver was doing. This would be the first spring since 1967 without him. Seaver had been a good friend and an even better teacher. Just by watching him work, Ryan learned what it took to excel in the majors: a combination of brains and hard work. Not that he was scared of work—it's just that Ryan never thought of baseball as work. He remembered what Whitey Herzog had told him in 1966—that he had never met anyone lazier. But by the time he left the Big Apple in 1971, Ryan had transformed himself into the hardest worker Herzog had ever seen. He would miss Tom Terrific and the White Rat, but not Gil Hodges nor the harsh New York press corps. All winter long, he seethed when he read how the Mets were crazy for trading him. But the California press wasn't much better, saying how foolish the Angels were for acquiring him. Every day there was something in the paper about how the Angels had traded their best and most popular player, Fregosi, for an unproven pitcher.

The Mets could fall back on an excuse: Ryan was inconsistent. Vietnam had been going full-bore and Ryan was in the reserves, which meant that every two weeks he had to return to Houston for military duty. That and the two weeks of duty every July and August really threw his pitching schedule out of whack. The military commitments kept him from establishing a routine and mastering his control. He wondered why the press never picked up on that. It didn't really matter much now, though; his soldiering was done, and now there were no more excuses.

As he inched closer to Los Angeles in his Volkswagen, the radio signals grew in strength. Charlie Pride kicked in with "Kiss an Angel Good Morning." Ryan sang along to stay awake, and he thought again about Ruth and what a special woman she was. The thought of her alone with the baby made him question his sense of responsibility. Reid was a handful, and while he could only be home a few hours every night, he knew that Ruth appreciated the company. Ryan refused to be like many of his teammates, who often neglected their wives. He couldn't ever be like them—carousing around till all hours of the night and acting like a bunch of schoolboys. He had a wife who was both beautiful and thoughtful, and who would follow him to the ends of the earth. That was better than money in the bank.

Today, Ryan maintains that the faith that both Ruth and the Angels put in him at that crucial juncture in his career was a Godsend. More than once he had thought about quitting baseball, but his spouse wouldn't let him. Morgan, Reese, and Torborg refused to give up on him, as well. The physical and mental work he was putting in was hard and repetitive, but Ryan knew he was earning a second chance with the Angels.

When the curtain raised on the 1972 season, Ryan was determined not to blow this opportunity. He won his first start, a 2-0 complete-game shutout against the Twins in which he struck out 10 batters. But then he lost his next two games, getting hit often and early. Manager Del Rice contemplated dropping him as a starter and moving him to the bullpen, but Morgan intervened. "Stick with him, he's coming around fine," he assured the skipper. "He just needs more work."

In late May, the breakthrough came. He began by shutting out the White Sox. Two starts later, he three-hit the Tigers, and three starts after that he two-hit the A's. The rhythm, consistency, and control that had eluded Ryan for so long finally became his ally. In his last start before the All-Star break, he posted the most impressive victory of his young major league career when he one-hit the Red Sox, striking out 16 while walking just one. After allowing a scratch single to Carl Yastrzemski in the first, Ryan retired the next 26 batters in a row, and at one point struck out eight straight. That was a record, and for the second time in his career, he also struck out the side on nine pitches. It was a masterful performance, arguably as good or better than any of his seven no-hitters.

However, the Angels were struggling with their own growing pains. At the break, they were eight games under .500 and in fifth place in the A.L. West. A

Ruth Ryan's support of her husband early in his career was instrumental in his eventual success. AP/WWP

rebuilding mode began after the Alex Johnson debacle of 1971, and the Angels had new faces at catcher, first, short, and two of the three outfield slots. The team was getting outstanding pitching from their rotation of Ryan, Wright, Messersmith, and May, but little offensive support. Ryan found his groove, but as the season wore on he lost several low-scoring games. Unfortunately, it would be a pattern Ryan would live with for several years with the Angels.

But Ryan's success brought an air of greatness to an otherwise mediocre team. As Ryan piled up the strikeouts, word traveled fast that something special was going on in Anaheim. The press picked up on his dominance, and stories began circulating nationally about Ryan's overwhelming fastball. Someone called it "Ryan's Express," after the popular Sinatra film, *Von Ryan's Express*. Suddenly, Jim Fregosi was all but forgotten. The Angels had a rising superstar.

Ryan kept pushing himself. Before games, it wasn't unusual to see him running long after his teammates had stopped, and on off days the pitcher jogged along the dry streambeds surrounding Anaheim Stadium or the streets around his home. He was determined to be in the best possible shape, betting that it would pay dividends down the road.

The secret to his success may have been discovered in early May of that season, when Ryan stumbled onto something that transformed his pitching forever. Like a spy behind enemy lines, Ryan slipped past trainer Freddie Frederico's door and made his way down the tunnel to a little storage area where the weight machine was kept. There were no free weights in the room, just a basic Universal weight machine with four stations. Hardly anybody knew about the machine or was even aware of how it got there, but it didn't really matter because nobody but Ryan used the contraption anyway.

Opening the door, he flipped the light switch and then quickly closed the door behind him, checking to make sure that no one had seen him enter. If Frederico knew what Ryan was doing, then the trainer would probably hit Ryan in the head with a dumbbell to knock some sense into him. Lifting weights was strictly taboo for pitchers. The conventional wisdom was that weights made your muscles tight, but Ryan had discovered just the opposite. In just a short time using the weights he had noticed an improvement in his stamina and flexibility.

After limbering up by stretching, Ryan began his circuit: three sets of 10 reps from the bench, military, lat machine, and leg presses. He didn't add too much weight—just enough to feel tension. The whole workout lasted about an hour. When he was finished, he quietly made his way back to the clubhouse.

Unbeknownst to Ryan, he had inadvertently begun a phenomenon that would someday revolutionize the sport. Within 10 years, every major league clubhouse featured weight rooms, and every player was encouraged to spend time there.

"In those days they didn't want pitchers lifting, so I had to do it on the quiet side," Ryan recalls. "I felt like there had to be other things you could do to strengthen yourself, that's why I started doing it. With the weights, we were a little before our time. It was new back then, and when we look back we can see the impact that it has had on the game. For me, that weight room in Anaheim established a foundation that I worked off of the rest of my career."

Starting in 1972, on the days Ryan wasn't pitching he also stretched, lifted, and ran. During batting practice, he remained on the bench studying the opposing team's hitters. No method of preparation was beyond the realm of consideration as long as it worked. Ryan's innately conservative thinking went out the window when it came to working out. Former catcher and roommate Art Kusnyer, who was there for Ryan's first two seasons with the Angels, gives a good example of Ryan's progressive attitude when it came to conditioning.

"One day there were these two hippies out on the field tossing Frisbees," remembers Kusnyer. "Turns out they were two buddies of Nolan's, and they were gonna talk to the guys about stretching. Back then when we stretched, we just touched our toes and did some sprints. Suddenly, Nolan's stretching in all these weird positions. As big and muscular as his legs were, to stretch like he could was amazing. It took a while, but the stretching caught on. Now everybody's doing it."

Ryan and Jimmie Reese also began an intense running regime. They worked long after the other pitchers, and the extra running gave Ryan the endurance to pitch into the late innings. As time went by, the two bonded and a deep friendship developed. Ryan eventually named his second son, Reese, in honor of his mentor and friend.

"Jimmie means a lot to my dad not only as a coach and a mentor but as a father figure," says Reese Ryan. "My dad lost his own father when he was 19 years old, and when he got to the Angels he was in his early twenties. He was young and fairly impressionable at that time, and Jimmie really had a big impact on him."

Says Nolan himself of those early days: "My history with the Angels was that I finished stronger than I started. A lot of that had to do with the condition I was in and because of my relationship with Jimmie."

Reese Ryan adds: "My dad believed that if the opponent was better or had more God-given ability than you, then there was nothing you could do about it. But he also believed there was no reason somebody should be in better shape or play harder than you. That was the way he played the game, and that was the way he lived his life."

But the training couldn't fix everything. If there was one demon that still lurked from Ryan's past, it was his sometimes atrocious control. In 1972, Ryan led the league in strikeouts with an astounding 329, the fourth-best mark in major league history and 79 better than his nearest American League competition. But he also led the league in walks with 157 and wild pitches with 18, and was among the league leaders in hit batsmen with 10. His occasional wildness led Oakland A's slugger Reggie Jackson to comment that a Nolan Ryan mistake could "kill you," a sentiment widely shared around the league.

Ryan had been hitting people with baseballs all his life. In high school, he broke a batter's helmet and the next batter's arm on two consecutive pitches. The opposing team refused to face him anymore. Wherever he had played, his wildness had followed—and sometimes preceded—him. If he was going to succeed at the big league level, Ryan had to discipline his arm.

After finishing the 1972 season strong—with a 19-16 record, 284 innings pitched, a 2.28 ERA, the fewest hits allowed per nine innings in the major leagues at 5.26, and a major-league best nine shutouts—Ryan finished eighth in the league in Cy Young voting, behind five 20-game winners, Luis Tiant, and Sparky Lyle. All in all, not too shabby for a 25-year-old on a fifth-place club that finished last in the American League in runs scored and ended the season with a 75-80 record. Some baseball historians argue that if Ryan had been on a contending team at that time then he would have had considerably more wins. But then again, if Ryan hadn't been with a team like the Angels, then it is doubtful he would have been allowed the luxury to work through his early-season struggles. The Angels gave him the needed room to nurture his talent.

If 1972 was not his greatest season, then it certainly was his most instrumental. The confidence and consistency that had eluded him in New York finally emerged in Anaheim. To show their appreciation, the Angels rewarded Ryan with a $54,000 contract for 1973, providing him with the emotional and financial stability he and his family had yearned for since Ryan first broke into the Mets rotation in 1968. The borrowed Volkswagen was returned, and in its place he purchased a new station wagon. With a boost in his confidence and his pocketbook, Ryan never again thought about quitting baseball.

The following season solidified Ryan as one of baseball's best pitchers. He exceeded everyone's expectations in 1973, going 21-16 in 326 innings for a team that once again finished under .500 and featured an anemic offense. He posted a 2.87 ERA, logged 26 complete games, tossed two no-hitters, and struck out 383 batters, breaking Sandy Koufax's single-season strikeout mark by one. Despite his efforts, Ryan was once again snubbed for the Cy Young Award, losing out to Jim Palmer, whose Orioles won 97 games that season.

As the two premier pitchers in the league, Ryan and Palmer often jousted for the prestigious award. One year, Palmer made some remarks that irked Ryan and resulted in bad blood between the two aces.

"Frank Tanana and some of the writers were saying I was politicking for the award, and some of the press asked what did I think?" Palmer recalled years later. "I said if 200 walks were criteria, I'm sure [Ryan] will win it. It was a silly remark and something I shouldn't have said. I always knew if you faced him you better be at your best. I've always understood that and have the utmost respect for him."

Ryan bears no grudges and maintains the slight in 1973 by the writers who voted for the Cy Young Award occurred because of an East Coast bias. "We were a small-market club and we weren't back east, and that's just the way it was," says Ryan. "Besides, we weren't a good club."

Ryan's first no-hitter of the 1973 season, a 3-0 victory over a solid Kansas City Royals club, came on May 15. Jeff Torborg was the catcher that day, as Ryan struck out 12 and walked three. On July 15, Ryan struck again against Detroit, this time with Art "Caveman" Kusnyer behind the plate.

"Nolan came up to me in the first inning and tells me there's some guy in the upper deck getting my signs and relaying them to the [Tigers] bench," recalls Kusnyer. "He said the guy was rolling up his pants leg for a fastball and letting it down for a curve. I say, 'How the hell can you see this? There are 15,000 people out there. What's he wearing, an orange suit or something?'"

Ryan insisted on changing the signs, and told Kusnyer he would touch the front of his hat for a fastball and the back of his hat for a curve.

"So he strikes out a couple guys and we get through the inning," Kusnyer continues. "The next inning he says he wants to change it to the back of the hat for a fastball and the front for the curve. Two pitches later, he forgot the sequence, and his next pitch hit home plate umpire Ron Luciano right in the knee. Luciano went down like a soft shit in the rain. I marched to the mound and told Nolan, 'Listen, screw this! I'm not catching a fastball with my forehead. From now on, I'm calling the signs and you can shake me off, okay?'"

As the game progressed it became obvious that Ryan had something special going. Matter of fact, Tigers manager Billy Martin stood on the front step of the dugout and constantly reminded Ryan of his no-hitter to jinx it. But one by one the Tigers continued to go down, overwhelmed by 100-mph fastballs and jackhammer curves that appeared as tiny as aspirins by the time they hit the catcher's mitt.

Kusnyer recalls an exchange that summarized the attitude of Tiger hitters that day. "Norm Cash struck out in his first at-bat and headed back to the dugout. Duke

Sims, who's on deck, calls out to him, 'How's he throwing?' All Cash said was, 'Don't go up there.'"

Through seven innings, Ryan had struck out 16, and the Angels were clinging to a 1-0 lead. They tacked on five runs in the top of the eighth, however, to pad the lead for Ryan. But then Ryan's arm began to stiffen and he lost the edge on his fastball. All of a sudden the Tiger bats were showing signs of life as they twice made solid contact against Ryan.

With two outs in the ninth and the no-hitter on the line, Ryan had only to retire Cash to end the game. Although Cash was in the twilight of his career in 1973, he was still a slugger to be feared, one who was capable of breaking up a no-hitter—and a shutout—with one swing of his bat. As an incentive, Cash had been drilled by a Ryan fastball earlier that season, and the memory of it was still fresh in his mind.

"I look over at Cash walking up to the plate, and he's got a table leg [for a bat]," recalls Kusnyer. "It was all square and knotted, and I say, 'You're not really going to use this, are you?' Nolan yells to Luciano, 'Hey Ron! Check his bat!' Cash looks at Luciano, who says, 'Get that thing outta here. You can't use that!' Cash said, 'I can't hit it with my bat, so what do I have to lose?'"

Cash went back to his regular bat, and promptly popped out to shortstop Rudy Meoli for the final out. In all, Ryan recorded 17 punch-outs, the most strikeouts ever in a no-hitter. What Kusnyer got out of the deal was five swollen fingers and a Pendleton shirt, compliments of Ryan.

"The following year," Kusnyer recalls, "for his third no-hitter he gave Tom Egan $500 and gave everybody else $100," Kusnyer recalls with a laugh. "Of course, he wasn't making a lot of money back then. But I still have the shirt."

The second no-hitter, considered by Ryan as the most overpowering of his seven, tied the record for most no-hitters in one season. Soon Ryan's face was featured in national publications including *Newsweek* and *Sports Illustrated,* both of which featured him on their cover.

By September, Ryan had already eclipsed Bob Feller's American League single-season strikeout record of 348, and had Koufax's 382 in his sights. Koufax had been one of Ryan's heroes. He had always admired him for his talent and integrity, so this record was particularly meaningful to him.

"Like Koufax, I was a strikeout pitcher, and it was very exciting to be in a position to surpass somebody you admired," Ryan says. "I felt very honored to be in that position, so obviously once I got close enough I was hoping I would get the opportunity to break it."

That opportunity came on September 27 in Ryan's last scheduled start of the season. If Ryan was to break Koufax's record, he needed 16 strikeouts against a dangerous Twins lineup that included Rod Carew, Tony Oliva, Harmon Killebrew, and a host of capable hitters. The Twins struck for three runs in the top of the first inning, but despite the rough start, Ryan was piling up the strikeouts. Through the first three innings, he had struck out five batters. He followed that up by striking out the side in the fourth, and then he punched out Carew for the second time to open the fifth. Heading into the seventh, Ryan had 10 strikeouts but still needed to finish the game with a flourish if he was going to catch—or break—Koufax's record. In the seventh, he struck out the side, getting Carew for a third time.

"He was just blowing the ball by people," recalls Carew. "His ball literally exploded. I remember he threw Harmon Killebrew a fastball that was up and in, and his eyes got big as saucers. He was just unbelievable that night."

Ryan was now within two of the record with two innings remaining. In the eighth, he struck out Steve Brye with the go-ahead run at third base to tie Koufax's mark. But in the process Ryan also tore his hamstring, leaving him in a world of pain. Between innings, trainer Freddie Frederico and Dr. Jules Rasinski iced and massaged the leg.

As the ninth frame opened, Ryan was hanging on by a thread. The appreciative home crowd was behind him on every pitch, cheering the strikes and booing when the Twins made contact. Four batters came to the plate in the inning, but Ryan failed to get the strikeout. However, his hapless teammates couldn't score in the bottom of the ninth, so the game went into extra innings.

The tenth inning got off to a poor start for Ryan when catcher George Mitterwald singled to left. But Ryan coerced the next batter to hit into a double play, and after allowing a single and a stolen base to left fielder Mike Adams, short-stop Jerry Terrell popped out to end the inning. Still, Ryan was one strikeout from owning the record.

The Angels went down in order in their half of the tenth, leaving Angels skipper Bobby Winkles with a tough decision to make. Fearing possible long-term injury, Ryan and Winkles both agreed that the 11th inning would be his last. Ryan reached two strikes on lead-off hitter Steve Brye, but Brye ended the at-bat by grounding out to short. Carew, who had struck out three times in the game, drew a walk and, with Oliva at the plate, broke for second. Catcher Jeff Torborg got off a good throw to second, but Carew slid in safely under the tag. The crowd booed Torborg mercilessly, as he almost recorded the inning's second out. Obviously, Angels fans were hoping to maximize Ryan's chances of breaking the record, and Torborg had almost subtracted another out from the equation.

Oliva followed with a fly to center field for the second out, which brought to the plate Rich Reese, who had pinch ran for Killebrew in the ninth. As Reese approached the batter's box, Winkles visited the mound to ask Ryan how he felt. Ryan, clearly exhausted, told Winkles he had enough left in the tank for one more batter.

Angels Hall of Fame broadcaster Dick Enberg, who was calling the game on the radio, described the scene thusly: "Ryan now has two strikes on Rich Reese… two-strike pitch is coming up, Ryan sets, here it is, SWUNG ON AND MISSED. …Nolan Ryan is the major league strikeout king of all time! … Ladies and gentle-men we have seen one of the finest young men to ever wear a baseball uniform record one of the most incredible records in major league history. 383 for Nolan Ryan!"

Ryan recalls how happy he was to not have to pitch any further on a bum leg: "The last two innings I had a real tight hamstring and was relieved that I got it done and didn't have to pitch another game [in order to break the record]. With the tight hamstring, you just don't know where that would have led."

To make the night even sweeter, the Angels sneaked in a run at the bottom of the 11th inning to give Ryan his 21st victory and cap what has to be one of the greatest seasons ever for an Angel pitcher. The fans, the press, and management all threw their arms round Ryan. On the last day of the season, the grateful Angels organization gave Ryan a special day in his honor and handed their superstar the keys to a new truck. Even better, they raised his salary to $100,000 a year, making Ryan one of the highest paid pitchers in the game. General manager Harry Dalton, the man who took the risk and traded Fregosi for Ryan, suddenly looked like a genius.

Ryan's resilience was continually put to the test by the Angels' mediocrity. This was never truer than during the three-year stretch between 1974 and 1976, when the Angels dugout featured a revolving door used exclusively by the team's managers. Three different managers were given a serious crack at the job during those three seasons, and the only thing they had in common was that none of them worked out. In 1972, Bobby Winkles, who led Arizona State to three College World Series titles in the Sixties, was added to the Angels' coaching staff. The next year, he was hired to replace Del Rice.

Winkles's major problem was trying to convince veterans like Frank Robinson to buy into his program. By 1973, Robinson was entering his 18th season in the majors, and was a certain Hall of Famer. More importantly, he was one of the Angels' few offensive threats. His 97 RBI and 30 home runs in 1973 were best on the team. The only other Angel to hit double digits in homers was Bob Oliver, with 18. The following season, Robinson led the team in home runs and RBI again, despite being traded to Cleveland in mid-September. Robinson was not the sort of player to take well to a rookie manager.

"I don't think it was a good match for him and the Angels," Ryan says of Robinson. "Winkles was accustomed to college kids and not accustomed to managing 162 games. Frank Robinson was as intelligent and aggressive a hitter as there was in the game. But with the type of ball club we had and the fact we were in a rebuilding mode, at that point in Frank's career he would probably have been better someplace else competing for a pennant."

The Angels fired Winkles midway through the 1974 as the team got off to a 30-44 start, and promptly hired Dick Williams, who had just won two World Series titles with the Oakland A's in 1972 and '73. Williams resigned as manager of the A's despite winning 288 games there during his three-year tenure. He was fed up with Oakland owner Charlie Finley's continual meddling with his team. Yankees owner

George Steinbrenner quickly attempted to hire Williams as his manager, but his bid was rejected when the still-meddling Finley claimed that Williams could not sign with the Yankees since his contract with the A's still had another year left on it. To start the 1974 season, the skipper responsible for the previous two World Champions was out of work.

However, Angels owner Gene Autry was able to gain Finley's permission to hire Williams, and by July the Angels had their new manager. Williams's winning ways did not carry over to the Angels, unfortunately. He got off to a rocky start, dropping his first 10 games as the Angels stumbled to a last-place finish in the American League West, 22 games behind the eventual World Champion A's.

The following season was no better. Employing a host of young players—seven regulars and five pitchers were 26 years old or younger—the Angels once again finished last in their division. Not used to losing, Williams became increasingly frustrated and so relentless with his young team that many of them disowned him. Among his more memorable moments were having his team take batting practice in a Boston hotel lobby with Wiffleballs; screaming so hard at rookie outfielder Dave Collins that he made him cry; and nicknaming his bullpen the "Arson Squad" because the relievers blew too many saves.

But the final straw that resulted in his dismissal midway through another tumultuous, losing season in 1976 was challenging third baseman Bill Melton to a fight on the team bus in July. When Williams heard singing and laughing in the back of the bus, he yelled sarcastically, "Quiet back there, all you winners!" Melton, who did not see eye to eye with Williams in part because Williams had left him off the All-Star team a few years prior when Melton was with the White Sox, did not take kindly to the comment. Probably under the influence of alcohol, Melton responded to Williams's remark by ripping a bus seat from its moorings and yelling "f--k you!" at the manager.

"You're suspended!" Williams shouted back.

"This is the happiest day of my life!" answered Melton.

At that point, Williams offered to meet Melton outside the bus. Cooler heads intervened, but the incident cost Williams his job. His reign—during which the team was aptly known as "The Hell's Angels"—lasted only one full season and parts of two others, and included two last-place finishes. Through it all, Ryan's good nature and patience were constantly tested.

"We were in that rebuilding process, and it was a deal where they were trying to mix in veteran players at the end of their careers with young players who were called up to the big leagues sooner than they should have been," Ryan recalls. "We were trying to be competitive, and it wasn't working because we didn't have enough talent. I don't know if they could have done anything differently because the [farm] system was depleted. Finally, what they did was go to the free agent market, and that's how they became competitive."

With a team all but resigned to losing, attention focused on Ryan and hard-throwing lefty Frank Tanana, who was just 20 years old in his rookie season of

1974. The tandem, dubbed "Tanana and Ryan and two days of cryin'," won 36 games in '74, over half of the team's eventual total. Ryan himself won 22 games that season and again posted an astronomical number of strikeouts with 367. For two years they were the best one-two strikeout duo in the majors.

Lefty Clyde Wright, who had the fourth spot on the Angels staff prior to Tanana's arrival in 1974, remembers the afternoon at Palm Springs when he realized his days as a starter were numbered.

"Tom Morgan and I were walking into the clubhouse and I hear this mitt poppin'," says Wright. "Turns out there's this kid named Tanana throwing down there in the bullpen. The mitt kept getting louder and louder and I looked at Morgan and said, 'Just tell me one thing—is that son of a bitch down there righthanded or lefthanded?' He said, 'He's left-handed.' And I said, 'I'll see y'all later.'"

Hard-nosed second baseman Jerry Remy and first baseman Bruce Bochte also were bright spots during this dark time, but center fielder Mickey Rivers was the team's only legitimate offensive star. One of the game's best base-stealers, Rivers supplied enough comedic relief to rival all the Marx Brothers combined. His playful sense of humor and Yogi Berra-like grasp of the English language helped the team endure the horrible mid-'70s. Ryan remembers Rivers as a free spirit who sang to his own tune.

"The first year I was there, he didn't show up at spring training for a week, and they kept wondering what happened to him," remembers Ryan. "They had sent a plane ticket for him to go from Miami to L.A., and even had someone at the airport to pick him up and bring him down to Holtville. Mickey never showed up, and for a week they never heard from him. When he finally got there, he said they had to change planes in Houston and they lost his luggage. The team asked, 'How did you lose your luggage when you have a ticket all the way to L.A.?' Mickey didn't really have an answer, so who knows what happened. But that's a Mickey deal. He got to Houston and decided he would stay a week."

Mickey's off-the-field antics aside, he was the team's most consistent contributor on it. In 1975, his last season with the Angels before being traded to the Yankees, the colorful Rivers hit .284 and swiped 70 bases. He was joined in the outfield by Leroy Stanton, whose 14 home runs and 82 RBI were easily team highs. The team's lack of talent and maturity was abundantly clear—especially on offense. In what was becoming a common annual theme, the offense was once again ineffective, finishing next to last in runs scored and hitting a league-worst 55 home runs, 39 less than the closest team. The pitching staff again shouldered the burden of keeping the team competitive. Ryan won 14 games, but due to injuries started just 28 games, 13 less than the previous year. Ed Figueroa picked up some of the slack by posting 16 victories, 16 complete games, and a 2.91 ERA. But it was 21-year-old Frank Tanana who was the Angels' best hurler that season, as he won 16 games, posted a 2.62 ERA, and struck out a league-best 269 batters.

Notwithstanding the Angels' mediocre play, Ryan continued to break records and grab headlines. Much as Bo Belinsky had done a decade prior, Ryan was keeping the national spotlight on the Angels despite their losing ways. To capitalize on Ryan's growing reputation, Angels publicity director George Lederer arranged a scientific test to be conducted by Rockwell International to discover, once and for all, the true speed of "the Ryan Express." Unlike today's radar guns, the Rockwell machine was precisely calibrated to give an accurate, consistent reading. During a night game against the White Sox on September 7, 1974, an eighth-inning pitch to Bee Bee Richard was clocked at 100.8 miles per hour, eclipsing Bob Feller's unofficial mark of 98.6. The Rockwell test naturally enhanced the Ryan mystique. If players didn't already have enough to worry about when facing the Angels ace, they now had to deal with the scientifically proven fact that they were facing the hardest-throwing pitcher in the history of Major League baseball.

More to the point, those same hitters had to accept the fact that Ryan was going to keep them off the plate—even if it took a 100-miles-per-hour fastball to brush them back. In today's game, throwing inside is a lost art, primarily because hitters feel they are entitled to the whole plate, and pitchers lack the control, guts, or both to keep hitters honest. Throwing inside is now considered by many to be an act of aggression. In Ryan's time, however, that concept was as foreign as steroids.

"I grew up in an era where you pitched inside," Ryan says. "Back then, a hitter had to decide what part of the plate was his, the inside or the outside, but he didn't get both."

Ryan believed in mutual respect between a batter and a pitcher, as well. Kusnyer says that modern hittters who like to stand around and watch their home runs sail over the outfield fence would have paid dearly for that arrogance if facing Ryan.

"Ryan's generation was brought up with the philosophy of 'I'm gonna show you respect, so in turn you show me respect.' These guys today, hopping up and down, doing the moonwalk and break dancing, wouldn't do that with Nolan. I guarantee it," says Kusnyer. "If they did, their next time up they wouldn't be hopping to first base—they would be crawling."

Ryan was also protective of his teammates as well as the plate. If a teammate was plunked by a pitch, the opposing team knew that Ryan was going to retaliate. It wasn't a matter of if, but when. This practice of sticking up for his team became known around the Angels dugout as "Ryan's Law." One example occurred when the Angels faced the Tigers in 1972. Detroit manager Billy Martin ordered his pitcher to drill first baseman Jim Spencer. Kusnyer was catching for the Halos that day, and as he was getting on his gear in between innings, Ryan told him, "The first guy is going down." That first, unlucky guy was Norm Cash, and when he got to the plate Kusnyer told him, "Tie your shoes on real tight."

"There must have been 40,000 people in the stands, and they all yelled, 'Look out!' at the same time," recalls Kusnyer. "That ball was coming at Cash so hard he looked like a skeleton. Before he could turn out of the way, the ball hit him so hard in the back of the elbow that he limped off the field. On his way off, he told his teammate who was waiting on deck, 'Tell Billy I'm done for the year.'"

When word got around the league that Ryan could be a "little bit crazy on the mound," he didn't deny it. The fear his fastball put into people was an asset he wasn't afraid to exploit.

"I was always aggressive," says Ryan. "I wanted them to think, 'This guy may knock me down.' If fear could be a factor, then I wanted it to be because it gave me the edge. My belief was that every fourth day that mound was mine. I had a job to do and that was to give us the opportunity to win a ball game."

Perhaps former teammate Don Baylor says it best: "Nolan had the kind of mentality that he would knock you down and kind of smile at you at the same time."

When Ryan brought his "A game" to the mound, the combination of his arsenal of pitches and his unwavering intimidation proved to be simply overwhelming for the opposition. On September 27, 1974, in his last scheduled start of the season, Ryan fired his third career no-hitter, against the Minnesota Twins. He walked eight Twins, but struck out 15. In typical Ryan fashion, he was gracious after the game and told the press, "I had made a silent goal to try and throw a no-hitter at home just to show the people I appreciate the way they have treated me."

Ruth Ryan had attended every Angel home game that season, but missed that no-hitter because she left for Alvin two days earlier to get their house in order for her husband's arrival. Although she heard the last few innings via telephone thanks to the efforts of the Anaheim Stadium switchboard operator, she vowed she would never miss another one. She didn't have to wait very long.

It was a sunny afternoon at Anaheim Stadium on June 1, 1975, and in order to get out of the heat Ryan avoided the dugout and sat on the staircase in the tunnel next to the bat room. It was shady inside, and the space would allow him a moment to re-group and go over the Oriole lineup. Under the leadership of Earl Weaver, the Orioles had maintained their trend of success from the Sixties and were perennial contenders for a World Series ring. The 1975 O's featured a potent offense that included Don Baylor and Ken Singleton in the outfield and Lee May at first. But heading into the ninth inning, Ryan was focusing on another three names: Al Bumbry, Tommy Davis, and Bobby Grich—the heart of the O's batting order.

Ryan made easy work of Bumbry, who hit a weak fly ball to Morris Nettles in left. Then Davis, a former two-time batting champ for the Dodgers, worked the count to 2-2 before pounding the next pitch up the middle. It looked like a bonafide hit, and the home crowd stirred in their seats. But second baseman Jerry Remy came out of nowhere to snag the ball—his body fully extended—and throw over to Bruce Bochte at first for the second out. The crowd went wild.

Ryan is congratulated by teammates after completing his fourth no-hitter in 1975. AP/WWP

All that stood between Nolan Ryan and his fourth career no-hitter was Grich, who sauntered up to the plate with a certain confidence. In right field, Leroy Stanton studied the position of the sun and readied his sunglasses just in case. Centerfielder Mickey Rivers appeared statuesque, knees bent in his stance. For once "Mick the Quick" was all business. Thinking it would be just like Grich to bunt, Dave Chalk moved in a couple feet at third base.

Ryan wiped the sweat from his brow, looked in to catcher Ellie Rodriguez for the sign, and fired a fastball. Grich was on the pitch but fouled it straight back for strike one. Showing the same patience that had rewarded him with walks in two of his previous at-bats, Grich laid off two balls before fouling off another pitch to even the count at two balls and two strikes.

Bochte recalls what happened next: "Everybody in the whole stadium was thinking the same thing—fastball. But instead out floated this 75-mile-per-hour change-up. Everybody just looked at it wide-eyed, including Grich, who watched as it went across the plate for strike three."

The stadium exploded as Ryan came off the mound. In the stands, Ruth Ryan's eyes began to overflow with tears as she made her way down the stairs to the field. She rushed to her husband and kissed him over and over again. At the age of 28, Ryan had already tied the Major League record for career no-hitters—set by Sandy Koufax—with his fourth.

In the clubhouse, champagne corks popped and someone borrowed four baseballs, and with a black felt pen wrote a big zero on each one. As Ryan—who'd had a tender elbow before the game and wasn't even sure he had his best stuff—held the four balls aloft, photographers snapped photos of the symbolic moment for posterity.

The game was Ryan's defining moment as a California Angel and one of Ryan's favorites. "I'm very proud that I have seven no-hitters and was able to throw four in a three-year span, but I would have to say the fourth one is the most memorable because it tied me with Sandy Koufax," Ryan says.

Comparisons between Koufax and Ryan have long been drawn, but although their values and personalities were similar, their pitching styles bore some differences. Norm Sherry, who caught Koufax with the Dodgers and later managed Ryan with the Angels, says both were unique in their own way.

"Ryan was a more physical pitcher," concludes Sherry. "He would use his legs and had a lot of drive and put a lot of terrific effort into throwing the ball. Koufax was more fluid and gave less exertion than Ryan. Because of his large hands, Sandy was able to get more backspin, and his ball had more life on it. Nolan held the ball deep in his hand and had a heavier type of action that would make the ball cut in and out and sometimes sink.

"People have always asked me who threw harder. My answer is when you throw like they did, what difference does it make? Hard is hard."

Koufax, whom Ryan calls the most overpowering pitcher he's ever seen, took home three Cy Young Awards and one MVP Award during his 12-year career. He also led the league in wins on three occasions, going 97-27 over his final four seasons. There was no shortage of praise heaped on Sandy's shoulders, whereas Ryan's success was occasionally met with skepticism by his detractors.

"In baseball, people are always trying to pull you down," says Ruth Ryan. "You get criticism from everybody, and at times you need to look out for yourself and be your own cheerleader. You hear and read things said about you, but you can't let that affect you. I think Nolan's stubbornness helped him, in part, to get through it."

His stubbornness also helped Ryan combat the numerous critics who didn't always realize there was more to the game than won-loss percentages. Intangibles come into play when judging a workhorse like Ryan, whose massive number of innings pitched was just as valuable as wins and losses. In five of his eight seasons with the Angels, Ryan topped 284 innings pitched. Only once did he fail to reach the 200-inning plateau, in 1975 when he threw 198 innings.

"People who say Nolan is a .500 pitcher don't know baseball very well," says Rod Carew. "Every time he took the mound, you had a chance to win. He was a staff saver. He didn't go out there and pitch two or three innings, he would pitch eight or nine. When he started, at first he would be throwing 95 miles per hour, and by the eighth inning he might be throwing 97 miles per hour. He usually kept our team in the game and gave us a chance to win."

Ryan's philosophy was to not concern himself with things he couldn't control. "I didn't worry about critics, because that is just what they are—critics. A lot of the time, the people critical of you really have no understanding of everything that comes into play. My attitude is, you can't worry about those things. You can drive yourself nuts worrying about everything that people say about you."

The things he could control, however, he took very seriously. Unlike today, when pitchers are only expected to throw six or seven innings, Ryan took pride in starting and finishing a game. In his day, pitchers were expected to go as long as they could. This is one reason his all-time strikeout record of 5,714 will likely never be broken. It's doubtful that any starting pitcher will ever average enough innings per start—yet alone pitch for as many seasons—as Nolan Ryan was able to do.

Reggie Jackson, who faced Ryan many times while with the A's and Yankees, recalls one game in which Ryan threw 212 pitches. "Never a whine [from him], nothing," says Jackson. "He would throw 150 pitches every game. Today, 120 is a lot of pitches. Nolan Ryan would throw 120 pitches in five innings!"

Throughout Jackson's 21 seasons, few pitchers impressed him both as a player and a person as much as Ryan did.

"Nolan Ryan is a good and humble man, so you're gonna feel good when he's around you," says Jackson. "It feels good to me if he calls me friend, because he's a Seal of Good Housekeeping. He has a quality image. ... It was a privilege as a player to have played against him."

The Angels struggled as usual in 1976, despite attempting to upgrade their offense by trading Rivers and Figueroa to the Yankees for All-Star outfielder Bobby Bonds, and Jim Spencer to the White Sox for third baseman Bill Melton. Bonds struggled to stay healthy, and when he was, he failed to find his power stroke, hitting a lowly 10 home runs in 99 games. The Angels once again finished last in the American League in runs scored, yet again dooming them to an under-.500 record.

However, with the arrival of free agency in 1977, the Angels finally began to improve as a team. With their first free agent signing of the offseason, they nabbed 27-year-old outfielder Don Baylor. The following day, they signed another Oakland outfielder, 29-year-old Joe Rudi. Seven days later, they signed All-Star second baseman Bobby Grich. The signings drastically improved a struggling offense and made the Angels contenders, at least on paper.

A healthy Bonds rebounded in 1977, tying Leon Wagner's franchise record with 37 home runs and driving in a new franchise-best 115 RBI. Baylor also began to blossom as a power hitter, clubbing an until-then career-best 25 home runs. But despite significant improvements in runs scored, injuries kept the Angels out of the divisional race, and they finished fifth for the second year in a row.

Undeterred, Autry continued the free agency binge in '78 with the big-money acquisition of rising star Lyman Bostock, who had hit .336 with 14 home runs for the Minnesota Twins the previous year. In another bold move, Bonds was dealt along with young outfielder Thad Bosley and pitching prospect Richard Dotson to the White Sox for pitchers Chris Knapp and Dave Frost, and a player who would become a regular for the Angels for more than a decade, catcher Brian Downing.

The signing of Bostock looked like a wise move for the Angels. Bostock was hitting close to .300 in September when fate stepped in and ended the rising star's life. After playing in a game against the White Sox in Chicago on September 23, Bostock was murdered in Gary, Indiana. While sitting in a back seat of a car, he was killed by a lone gunman in a case of being at the wrong place at the wrong time. The tragedy overshadowed the Angels' first solid finish in years. The team won 87 games, tying for second place in the division. Rookie third baseman Carney Lansford hit .294, while Baylor put together an impressive season with 34 home runs and 99 RBI.

To make up for the loss of Bostock, Autry got busy in the offseason. In December, he traded utility player Ron Jackson and designated hitter Danny Goodwin to the Twins for outfielder Dan Ford. However, it would be a second deal that offseason with the Twins that would truly define the 1979 Angels. In early February, Ken Landreaux and three others were dealt to the Twins for seven-time batting champ Rod Carew, making the Angels one of the most star-studded teams in baseball. Within two days of the trade, Angels season ticket sales had already increased by several thousand.

In January of 1979, Ryan told general manager Buzzie Bavasi that he was happy with the Angels and had no intention of becoming a free agent after the '79 season. He requested a three-year contract extension that would see his salary raise 33 percent to $400,000 per year, plus a $200,000 bonus. Bavasi wrote back that he wouldn't negotiate contracts until the season was completed, which placed Ryan's request on hold. Stung by Bavasi's indifference, Ryan promptly signed with an agent, and told Bavasi the Angels had to decide by the spring or he would seriously consider free agency. By May, however, Ryan had more significant concerns on his mind.

On May 8, while in Boston for a series against the Red Sox, Ryan received word from his wife that their oldest son, Reid, had been struck by a car in front of their Villa Park home, and was in intensive care at Orange County Children's Hospital. Ryan took the first plane home to California and was at his son's bedside the next morning. Reid had suffered a broken leg and damage to his kidney and spleen. Ruth and Nolan took turns at the hospital, and through a lot of tears, prayer, and the efforts of the medical team, Reid pulled through.

"Every day he would stop by and see me before he went to the ballpark," Reid remembers. "He would always bring me coloring books and jig-saw puzzles or little novelty batting helmets that he picked up on the road. He always spent time with the other sick kids, too, and those visits meant a lot to them."

With Reid on the mend, Ryan's agent, Dick Moss, dropped by Bavasi's office in July to check on his client's status. When Bavasi asked how much they wanted, Moss wrote down $1 million a year for two years, and $700,000 for a third. Bavasi nearly had a coronary.

"I'm from the old school where your record indicates how much you get," Bavasi later said. "For those first two years I was there [in 1978 and 1979], our ball club was over .500, but Nolan's record during that time was under .500. He was 26-27 for those two years. I had fellas who were 11-8, 12-4. What am I going to do with them if I give Nolan all the money?"

Part of the problem was that Bavasi was used to playing hardball with players, and actually thrived on it. When he was with the Dodgers in the 1950s and '60s, management held all the clout. With the onset of free agency, the rules had changed; but Bavasi wasn't willing to change along with them.

"Buzzie came from the Koufax and Drysdale era and had a hard time with the possibility of a pitcher making a million dollars a year," recalls Ross Newhan. "The disagreement was more than money, however. I think he and Dick Moss got into somewhat of a personality disagreement."

Ryan went 16-14 in 1979, but posted a 3.60 ERA and along with Dave Frost, who also won 16 games, anchored the Angels rotation. But for once, it wasn't the Angels pitching staff that was remarkable—it was the offense. Finishing tops in the league in runs scored with 866, the Angels featured a consistent group of hitters who could hit for average and power. Baylor didn't miss a single game en route to smashing the franchise record for RBI with a league-leading 139. He also contributed 36 home runs, 120 runs scored, 22 stolen bases, and a .296 average, making him an obvious choice for the MVP Award. However, he had a little help from his teammates. Carew, playing first base, hit .318, but was bested in average by Downing's mark of .326. In stark contrast to Angels teams of the past, the 1979 club featured four players who hit 20 or more home runs. Both Grich and newcomer Dan Ford broke the century mark in RBI with 101. Eight of the team's nine regulars hit .280 or better as the Angels featured the most effective offense in franchise history.

With just 88 wins, the Angels held off the Royals, Rangers, and Twins for the A.L. West crown, their first in 18 seasons. But they lost 3-1 in the American League Championship Series to a superior Orioles team that won 102 games in the regular season.

In eight seasons with the Angels, Ryan had helped lead the team from obscurity to serious contention. And he had conducted himself with the utmost class, professionalism, and dignity. The fans, press, and ownership loved him unconditionally, so even though Ryan was without a contract heading into the 1979 offseason, there was little speculation that the ace would not be back with the Angels in 1980. Ryan would have been content to play out the rest of his career in Anaheim, which he proved by purchasing a new home in nearby Villa Park, California.

But Bavasi ruined all that in the offseason by making some disparaging remarks about Ryan in the press, the worst of which was his off-hand suggestion that Ryan could easily be replaced by a couple of 8-7 pitchers. That was the final straw for Ryan. He put a "for sale" sign in front of his new Villa Park house, and told Moss to file for free agency. Later that winter, after he signed a contract with the Houston Astros for $1 million a year for three years, Ryan took out a full-page ad in the *Orange County Register* thanking Angels fans for their support and kindness.

Many have wondered how the Angels organization could ever let this happen. How could Autry lose his star player, a once-in-a-lifetime pitcher and someone he trusted and admired? Newhan later admitted it was the franchise's "biggest mistake."

"Gene had put a lot of faith in the people he had working for him," recalls Newhan. "Should he have stepped in? Probably, because Nolan was one of his favorites and maybe he should have told Buzzie, 'Let's not lose him. Go to any length that is reasonable.' It was unfortunate. Up to that point, he was probably the biggest attraction in Angels history."

It's easy for an Angels fan to look back and wonder, "What if...?" In both 1982 and '86, the Angels came within one game of winning the pennant. Would Ryan's arm have made a difference? Nobody knows for sure, but obviously his presence would have been huge.

Bavasi admits that if he had it to do over again, he would have dealt with Ryan directly and not through his agent. He still maintains, however, that contract negotions should be based on record, pure and simple. Ryan won 138 games for the Angels and lost 121. On a team with a competent offense, his win total would have likely been significantly higher.

The Ryans eventually came to see the move was for the best.

"He didn't want to leave," recalls Ruth Ryan, "but it became a matter of principle. He really wanted to be with an organization he felt appreciated him. It was unfortunate, but Buzzie was doing his job, and I don't know if we handled things the right way or wrong way. But once it happened, it happened. You just have to look ahead. You don't look back."

Ryan himself is characteristically gracious and to the point. "I don't have any hard feelings or animosity toward anyone," he says, "because I'm a believer that everything will work out for the best, and it did for me."

Ryan pitched for 14 more seasons, recording three more no-hitters and 157 victories. Autry tried in vain to get Ryan back when he became a free agent again in 1988, but Ryan opted to stay in Texas, mainly because he didn't want to uproot his children again. He entered the Hall of Fame in 1999 with kind words for Autry, the Angels organization, and its fans.

Ryan claims his longevity was a combination of genetics, work ethic, positive attitude, and good health. But according to his son, Reid, there were more complex factors figuring into his father's determination. He claims his dad had a unique philosophy ingrained in him by his parents, who were reared in the Great Depression and had worked hard all their lives. Like many who suffered through that era, Ryan's parents took nothing for granted.

"The Ryans are a very serious family," says Reid. "My parents look at their parents who sacrificed for their kids, and sometimes they feel guilty about enjoying life. I think that is one of the reasons my dad played so long. He understood clearly what his parents went through and how tough it was for them to support their family. His philosophy has always been, 'When the sun comes up you go to work, and when it goes down you keep working, and every opportunity that you have be thankful that you have it.' Even now we say, 'Hey, Dad, you're 50-something years old, why don't you just relax and not fly out to New York and do that card show or these commercials?' In the back of my dad's mind I know he's saying, 'I can go to an appearance and make more money than my father made in a whole year of working two jobs.'"

According to his eldest son, baseball satisfied Ryan's competitive needs, but more importantly supplied a means for endeavors closer to his heart.

"Baseball did not define him," adds Reid. "To him it was a job, and although he enjoyed playing, his first love and passion was the cattle business. When the season ended he always went back to ranching and to the family and to the things he really enjoyed. That way, when the baseball season came around, he was always fresh and ready to go."

Reid also maintains that a change of scenery was also a big factor for his dad's longevity. "Part of the fun for him was changing clubs and leagues. I don't think he could have played 27 years with just one club. To him, new teammates and new family situations made things interesting."

Rangers equipment man Zack Minasian, who was with the team when Ryan was a Ranger from 1989-1993, says that Ryan's rare competitive spirit enabled him to raise his game to a higher level.

"He mentioned the word 'challenge' a lot, and that word meant everything to him," recalls Minasian. "When you gave him the ball, you were challenging him to go out and beat that other ball club, and that's what he did. Some guys shy away from challenges, but Nolan thrived on it. He loved going against the best. That's what fueled him."

But by Ryan's own admission, all that ended when he hung up his glove.

"Am I competitive today? No, I'm completely burnt out on it and don't have any interest in competing in anything," says Ryan. "I had to do it for a living, and it took a lot of effort and preparation for me to get into that state of mind to be aggressive and competitive. That's just not something I want to do anymore."

Upon retirement, Ryan dove headlong into his ranches and joined his sons and daughter Wendy in buying a Houston Astros Double-A affiliate team, which they relocated to Round Rock, Texas. They named their new team—now a Triple-A team—the Express and helped build Dell Diamond, a state-of-the-art ballpark. In

2004 the family built another facility, which presently houses the Astros' Double-A affiliate in Corpus Christi. As much as he loved remaining connected to baseball, the opportunity to work with his children is the greatest satisfaction for Ryan.

"Baseball has given us everything we have," says Reese Ryan, who serves as chief financial director for the two clubs. "What we're trying to do here is to give something back. We've been able to move baseball into two markets that have been absent from baseball for a long time, and that's a pretty neat deal."

According to Ruth, having several grandkids around has taken a little bit of the edge off her husband. But, she adds quickly, he still possesses the same qualities that attracted her to him in high school. Despite all the fame and financial rewards that went hand in hand with Ryan's career, his core values have never changed, says the man himself.

"I always thought just because I was blessed with the ability to throw a baseball and have some neat things happen to me, that it didn't really entitle me to think that I was any better than anybody else and act any differently," says Ryan. "Even though those things happened to me, I am still who I am. That was just my attitude."

As far as his baseball legacy goes, former Major League pitcher Orel Hershiser, who played against Ryan in the mid-Eighties, provides this assessment: "As professionals, we see a lot of guys who have tremendous talent and we see a lot of guys waste tremendous talent. The greatest compliment I can give Nolan is the fact that when blessed with that much talent, he paid the debt right back. Even though he reaped the benefits of fame, accomplishment, and wealth, along with the great enjoyment of playing this great game in front of a world-class audience, he also took on the additional responsibility of saying, 'I'm going to be a true professional. I'm going to be a role model. I'm going to do this right. Not only for me and my family and my team, but for all of baseball to enjoy.'"

Ironically, Ryan's next-to-last performance of his 27-year career came on September 17, 1993, at Anaheim Stadium. Sadly, it would be his final start before suffering a career-ending arm injury in the first inning against Seattle the following week. In a weird twist of fate, the baseball gods chose Anaheim as Ryan's last defining moment.

From the size of the line, one might have surmised that the Rolling Stones or the Pope were in town. It wound five rows deep around the front of Anaheim's Doubletree Hotel before curling into the street. But the people in line weren't there to experience rock 'n' roll or religious nirvana. Instead, they carried cards, balls, gloves, plastic helmets, and photos to hand over to a balding, middle-aged gentleman from Texas who 15 years earlier had played baseball for the Angels. When spoken to, he would answer graciously and with a smile as he signed his name—Nolan Ryan—over and over again.

The autograph session was a totally impromptu affair, not the brainstorm of a publicist. Whether Ryan saw it as his responsibility or a civic duty to hold the signing, only he knew. Maybe it was just the simple pleasure he got from making people happy. When his ride pulled up in front of the hotel to take him to the ballpark, Ryan politely informed the driver that he would need a few more minutes before he was ready. But in fact he would need another hour before he was ready to drive away, for there were still more people in line.

As his car made the turn down State College Boulevard to the stadium, Ryan couldn't help but notice how the area had grown since he left. At the stadium he dressed and met with some national and local sportswriters. Then he ventured outside, where hundreds more fans, pens in hand, eagerly awaited the chance to get his signature.

There was a slight stirring in the crowd when he finally made his way to the bullpen for his pregame warmup. Then, as he returned to the dugout, something wonderful happened. As if on cue, everyone in the stadium stood and cheered. The standing ovation went on for five minutes, and accompanied him the entire way back to the bench. Before he disappeared into the dugout he modestly doffed his hat, then took a seat on the bench and prepared to take the Anaheim Stadium mound one last time.

He pitched another gem that night, tossing seven strong innings, striking out five, and allowing just one unearned run. In the seventh inning, he whiffed Greg Meyers for his 5,714—and final—strikeout of his career. Ryan was 46 when he formally retired five days later due to a chronic elbow problem. He would have to wait until 1999 for his call from the Hall of Fame, but the wait was but a mere formality. During his 27 years in the majors, Ryan won 326 games, tossed seven no-hitters, and set over 50 major league records. No one else in baseball history had ever thrown so hard and for so long.

11

"GROOVE"

DON BAYLOR

*F*rank Robinson stood in the center of the Orioles clubhouse eyeballing the local sports section when he suddenly stopped reading, grabbed a bat from his locker, and began pounding it on a wooden table.

BAM! BAM! BAM!

"Listen up, everybody! I want you guys to hear this," shouted Robinson. "A writer asked someone in this room, 'How do you expect to break into the line up when you have Merv Rettenmund, Don Buford, Frank Robinson, and Paul Blair playing in front of you?'"

Robinson eyed the 40 or so players around him and then turned back to the article. "Here's what he said: 'Once I get in a groove it really doesn't matter who is out there. ... I should be able to play.'"

Robinson surveyed the room and spotted 21-year-old Don Baylor sitting in the corner doing a pretty good imitation of a guy trying to disappear from sight. Turning to the team, Robinson smiled. "Pretty brash words for a rookie, don't you think?" he asked.

Although just a rookie, Don Baylor was savvy enough to know if he spoke up, his teammates would be all over him. He might even be brought up before Baltimore's infamous Kangaroo Court, in which Robinson, with his mop wig and air of superiority, served as the sole judge and jury. Since Baylor had no intention of digging a deeper hole for himself or his wallet, he just sat there defiantly and braced for the pot-shots surely headed his way.

But the silence was deafening, and continued on for what to Baylor seemed like an eternity. Finally it was broken by shortstop Mark Belanger.

"Groove," said Belanger. "I like it, boys. That name's gonna stick."

"*Groooove!*" echoed the excited clubhouse.

Baylor had opened his mouth and announced to the world how good he was, and now Robinson had extended the invitation to back it up! It was a daunting position for a newcomer to be in, but Don Baylor was used to challenges and even adversity. He'd been up against it all his life.

Twelve-year-old Donnie Baylor was nervous on the first day of school. How would he react when called on to introduce himself to his classmates? Would he stumble and mix up his words, or freeze and say nothing? When the time came to make the announcement, Donnie swallowed hard and rose from his seat.

"Don Baylor," he said clearly and succinctly.

As he sank back in his chair he noticed a few smirks, but for the most part the room remained silent. In choosing to become one of the first of three African-American children to integrate O' Henry Junior High School in West Austin, Texas, Baylor had opened himself up to all kinds of scrutiny. He had voluntarily crossed a wide racial barrier—one that was not simple to breach in 1962—and in doing so became a moving target. His brothers, cousins, and friends had all chosen differently. They preferred 40-minute bus rides every morning from Clarksville to East Austin's all-black Kealing Junior High, five miles away. But Donnie opted for the four-block walk into West Austin and the new world he hoped would offer alternatives to trade school or a black college.

The hazing and catcalls began almost immediately, but his classmates soon found out that Donnie Baylor was no pushover. When another student called him "nigger" to his face, Donnie chased the frightened youth all the way to the auditorium and tackled him so hard that they skimmed across the stage and got tangled up in the stage curtain. Donnie would have knocked the kid's head off had he not been pulled away. The principal turned a blind eye to the provoker and gleefully punished Donnie. But the incident did wonders for Baylor's credibility. When word got around that the black boy from the other side of the tracks came out swinging when provoked, no one dared to push his buttons or call him demeaning names to his face again.

When Baylor went to all-white Austin High School three years later, some of his biggest adversaries were his coaches and teachers. When he went out for football, Baylor had to literally beg for a uniform. As a sophomore in baseball, despite batting .345—best on the team—he had to wait for his junior year and a new coach to finally become a starter.

The ball field wasn't the only place Baylor was confronted with racism. It was a school custom to have the cheerleaders escort the varsity football players to their classes on game days, but Baylor didn't qualify for the star treatment because his skin was a darker color.

Baylor found the strength to persevere back home in Clarksville, with the help of his family, friends, and a 100-year-old church.

His wife, Rebecca, reflects on those challenging times: "He had to fight, literally and figuratively, just to play ball. Growing up poor, especially as the oldest child, and in a racist environment, he learned early on that he had to fight to get and protect what he wanted. The resolve to accept and face a challenge never left him. He may be the product of a household with an abundance of discipline, pride, and love. If color was what separated folks, it was family and faith that united them, and the Baylor clan had plenty of both."

Amazingly, Baylor never lost the openness and good-heartedness instilled in him by his church and family. They insisted each person be measured individually. Baylor took that advice to heart, and it enabled him to eventually have friends of all races.

Throughout his high school athletic career Baylor continued to work hard, and when he finally got his chance to strut his stuff, he excelled. Unlike other coaches, Frank Seale, his high school varsity baseball coach, made sure that Donnie got a fair shake and did everything in his power to see him reach his full potential. Baylor says that Seale greatly aided him in reaching the next level.

As a tight end in football, Baylor possessed speed and amazing hands. In baseball, he could just flat-out hit. Legendary Texas Longhorns football coach Darryl Royal recruited Baylor as an end, but insisted that he only play football. While football was the king of sports in Austin, Baylor's passion was baseball, and when he was selected number two by the Baltimore Orioles in the 1967 free agent draft, he chose to bypass college altogether and pursue his dream. As he pursued his dream in the minor leagues, Baylor kept the lessons he learned in Clarksville close to his heart. "Clarksville is my foundation," he'd always say. "It's what I am."

In 1967, Baylor joined the Bluefield Baby Birds of the Appalachian Rookie League in West Virginia. There he was indoctrinated into the Orioles way of playing baseball, and that's where he first met a scrappy infielder named Bobby Grich, from Long Beach, California.

"I went to Bluefield and the very first guy that came up and shook my hand was Donny Baylor," recalls Grich. "He was the number-two draft choice and I was number one. He was black, I was white, but he introduced himself with a big smile and said, 'Welcome to the team, man!' From that moment on, he and I hit it off, and we've been the closest friends ever since."

Some people couldn't figure the unlikely friendship, but there was a big common denominator. "He was a surfer from Long Beach and I was a browneck from Austin, Texas," says Baylor. "But he was colorblind, and so was I."

Both men excelled, with Baylor leading the league in hitting, runs scored, and stolen bases, while Grich raised eyebrows with his tenacious play. As the two earned raves for their individual play, they were continually lectured on the concept of team play and pushed to further develop their fundamentals—both of which were considered top priorities by the Orioles.

When Baylor joined the Orioles for spring training the following year, he learned quickly that there was one man in camp from whom all others took their cue: Frank Robinson. On a team that included Boog Powell, Brooks Robinson, Davey Johnson, Jim Palmer, Dave McNally, Mike Cuellar, and Paul Blair, Robinson was unquestionably the field general. Baylor soaked Robinson up like a sponge, emulating everything he did right down to the bat he used.

"He was just like Frank," observes former Orioles teammate Elrod Hendricks. "He imitated the way he ran the bases and how he stood right on top of the plate. If the ball came at him he'd just let it hit him and walk to first, then bust the second baseman to bits when he slid into second—just like Frank did. When Frank had Donnie down in winter ball, he showed him how to hit on the plate, which was apparently what he wanted to do anyway because Frank hit right on the plate. And he wanted to be just like Frank."

Baylor admits Robinson made a huge impact on him and says his apprenticeship served him well. "Through Frank I learned what leadership was all about," recalls Baylor. "I could tell he was tough by just watching him. Whether it was sliding into second or the way he stood on the plate, his attitude was, 'Just jump on my back.' All of that appealed to me, so I did my best to emulate that style."

Baylor was named Minor League Player of the Year in 1970, but because of the depth of talent in the Oriole organization and the fact that Baltimore was winning over 100 games a season, he had to wait two years to join the big league club.

Hendricks recalls the day during winter league in 1971 when Baylor proved to everyone he was ready. "Doyle Alexander was pitching, and he gave up a hit that caromed off a cement ridge in the outfield that was used for track and field," remembers Hendricks. "It hopped over Baylor, who had to hustle just to get the ball in and hold the guy to a triple. After the inning was over Alexander came charging back to the dugout, threw down his glove, and accused everybody on the team of dogging it.

"'You're all gutless bastards!' screamed Alexander. 'If you guys don't want to play, get the hell out of here!'

"'You talking to me?' Baylor asked incredulously.

"'Yeah!' responded Alexander.

"'I just saved you a run, asshole! We're busting our butts out here! You're the one giving up all these goddamn line drives, not us. I'm gonna kick your ass!'

"Baylor was ready to go to war!" says Hendricks. "Robinson had to use all his strength to restrain him. The veterans gained a lot of respect for Baylor from that point on. All of a sudden they said, 'Hey, this guy means business, this guy wants to win and he's not gonna take crap from no one.' He never had any more problems after that."

Baylor was earning respect from his teammates on the field as well as in the dugout. He would straddle the plate, and if the ball came inside he'd let it hit him. In his six seasons with Baltimore, Baylor established himself as one of baseball's toughest and most aggressive players. Just like Robinson, he adopted a "win at any cost" attitude and routinely led the league in the "hit by pitch" category. By the time his career ended, Baylor had set a new major league record by being hit 267 times in his career.

Being the hard case that he was, Baylor never let on if the beaning hurt—except once. On a cold day in Baltimore, Nolan Ryan hit him with a fastball on the wrist.

Recalls Hendricks gleefully: "Normally, he'd just go down to first base and not rub it. But he got halfway down to first and said, 'Screw this!' He called to our trainer, 'Come here, man! Put something on this damn thing!' He never wanted the pitcher to know that he was hurt, but that day he gave in to Nolan."

According to Hendricks, Baylor also shared another characteristic with his mentor, Robinson. "Maybe it's a Texas thing, but those two guys had very short tempers, hair-triggers," Hendricks says. "The difference was, Baylor let you know he was pissed, whereas Frank, he would never let you know until he was ready to explode; and by then it was too late."

In the spring of 1976, Baylor was sent to Oakland for Reggie Jackson. Upon getting the news from manager Earl Weaver, Baylor broke down and cried. "It was as if my family had kicked me out of the house," Baylor admits. "I was heartbroken."

After posting the best numbers of his young career in 1975 with 25 home runs and 76 RBI, Baylor slumped with Oakland in 1976, batting .247 with just 15 home runs. However, he did showcase another element of his game, increasing his stolen base total from 32 in 1975 to 52 stolen bases the following year. But the A's were in transition, and fearing the onset of free agency, owner Charlie Finley was anxious to get something for the key members of his three-time championship team while he could. Finley's indifference provided Baylor with the opportunity he needed to get out of Oakland, and in the fall of 1976 he joined the inaugural roster of players available for free agency.

Although he detested the emergence of free agency, Gene Autry realized a new era had dawned in baseball, and he was prepared to take full advantage of it. When word got out that Baylor and several others were on the market, Autry ordered general manager Harry Dalton to take immediate action. In a three-week flurry, Dalton signed Baylor, Joe Rudi, and Bobby Grich to the team.

Baylor negotiated a $580,000 signing bonus on top of his salary of $1.6 million over six years; suddenly he was one of the highest paid players in baseball. However, as he soon realized, with all that money came the pressure to perform. Baylor was shocked when he discovered that the winning attitude ingrained in him at Baltimore was virtually nonexistent with the Angels. With the exception of just a handful of players, Baylor joined a clubhouse totally indifferent to winning—something he simply couldn't accept. Part of the problem was the Angels didn't have a lot of talent to work with. Managers Norm Sherry and Dave Garcia—Sherry's eventual replacement—didn't help matters by letting players walk all over them.

Despite the inflow of free agents, the Angels struggled in 1977. In April Grich hurt his back moving an air conditioner and spent a significant part of the season on the disabled list. Then a broken wrist ended Joe Rudi's season in late June. At the time, Rudi was on pace to drive in over 100 runs. That left Baylor with the unenviable task of carrying the free agent load all by himself. The team's slow start put a damper on the whole season, and fans needing someone to blame chose Baylor because of all the zeroes on his paycheck.

"I remember coach Del Crandall preparing me for the game every day with a 'Booooo!'" Baylor recalls ruefully. "Then I'd go outside and everybody in the stands started in on me. It was brutal!"

To add to his woes, an old football injury to his shoulder resurfaced, hampering his throwing. The combination of a weak arm and struggling bat made him a prime candidate for designated hitter—a role Baylor did not covet but was forced into for nearly half of the season. He prided himself on his all-around play, and it was hard to accept being perceived as only an offensive threat.

"Dave Garcia told me, 'If you were managing this team, who would you want to play leftfield? Don Baylor or Joe Rudi? Joe was a Gold Glove left fielder, and if you're a manager you've got to be truthful.'" Baylor recalls. "I said, 'Okay, I'll be designated hitter.'"

But losing his status as a defensive asset left him depressed and affected his hitting. Baylor struggled until mid-July, when his old mentor, Frank Robinson, joined the club as a batting coach. Robinson told him not to pressure himself by trying to carry the team. He could help more by playing within himself. Under Robinson's tutelage, Baylor flourished: In one 13-game stretch, he smashed six homers and collected 17 RBI.

Despite Baylor's late resurgence, the Angels finished 74-88 in 1977, 28 games behind the league-leading Kansas City Royals. Baylor's .251 average and 75 RBI were respectable, but a far cry from what Autry expected from his newest millionaire.

"I knew I was gonna have to win the fans back after '77," Baylor says. "I hit 25 home runs that year and still got hammered pretty good by the press. But the tough times I went through made me stronger. I could have cried about it, but instead I committed myself to turning it around."

The big bucks Autry doled out to Baylor and the other free agents—plus years of carefree spending—left the franchise in a serious financial bind. To help remedy the situation, Autry hired former Dodgers general manager Buzzie Bavasi, whose reputation for frugality was widely known.

"When I got there, the secretaries had secretaries, and it was a joke," Bavasi recalls. "I planned on staying one year, but after I got there Harry Dalton was offered the GM job from Milwaukee, and Gene asked me to stay on."

Bavasi figured his reputation as a cheapskate was an asset and even insisted that the press call him "El Cheapo" so no one would expect anything more. He clamped down everywhere. He streamlined the front office, limited free tickets, and even pulled new balls out of players' lockers. Together with team vice president Red Patterson, who Autry had also brought over from the Dodgers, Bavasi guided the team back in the black.

Bavasi's early moves were among his best. To satisfy the Angels' need for a catcher, he traded aging slugger Bobby Bonds to the Chicago White Sox for Brian

Don Baylor's potent bat and strong leadership helped the Angels to their first divisional title in 1979.
Lou Sauritch/Sauritch Sports Photography

Downing, who went on to a long and distinguished career with the Halos. Then Bavasi signed hard-hitting free agent Lyman Bostock from the Minnesota Twins.

Baylor salivated at the thought of the talented Bostock hitting ahead of him in the line-up, but Bostock had trouble adjusting to his new surroundings. He struggled so badly in April that he actually refused his paycheck. Autry, who made it a point to make regular clubhouse rounds, almost went down like one of the bad hombres in his old movies when Bostock handed him back his check at the end of the month.

"I don't deserve it," Bostock told Autry. "I didn't come over here to hit .150. Don't pay me until I get better."

Baylor says the check ended up being donated to charity, and Bostock started hitting .400 from that day forward. But even with the lineup producing runs and the team playing relatively well, Garcia's passive managerial approach was causing a strain in the clubhouse. Midway through the season Bavasi fired him with an eye to finding someone more in tune with the new spirit of the club.

"I read in the paper one day that Jim Fregosi made two errors in Pittsburgh, and the next day he was our manager," Baylor recalls.

Fregosi's career had languished since he was traded from the Angels to the Mets in 1971. He never regained his form at the plate and had been reduced to the status of a mere journeyman. He was only playing part time for Pittsburgh when Autry asked him to become the Angels manager. With Fregosi at the helm, an attitude shift was immediately apparent. No longer did the Angels rush out of the clubhouse as soon as the final out was made. The trio of Bostock, Baylor, and Grich galvanized the team with a cohesiveness not present for years. The recharged Angels were loose yet focused, all of which stemmed from Fregosi's leadership.

Fregosi told Baylor it was his job to put the best defensive team possible on the field, but agreed to play him in the outfield whenever the situation presented itself. Fregosi also detected something in Baylor that until then had been brimming just beneath the surface—that he was a natural leader. In a show of confidence, the manager told Baylor he was counting on him to show the Angels what it took to win.

Fregosi's assets also included his age. Only 36 years old, he could relate to the players, one of whom—first baseman Ron Fairly—was actually his senior. Baylor recalls a good example of Fregosi's winning affability.

"Grichie was always looking in the stands, and one day he spots this blond in the family pass section," Baylor remembers. "He gets one of the clubhouse kids to take her a note. He writes, 'My name is Bob Grich. I'd like to take you out. Please give me your number.' She writes back, 'I'd like to give you my number, but I'm married to the manager, Jim Fregosi.' Jimmy got a bigger kick out of it than anybody, and it just got better from there."

The Angels and Baylor stayed hot, and by September 1 were still in the hunt, only a game behind the division-leading Royals. Three weeks later, the Angels—still holding on to the slimmest chance of making the playoffs despite trailing the Royals by five and a half games—headed into Chicago for an important three-game series with the White Sox. With the team understanding that a loss—any loss—might end their playoff hopes, a tragic event occurred that permanently and significantly shifted their focus.

On September 23, 1978, Bostock, riding in a car with friends in Gary, Indiana, was shot to death. Police identified the assailant as Leonard Smith, the estranged husband of a passenger in the car, Barbara Smith, who was a childhood friend of Bostock's. Smith had been stalking her, and when Bostock's uncle, who was driving the car, pulled up to a stoplight, Smith fired a shotgun point-blank into the back of the car. She was hit by one pellet, while Bostock, sitting next to her, caught the full force of the round in the face. The likeable and gregarious athlete was dead at age 27.

Earlier that day, the Angels had lost 5-4 to the White Sox at Comiskey Park. Bostock had a lot of friends from Gary, his hometown, in the stands. Baylor recalls that his friend went up to bat in the ninth inning with the winning run on base and two outs, and then grounded out to end the game. "He was so pissed I'm not sure if he even took a shower," says Baylor. "The last time I saw him was after the game when he dashed by me wearing a sport coat and dripping wet from sweat or a shower. I asked him, 'Where you going?' But he didn't say a word. He just bolted by. That was the last time I ever saw him alive.

"After the game I joined Rudi, Ryan, and Remy at Eli's for some music and dinner, and when we got back to the hotel our phones were ringing off the hook. Turns out it was Buzzie calling, saying Lyman had been shot. The news spread like wildfire, and within a few minutes everybody knew. We asked Buzzie where Lyman was. We wanted to go see him. But Buzzie said we couldn't go there because he had over a hundred [shotgun] pellets in his head and they didn't expect him to live.

"We were all stunned and sat out in the hallway just staring at the walls. Hotel guests walked around us, on us, and over us, but we didn't even notice. We just sat out in the hallway and cried. We couldn't believe it. It was the worst night I ever had in baseball.

"No one really slept that night, and the next morning my head was killing me so I walked down to Walgreen's to get some Excedrin. We had just lost a teammate but, damn it, we still had to play a ball game! So off we went. It was Sunday and I got to the park early, and when I got there there was some damn photographer and he was taking a picture of Lyman's empty locker. I threw him the hell out.

"Our clubhouse was just like a morgue. We had no batting practice, or anything. Max Patkin, the baseball clown, was supposed to perform that day. He came in and told me, 'My fee is $5,000, but I don't want to go on.' He refused to do it out of respect for Lyman.

"I felt I had to do something for him, so I homered. No batting practice, no warmups, I just swung and it went out. To this day I still don't know how I got around the bases, my legs just felt so heavy. When I got back to the bench our equipment man, Mickey Shishido, came up to me. 'That was for Lyman, wasn't it?' he said. 'You hit that one for Lyman.'

"Even after all these years, every time I go back to Chicago I think about him. It was the end of the season and we were [still in the race], but after that happened the guys just wanted to get the season over with.

"Losing Lyman was a hard one. He was a great player. But losing a friend and a teammate, that was the worst of it. It was a brutal day, an absolutely brutal day."

The Angels actually won four in a row after Bostock's passing, and five of their final seven games, but the first-place Royals went 5-3 to finish the season and seal the divisional title. The Halos finished five games out, in a tie with the Rangers.

During the offseason, Bavasi made a bold move in trading for the Twins' 12-time All-Star Rod Carew. When Baylor heard the news he was ecstatic. With Carew in the lineup in 1979, he knew the Angels had a decent chance of going all the way. During the 1978 season, Baylor had missed the century mark in RBI by just one, and during that offseason that single RBI gnawed at him continuously. He used that—coupled with the arrival of Carew—as motivation.

"I started running and working out before Thanksgiving, running every day, no matter where I was," remembers Baylor. "And the whole time the sound I was running against was, 'I'm gonna drive in a hundred, gonna drive in a hundred, gonna drive in a hundred.'"

If there was ever a year that a player put it all together and led his team to the top, it would have to be Baylor's 1979 season. Groove hit the ground running and never looked back. In April, a notoriously bad month for him, Baylor set a league record with 28 RBI as the Angels cruised to a 15-8 start compliments of a 10-game win streak. By the All-Star break, he had collected 23 home runs and 85 RBI, earning a spot on the All-Star team alongside teammates Carew, Downing, Grich, Ryan, and Mark Clear. During the month of July, Baylor topped his RBI total from April with 34, and tacked on 11 home runs. He was simply a hitting machine with runners in scoring position, notching a .330 average in such situations for the season. On August 8, he passed the century mark for RBI, reaching his offseason goal with 47 games still to go. By season's end, Groove had collected 139 RBI, 36 home runs, and two "Player of the Month" awards. Amazingly, he struck out just 51 times in 722 plate appearances. It was the greatest offensive season in Angels history.

"Donny carried the whole team on his back," claims Carew. "He came through with the big clutch hits and home runs all year. He was the straw that stirred the drink."

Adds Bobby Grich: "Everything he did in '79 was about the team and winning. He was a quiet leader who never wavered. No matter who was on the mound, no matter what the situation was, he was just like a rock, a Texas rock."

Ryan also has nothing but praise for Baylor's leadership. "Don Baylor was as tough a guy as you'd want to play with," says Ryan. "An extremely fierce competitor—he was the type of teammate you wanted to have because of his desire to win and commitment to the game."

Baylor feels the season's turning point was a big weekend sweep in July of the World Champion Yankees. After that a new spirit invigorated the Anaheim fans. "That series gave us credibility," says Baylor. "That's when the fans really started believing, and 'Yes We Can!' became our battle cry."

The "Yes We Can!" chant started with a few isolated fans during the Yankee series and quickly evolved into a regular, roaring chorus of 40,000-plus. When the team was behind in the late innings, instead of fans reaching for their car keys and streaming to the parking lot, they would remain in their seats and begin the chant.

Players who made an exceptional hit or a defensive gem got called out of the dugout for curtain calls and thunderous ovations. Suddenly, come-from-behind victories became regular occurrences. By late summer, the usually laid-back Anaheim Stadium had turned into Party Central.

All that was left to do was clinch the division. Heading into September, the Angels were still battling it out with the Royals and Twins. As the final month wore on, the Halos began to distance themselves from the pack, building a steady three-game lead that grew to four games with a week to go on the schedule. On September 25, Frank Tanana got the Royals' Darrell Porter to ground out to seal a 4-1 victory and clinch the Angels' first Divisional Championship in front of the home crowd. The 18-year drought had officially ended, and Autry finally had himself a winner.

The Angels' reward for winning 88 games and the division was to face off against Baylor's former team, the Baltimore Orioles, in the American League Championship Series. In Game 1, held in Baltimore, Nolan Ryan took on his old nemesis Jim Palmer. Ryan pitched seven strong innings but left with the game tied 3-3. Palmer went nine innings, and closer Don Stanhouse pitched a scoreless tenth to set up a three-run rally by the O's in the bottom of the tenth. John Lowenstein hit a pinch-hit, three-run homer off of reliever John Montague to end the game.

Game 2 appeared to be over quickly, as the Orioles jumped all over Dave Frost, a reliable workhorse for the Angels during the regular season, in the first and second innings. By the end of the third, the Angels were already down 9-1. But California didn't quit against 23-game winner Mike Flanagan, scoring one in the sixth and seventh innings, and three in the eighth to enter the ninth down 9-6.

With Stanhouse back on the mound in the ninth to save the game for Baltimore, Larry Harlow began the inning with a walk. He was forced out at second on a ground ball hit by Rick Miller. Willie Davis, batting for Dickie Thon, smacked a double to left that set the table for Carew to bat with runners at second and third. Carew hit a ground ball to second, and the Orioles, conceding the run, allowed Miller to score to bring the Angels within two runs of tying the game. Carney Lansford then singled home Davis, and Dan Ford followed with a single to right as both runners advanced on the throw to third.

This brought Baylor to the plate with the go-ahead run on second—but first base open. Orioles manager Earl Weaver—knowing Baylor better than most from his long stay in the Orioles organization—made the easy call to intentionally walk Baylor, loading the bases for Downing. With two outs, and the bases juiced, Stanhouse slammed the door shut, getting Downing to hit into a force out at third base to end the game. Orioles 9, Angels 8.

The Angels had more magic up their sleeve in the best-of-five series. Playing in front of their home crowd, they scored two in the bottom of the ninth to win Game 3, 4-3. But the Orioles pitching was simply too good in this series, and Scott McGregor pitched a complete-game shutout as Baltimore took Game 4, 8-0, and won the series, three games to one.

"We were outtalented in '79. The Orioles had a better team and better pitching," Baylor admits. "Overall, they played better as a team. They got the hits when they needed them, and Weaver pushed all the right buttons and it worked for them. We were inexperienced and it showed."

Baylor had finally disciplined himself to become a team leader, and it transformed him into one of the premier players in the American League. He was the full embodiment of the Robinson doctrine he had learned as a young Oriole: take no prisoners. On the base paths he was an aggressive runner who knocked down infielders on double plays like bowling pins. At the plate, he was a tough out. He walked almost as often as he struck out, and he was never afraid of taking one for the team. "Whatever it took to reach base"—that was Groove's motto. He called his approach "controlled aggression."

"Controlled aggression is a game face, a mindset," Baylor says. "The peripheral things that you see on the side, such as fans cheering, you're hearing all of that, but you're still locked into what you're doing. You're under control, your teammates look at you not as this wild, crazy man, but as a steady and consistent presence who puts his team ahead of himself."

Baylor's system was not exactly democratic. Some players received preferential treatment and some ex-teammates were exempt.

"Players who played in our division, guys like Freddie Patek, if they came across the bag they'd better get out of the way, because they were gonna get hit pretty hard. I was coming through and I wasn't going to take any prisoners. Guys like [Mark] Belanger, [Cal] Ripken, and Grich, guys I've known all my life, I wasn't going to tear their kneecaps out. When I hit them I'd still help them up and pat them on the back. Those other guys, I might leave lying there."

In November of 1979, Baylor went to Japan for an All-Star tour featuring Major League players. He had just returned to the States and was driving from the airport listening to the Angels' flagship station KMPC on the radio when the announcer said he was dedicating the song "My Special Angel" to Baylor, and predicted over the airwaves that Baylor was going to take MVP honors.

Later that afternoon, Baylor learned he had beat out the Orioles' Ken Singleton for American League MVP honors. It was the first time an Angel had ever won the prestigious award. It would be another 25 years until the next Angel, Vladimir Guerrero, would win the award.

Buzzie Bavasi broke precedent when he requested that Baylor receive extra compensation as a reward for his feat. "I got Gene to give him $50,000," says Bavasi. "They all thought I was crazy. When I was with the Dodgers, if one of our players won the Cy Young Award, all he got was a motion picture camera."

Awards aside, the Angels had business to take care of—namely defending their division crown. The team went the wrong direction from the word "Go" in the offseason, however, as Ryan filed for free agency on November 1. After losing their ace pitcher, the team then dealt a key part of their '79 offense—designated hitter-first baseman Willie Aikens to the Royals for outfielder Al Cowens. Cowens was terrible at the plate, and was promptly traded in May for Tigers first baseman Jason Thompson.

As was the case too often in the past, the Angels were unable to build upon their success in 1980. The Halos' ascent in '79 turned into a free fall in 1980. Injuries decimated the team. In April, Baylor broke his wrist on a checked swing, and by May he and seven others—including Downing, Rudi, and Ford—were all on the disabled list. The only offensive highlights were the always-impressive Carew, who at age 34 had another fine season by hitting .331, and newcomer Jason Thompson, who hit .317 with 70 RBI in 102 games with the Halos.

Pitching highlights were even harder to come by. Bavasi tried unsuccessfully to fill the void left by the departure of Ryan by signing Bruce Kison, who was largely ineffective. None of the 10 starting pitchers on the opening-day roster finished the season with a winning record, including Tanana, who was the closest at 11-12. The Angels finished in sixth place, 31 games behind the division-winning Royals and 23 wins worse than in '79. Autry called the 1980 club "the worst in 20 years."

The injury-plagued Baylor managed only five home runs and 51 RBI. Usually injuries didn't deter Baylor. Despite the physicality of his play, Baylor can only recall being on the designated list once or twice in his entire career. For the most part he avoided the training room and played through injuries, including a separated shoulder, a pulled hamstring, and a broken hand.

Due to his wrist injury, Baylor's efforts to negotiate a new contract after the 1980 season went for naught. Since he first signed with the Angels in 1977, salaries had escalated considerably, and Baylor felt he should be paid at the same level as other stars of his caliber. But whenever Baylor's agent approached Bavasi with a proposed contract extension, he was met with the same wait-and-see attitude that Nolan Ryan had received the year prior. Bavasi didn't learn from past mistakes, and in the spring of 1981, Baylor's relationship with the general manager went south.

A few days before the 1981 season began, Bavasi was talking to a reporter when the Angels GM spotted a copy of the new team program that featured Fred Lynn, Baylor, and Carew on the cover. "What's Don Baylor doing between those two hitters?" Bavasi joked. When the comment was printed in the *Los Angeles Times* the next day, an incensed Baylor headed straight to Bavasi's office and threatened to quit.

But Bavasi and Gene Mauch, director of personnel, played on Baylor's sense of loyalty. Bavasi claimed the whole thing was blown out of proportion and that he had great respect for Baylor's ability. "Don was sensitive, but he had a right to be," Bavasi later said. "I've always said if I had nine Don Baylors, I wouldn't need to worry about anything."

But Bavasi had plenty to worry about as the 1981 strike-shortened season got underway, despite all the offseason additions. In December, he dealt Lansford, Miller, and Clear to the Red Sox for All-Star shortstop Rick Burleson and veteran third baseman Butch Hobson. Then, in late January, he traded with Boston a second time, this time sending Tanana and Rudi for All-Star outfielder Fred Lynn and pitcher Steve Renko. As the season prepared to start in April, Bavasi struck twice more, acquiring pitcher Ken Forsch from the Astros for Dickie Thon, and catcher Ed Ott from the Pirates for Thompson.

But all the player movement was a moot point, as 1981 was another disappointing season for the Angels and Baylor. The team struggled to stay at .500 for the first two months. An 8-3 record in June finally catapulted the team to 31-29 when the strike began on June 12. The mediocre start had Autry in anything but a singing mood. He publicly tore into his club, distancing himself from his surrogate son Fregosi in the process. Baylor saw the pressure Fregosi was under and figured the manager's dismissal was imminent. Lacking the courage to face his skipper directly, Autry left Fregosi hanging before replacing him with Gene Mauch on May 28. Just 14 days later, the players launched a 50-day strike. When the season finally resumed in August, the Angels continued their slide, at one point losing 14 out of 15 games in early September.

Baylor remained healthy during the shortened season, and while his power numbers were solid, he hit just .239 on the year. Moving to the outfield, Downing struggled at the plate as well, as did new acquisitions Ott, Hobson, and Lynn. Lynn, in particular, was a huge disappointment, hitting only .219 on the year. The revamped pitching staff—featuring 20-year-old Mike Witt, Forsch, Renko, and Don Aase as closer—were decent. But no one was kidding himself come season's end—major changes were on the way.

Part of Autry's uncharacteristic behavior was because of the passing of his wife, Ina, in 1980, which left Gene in a state of depression. That changed when he started dating banker Jackie Elam. They eventually married and, acting on Gene's wishes, the new Mrs. Autry took over the daily business of running the club. Seeing that the club was constantly losing money, she insisted the team stop signing expensive free agents and start the process of rebuilding the club from within.

Before the spending spree ended, however, there was one more free agent just too good to pass up. Both Autry and Bavasi believed that Reggie Jackson was just what the team needed to turn things around. In January 1982, Bavasi signed Jackson to a four-year contract, making the Angels the only team to have four former MVPs (including Lynn, Carew, and Baylor) playing on the same roster. When Bavasi added catcher Bob Boone, shortstop Tim Foli, and third baseman Doug DeCinces to the mix, suddenly the Angels were back on the right track.

Baylor re-emerged in 1982 with a vengeance. In addition to 93 RBI and 24 home runs, he collected 21 game-winning hits. Baylor was now the veteran on the club, and he stepped up like never before.

"He became our go-to man in '82," Carew recalls. "After hitting a home run, he told the others in so many words, 'Jump on my back and I'll take you with me.'"

Reggie Jackson also acknowledged Baylor was a natural leader. "He had a great physical presence, was level-headed, and had a good feel for people," says Jackson.

Four MVPs united as teammates in 1982 (left to right): Fred Lynn, Rod Carew, Reggie Jackson, and Don Baylor. Courtesy of Mel Bailey

"Some guys are touted as a leader by their teammates and the press, and he certainly was one of them."

Riding on Baylor's broad shoulders, the Angels led the A.L. West by the slimmest of margins at the All-Star break. The race remained tight down the stretch, with the White Sox figuring into the mix as well. The '82 Angels featured a balanced attack, able to outpitch or outscore opponents. On the offensive side, newcomer DeCinces smacked 30 home runs and drove in 97 RBI while hitting .301. But in this potent lineup, DeCinces blended in. Jackson led the team with 101 RBI and a league-best 39 home runs, Carew finished third in the league with a .319 average, Lynn rebounded to hit .299 with 86 RBI, and Downing added 28 homers and 84 RBI. On the pitching side of the equation, veteran Geoff Zahn won 18 games, leading a solid staff.

The Angels swept the Texas Rangers in their final series of the season to claim their second divisional championship with 93 wins. They marched into the playoffs against the Milwaukee Brewers feeling they were a much more mature and experienced club than in 1979. Nicknamed "Harvey's Wallbangers" after manager Harvey Kuenn, the Brewers were a hard-scrabble bunch that played like throwbacks to an earlier era. Robin Yount, Paul Molitor, Ted Simmons, Ben Oglivie, and Cecil Cooper, along with home run co-champ Gorman Thomas, made for a formidable offense that easily outdistanced the A.L. in runs scored and home runs. And with veteran pitchers like Pete Vuckovich, Mike Caldwell, Rollie Fingers, and Don Sutton, the Brewers were no slouches on the mound, either.

The best-of-five series started in Anaheim, and behind a pair of complete games from 39-year-old Tommy John—acquired from the Yankees in August just a day before playoff rosters had to be set—and Bruce Kison, the Angels won the first two games, 8-3 and 4-2. Needing just one win to advance, they headed to Milwaukee confident they could win one more game and clinch the franchise's first pennant. But the Brewers were confident heading home as well, and Sutton stepped forward to lead them to a 5-3 victory in Game 3.

"The Brewers came to Anaheim flat as a door latch, and we just walked all over them," recalls Grich. "But by the time we got to Milwaukee, they were all rejuvenated. Don Sutton pitched Game 3, and it was overcast and tough to see the ball. Everyone came back to the dugout saying, 'I couldn't see the ball.' If they had turned on the lights, I think we would have won that game. Sutton was throwing 82 miles per hour and couldn't break a pane of glass. We should have hammered him, but that was their great equalizer then, not turning the lights on on a gray, overcast day."

The following day manager Gene Mauch, in what proved to be a controversial move, started Tommy John on only three days' rest. John was hammered for six runs, failing to make it out of the fourth inning. Meanwhile, Moose Haas held the Angels hitless for five innings, and they were behind 7-1 before an eighth-inning grand slam by Baylor made it 7-5. The Brewers scored twice in the bottom of the frame, however, and held on to win 9-5.

The fifth and decisive game was by far the most memorable of the series. Starter Bruce Kison left the game in the fifth with the Angels leading 3-2. Mauch turned the game over to dependable reliever Luis Sanchez, who allowed the Brewers to load the bases in the seventh. Mauch was left to make a fateful decision that Angels fans still debate to this day. Due up for Milwaukee was Cooper, a hard-hitting left-hander. Mauch had the choice of removing the right-handed Sanchez, who was struggling, and bringing in lefty Andy Hassler, whose hard slider was particularly nasty for left-handed hitters. The prudent move would have been to go with Hassler, but Mauch chose otherwise, sticking with Sanchez.

Baylor, who had played against Cooper in high school, picks up the action: "Coop's looking at me from the on-deck circle, and I'm nodding my head because I know Mauch is gonna make him face Hassler. I know he's done his homework and knows Hassler's reputation against lefties. Coop keeps walking towards the batter's box, and when he realizes Gene is gonna stay with Sanchez he can't believe it. Sure enough, on the second pitch from Sanchez, Coop gets a base hit to left that drives in a couple of runs to win the game. Needless to say, guys were in shock."

Simmons, a switch-hitter, stepped to the plate following Cooper, and Mauch made the call to the bullpen to bring in Hassler, who struck out Simmons to end the inning. The damage was already done, however; The Brewers led 4-3 heading into the eighth. The second-guessing of Mauch began immediately and hasn't stopped since. But Baylor, who has since managed himself, refuses to pile on.

"Gene Mauch had managed thousands of ball games," says Baylor, "so who am I to question his call? He didn't have the luxury to check with 45,000 fans and ask them what they thought. Sometimes you go with your gut, and at the time that's how he felt. As a manager, you go by hunches, and sometimes it works and sometimes it doesn't. Hassler threw his slider down and hard, and Gene probably felt he was going to throw a wild pitch. They had a man on third, so I figure he was defending against that more than anything."

Baylor recalls that the fallout from that game was intense. "The team said, 'We'd like to re-evaluate Gene Mauch,'" Baylor said. "Mauch replied, 'You don't have to re-evaluate me—I resign.' I became a free agent and went to the Yankees. And Mrs. Autry came out of all that with a lot more power."

Choosing to leave the Angels via free agency was one of the toughest decisions Baylor ever faced, but he realized that with Bavasi set in his ways there was simply no other way to go.

"I wanted to stay," recalls Baylor. "I would have even taken less money; but it just wasn't in the cards. I really felt kindred to the Angels. The biggest regret I have was failing to bring a championship to this club."

History has also proved that losing Baylor to free agency in 1983 was a mistake. His career was far from finished, and his presence and power helped to fuel three teams—Boston, Minnesota, and Oakland—into the World Series. There is no telling how the Angels would have fared had they kept him. Like Ryan before him, Baylor, who is well remembered to this day as the engine behind the Angels' first two divisional championships, was allowed to leave early—well before his usefulness was used up.

Baylor's skills as a team leader made him a strong managerial candidate, and in 1993 he became the first manager of the expansion Colorado Rockies. One of his greatest experiences, he says, was to see 80,000 people at the first ball game at Mile High Stadium. "It was breathtaking," he remembers. "The Rockies attracted four million fans that first year. As it turned out, they were dying for baseball."

He managed there for six seasons, winning Manager of the Year in 1995. In 2003, following a three-year managerial stint with the Cubs, the New York Mets hired him as their bench coach. In 2002, he had began feeling excessive fatigue but put off seeing a doctor, blaming the fatigue on his increasing age and the usual grind of a baseball season. However, tests taken during a 2003 spring training physical showed flag-raising abnormalities in his cell counts. Subsequent testing disclosed multiple myeloma, a cancer of the blood that destroys the bone marrow. Red and white blood counts became Baylor's chief concern from that point forward; for Baylor, the battle for life trumped the battle on the ball field.

Still, he was present and accounted for throughout the 2003 season. Chemotherapy throughout the season allowed Baylor to not miss a day of work. In the offseason, after more chemo and additional therapy, Baylor underwent a stem cell transplant. The procedure was a success, and by late March he reported to spring training camp in Florida for his second year with the Mets.

Groove treated the cancer as he did opposing pitchers during his 19-year career—without mercy. "I used to always tell our cystic fibrosis kids to be strong, and then it was my turn," Baylor says. "Now I had to go out and do that myself."

In 2005, Baylor became the Seattle Mariners' batting coach. That February he celebrated the anniversary of his stem cell transplant, and his cancer has been in remission ever since.

He considers winning the 1979 MVP Award and the prestigious "Roberto Clemente Award" in 1985, as his greatest baseball achievements. The latter is for community involvement and was presented for his work with 65 Roses, a nonprofit group aiding youngsters with cystic fibrosis. Since the 1970s, it has raised millions of dollars for research from annual golf tournaments and fundraisers.

"I try to balance what I do on the field with what I do off the field," says Baylor. "65 Roses gave me that opportunity, and working with the kids there has been pretty special."

For men like Baylor who know, love, and respect the game, there should always be a place in major league baseball. That competitive fire that has been with him since Clarksville still burns, and whether it's helping players to do their best or teaching kids to fight against life-threatening diseases, Baylor is still taking no prisoners and doing whatever it takes to win.

12

THE ARTIST'S ARRIVAL

ROD CAREW

*T*he passengers in the "Colored Only" section on the train bound for Panama City, Panama, were boisterous in anticipation of the big prizefight in town later that night. Smoke from their cigarettes and cigars mixed with the engine's exhaust, making the air in the car unpleasantly dense for the few passengers sober enough to notice.

Partying was the last thing on the mind of Olga Carew. Earlier that day she had felt her baby move downward, and she knew it was time. Her husband, Erick, wanted her to go to the clinic near their home in Gatun, but Olga refused. The rooms in Gatun were filthy and full of rats. She wanted to have the baby in Panama City, where the infant mortality rate was much lower. After she threatened to take the train alone, Erick relented, and off they went.

It was only 40 miles to Panama City, but to Olga it seemed like 400. The train was old and rickety, and it felt as if the couple were riding in a cement mixer. When it became obvious that the baby had no intention of delaying its arrival till Panama City, Olga panicked. Erick tried to comfort her, but the old wooden seats did little to smooth the bumpy ride. Luckily, a registered nurse was seated nearby. Margaret Allen had assisted at several births and offered to help. It didn't take her long, however, to realize that she couldn't do it alone.

"Get a doctor now!" someone shouted. The cry went through the cars and made its way to the "Whites Only" section in front, where first-class passenger Rodney Cline was sleeping. Someone noticed his medical bag and nudged him awake. He made his way to the back of the train, where he joined Margaret Allen in bringing Olga Carew's baby boy into the world.

Afterwards, Olga tearfully thanked him and named her new son in his honor. On October 1, 1945, Rodney Cline Carew made a memorable entrance into the world, met with cheers and cries from a sporting crowd.

With bleak trepidation, eight-year-old Rodney Cline peered out of the window at the big grassy field in front of his parents' apartment in Gamboa, a town in Panama's Canal Zone bordered by tropical rain forest. He expected his father to arrive home soon and knew that he would be able to tell by his father's posture if he was in for a whipping. When Erick Carew had had a bad day, he would be hunched over, his face a twisted scowl. He would slam the door and go straight for the large belt on the living room chair. "Cline!" he would shout, "Get your ass over here and face the wall."

The beatings were almost a daily ritual, but Rodney never considered running away. After all, this was his home, and Erick was his father. So he just resigned himself to the situation. Most children would have been destroyed, falling into depression and drugs, or perhaps becoming violent themselves. But Rodney was not a typical child. He was blessed with an optimism and faith instilled in him by his mother, who always told him that things would get better and encouraged his greatest dream, the one that consumed his every waking hour. Rodney saw himself one day playing professional baseball, and as long as he stayed focused on that goal, his father would never break him.

So he endured the beatings, and then limped outside, grabbed his baseball made of tape and newspaper, and flung it for hours against the brick wall near the side of the apartment. The exertion distracted him from the pain. He'd fling the ball until it fell apart, and then he would find more tape and paper and make another one.

That Rod Carew became one of baseball's all-time great hitters is nothing less than a miracle.

An abusive father wasn't the only obstacle he had to overcome. The Canal Zone in 1946 was segregated: Black people had separate schools, theaters, bathrooms, and drinking fountains, and were not welcome at all in white society.

"We were poor, but not impoverished," Carew recalls of his days growing up. "I had a pair of shoes that would have to last me till they wore off my feet. I had two or three pairs of pants I had to alternate every day for school. There were times my dad would bring food home and he'd put his name on it and you couldn't touch it. But we never starved. If I was really hungry I could go into the woods and get mangos and coconuts to eat."

Rodney's saving grace was baseball. On the ball field, he could be himself. By age 12, he was playing baseball seven days a week. He'd make a bat from a broomstick, carve the name Jackie Robinson or Mickey Mantle on the handle, and practice by smacking bottle caps instead of baseballs. His glove was made out of newspaper, tape, and canvas, and a ball was anything he could roll into a sphere and wrap with tape.

Everything he knew about Major League Baseball, Rodney learned from listening to Armed Forces Radio. He used his imagination and created his own concept of hitting, which led to the original and unorthodox style he later employed.

"As a kid, not seeing hitters certainly helped me. I visualized some of the things they were doing and it forced me to be creative and come up with my own approach to hitting. I don't know why hitting came so easy. All I know is that I was so much better than anybody else. I was good as a kid coming up, and it just continued from there."

Despite his talent and promise, Rodney received no support from his father. Erick even refused to sign him up for the local Little League. But his aunt's husband, John French, was head of the Little League, and he signed Rodney up, got him the proper equipment, and even hired him to paint the Little League park to earn enough money for a uniform.

It was instantly clear that Rodney was light years ahead of the other Little Leaguers, so French put him in the adult league with players twice his age. When Rodney surpassed them, French enrolled him in still tougher leagues to play with Panama's elite players. It was there on the rough-cut diamonds and rocky fields in Panama's rugged interior that Rodney honed the tools that would elevate him to the top of the game.

Meanwhile, things at home worsened. Erick's drinking drove him to insane furies, and one night he came home, beat Olga, and then started on Rodney before passing out. His son looked at his slumped over father and then thought about the machete in the shed next door.

"That night I wanted to chop him up—that's how angry I was," Carew recalls. "But then I said to myself, 'What good would that do? I'd just end up in jail.' That's when I decided to persevere. I could have turned and gone in the direction that 80 percent of abused kids go, but what saved me and separated me from them was that they didn't have the dreams and goals that I did. From that moment on, I said I was going to endure everything he dished out because I knew where I was headed. The dream of baseball permeated everything, and that's what got me through."

In 1962, Olga had endured enough for both of them. She left Panama to live with relatives in New York City, and later that fall she had earned enough to send for Rodney and his siblings. They lived together in a small apartment, and for two years he learned English and did odd jobs to support the household.

"This is it!" Uncle Clyde told his 16-year-old nephew as the subway lurched to a stop at the 171st St. Station in the Bronx. Exiting the train, Clyde led Rodney down an endless maze of steps. When they emerged outside they were face to face with a massive concrete wall that rose from the pavement like a Sphinx.

Knowing his nephew's love for baseball, Clyde was surprised to see Rodney's reaction. To most youngsters Yankee Stadium was an impregnable fortress, a distant palace reserved for the baseball gods. But Rodney did not seem impressed—at least not outwardly.

Uncle Clyde had kept watch over Rodney as the boy adapted to his new American surroundings. He looked on as Rodney had mastered English and survived living in a rat-infested apartment. Now he watched his nephew circle the hallowed stadium and was perplexed by his lack of outward emotion. Occasionally he would brush his hand against the rough stucco walls or peer dreamily into one of the fenced off entrances, but for the most part he seemed strangely quiet.

Then Rodney spoke in a voice filled with quiet certainty. "I'm gonna be playing in here one day," he said. Clyde didn't respond right away but continued to walk, letting the words his nephew told him seep in.

"Don't let anything stand in your way then," Clyde finally responded.

"What do you mean?" asked Rodney.

"I mean nothing!" shouted his uncle. "Not girls! Not parties or drugs! Nothing! If baseball is what you want to do, don't let anything stand in your way."

As they continued on Rodney noticed two city league baseball fields on the other side of the street.

"This must be the center of the baseball universe," he thought to himself. Feeling closer to his destiny than ever before, Rodney started to run, possessed by a nonsensical burst of energy that he could not contain. He was certain that some guiding force had placed him there to show him his future.

"I got what it takes. I know it!" Rodney declared as he leaped against the fabled deco wall. "I really do!"

"Then discipline yourself," replied his uncle. "Don't let anything get in your way. I mean it—nothing!"

The older man and the boy continued around the stadium in silence, while Rodney reflected on his uncle's words. What he didn't realize was that soon these very grounds would serve as a critical stepping-stone to his dreams. For now, however, he was content to look on and soak up his uncle's hard wisdom.

Because of his commitment to the family, it wasn't until his senior year in high school that Rodney got the opportunity to play baseball again. To his disappointment, he was cut by the high school coach, a move one of Rodney's classmates thought so unfair that he invited Carew to join his weekend City League team. Carew decimated City League pitching, and word spread quickly about the gangly kid from Panama on the Cavaliers who could hit rockets and run like a deer. In no time, professional scouts began showing up in droves, including a tenacious birddog from the Minnesota Twins named Herb Stein.

Stein was so blown away that he importuned Twin's owner Clark Griffith to come down from Minnesota and take a look for himself. Griffith saw Carew go eight-for-nine in a doubleheader, and instructed Stein to arrange a tryout when the

Twins came to New York the following spring. In April of 1964, 17-year-old Rodney got another look at Yankee Stadium—this time from the inside.

Twins trainer Doc Lenz sized up the youngster standing before him and then walked over to Tony Oliva's locker, pulled out a gray No. 6 jersey and a pair of pants, and handed them to the kid. After donning the uniform, Carew headed down the long tunnel to the field. No sooner had he arrived than he heard shouts of "Hey, Oliva! Hey, Tony! What's going on?" The startled Carew looked around to see who everybody was yelling at. A grinning Tony Oliva jogged over and explained in Spanish that he was wearing his shirt. Oliva told him to relax and take some balls.

Carew ambled over to the infield where he was met by All-Star Cuban shortstop Zoilo Versalles.

"What position do you play?" barked the future MVP.

"Second base," Carew answered nervously.

"Good! You can no play shortstop," responded Versalles. "I been here a long time *keed,* so forget about shortstop!"

Rodney strolled over to second and after taking a few grounders was called to the cage to hit. For two rounds line drive after line drive exploded off of his bat. By the third round he was pumping balls into the seats with such ferocity that he was told to stop.

"Get him out of there!" manager Sam Mele called to his coaches. "I don't want the Yankees seeing him!"

A coach informed Carew that his tryout had ended. Rodney returned to the locker room where he neatly folded his uniform and returned it to Lenz. For his efforts he received an autographed ball and a ticket to the game. He tried to watch a few innings but was so excited by the whole experience that he left early to inform his mother of the day's events.

One month later, on the night that Rodney graduated from George Washington High School, he signed a contract to play professional baseball with the Minnesota Twins.

Upon reporting to the Melbourne Twins of the Cocoa Beach League, Carew quickly discovered that the minor leagues were not exactly everything he had dreamed about back when he was tossing rag balls against the building in Panama. For one thing, he was very homesick for his family. For another, he encountered racism as virulent and vile as any he had experienced in his home country.

"We were playing a night game in Leesburg, Virginia, and the fans were heckling me because I was tearing the cover off the ball," Carew recalls. "About the fifth inning I was sitting at the end of the dugout when someone from the stands brought this little black cat and dropped it down next to me. As the cat came up to me I heard somebody say, 'Here nigger, here nigger!' My mind went back to Jackie Robinson. Someone had done that to him, too. So I didn't do anything, I just put my hand on the cat and shook my head at them, just like Jackie would have done."

Carew's apprenticeship in the minors was brief. Clark Griffith had put him on the fast track, and within two years he was a Twin. Carew hit .292 during his rookie campaign in 1967, was selected to the league's All-Star team, and was named AL Rookie of the Year. By 1969, Carew had established himself as one of the best second basemen in the game. In addition to helping the Twins win a divisional championship under skipper Billy Martin, Carew's .332 average was good enough to win the first of his seven batting titles.

More importantly, however, the '69 season proved to be a turning point in his approach to the game. That's when a Twins teammate named Sandy Valdespino suggested that with Carew's speed he could be a great bunter. Valdespino helped Carew master the drag bunt, which became a big part of his game. Soon he was averaging 25 to 30 bunt hits a season. Carew's success inspired other young speedsters such as the Athletics' Bert Campaneris and the Astros' Joe Morgan to follow suit.

Martin was pleased with his prodigy, but he knew Carew was capable of more. Not since Jackie Robinson had a player like Carew come on the scene with the nerve to steal home—and the skill to pull it off. Stealing home had become a lost art, but the gutsy play demoralized the defense, which was right up Martin's alley. The leading base stealers of the era, Lou Brock and Maury Wills, rarely attempted it. Martin worked with Carew all spring, and in 1969 Rod stole home six times, tying Ty Cobb's American League record. Through hard work, natural ability, and plenty of study, Carew had revitalized two of baseball's lost arts in one season.

But he is perhaps best remembered for another unique aspect of his game—his continually morphing batting stance and his unorthodox style of hitting. Carew spent years refining his swing, and it was his future teammate and friend, Nolan Ryan, who was responsible for encouraging him to further develop his swing. Before Ryan came to the American League in 1972, Carew had been able to handle any pitcher he faced. But when he found himself futilely flailing away at Ryan's 100 miles-per-hour fastballs, Carew decided his stance at the plate needed an immediate overhaul.

"Nolan made me start looking at myself," he says. "When I came up to the big leagues, I would hold my hands straight up and hit anybody. But I couldn't hit Nolan, because he'd overpower me upstairs. So I started crouching, and noticed I could see the difference in his fastball when I was down better than when I stood straight up. From then on I was able to handle his fastball a little bit better."

Soon Carew developed several different stances for different pitching styles, all deviating from his basic flex stance. His unorthodox approach frustrated pitchers,

Rod Carew revolutionized the game with his mastery of the drag bunt and his aggressive style of play. Lou Sauritch/Sauritch Sports Photography

who found it nearly impossible to find a pattern when pitching to him. Carew's improvisational style took his hitting to a level few have attained since. Suddenly "scientific and artistic," words rarely used to describe ballplayers, became commonplace whenever writers searched for the proper description.

Carew thought outside the box when it came to hitting. When stepping into a pitch, most hitters land flatfooted on their forward leg, which usually results in a slight jarring movement. Carew surmised that by landing on the ball of his front foot instead, it would lessen the jarring movement and enable him to get a better look at the ball. It may sound simple, but for a hitter this is an extremely difficult task. Carew mastered it, however, and credits that technique for part of his success at the plate.

"I could stand in the box any number of ways and hit," he recalls. "I could make a change from pitch to pitch and find comfort in it, because I had done it during extra batting practice. I had six different stances and could change at any time. Needless to say, it made me far, far different!"

Carew's work ethic was impeccable. Much like Angels outfielder Alex Johnson, the batting cage was Carew's office, where he spent countless solitary hours perfecting his swing and practicing his bunting. He became so proficient at bunting that he would place towels down the baselines and bunt ball after ball on—or within inches—of them. Carew used the field like a billiard table, seemingly placing the ball wherever he wanted. Bruce Bochte, the Angels' first baseman from 1974-'76, remembers that Carew could maneuver his bat in such a way that his ground balls achieved maximum backspin, causing them to scoot beyond the infielder's reach.

"We used to call him 'Scooter,'" Bochte says. "What he did was uncanny."

Carew's philosophy at the plate was simple: His model for success was to follow the ball all the way in to the plate and then react to it. To Carew, the flight of the baseball actually told a hitter what part of the field he should try to hit it to, and what sort of a swing he should use.

"Your bat does not go through the hitting zone the same on every pitch," Carew explains. "The angle on it changes somewhat, depending on the location of the pitch and the height. If the ball is on the outside corner, I might roll over and hit a ground ball, so why not take it the other way? A pitch on the inside tells me I have options: I can pull it or I can take it to center field or left. A high fastball tells me that I've got to get on top of the ball."

In addition to making adjustments—sometimes several within a single at-bat— Carew maintained his focus in the batter's box. "I tip-toed into the batter's box. I didn't want anyone to know I was there," explains Carew. "I needed a silence in there with me—I didn't want to be disturbed. I didn't want the catcher or the umpire to talk to me, because I didn't want them to take my focus away from the guy on the mound. I was all focus up there."

Part of Carew's focus also revolved around remaining one step ahead of the pitcher. "I studied pitchers. I knew how pitchers were going to try and get me out," he says. "I kept notes and always referred to them when I was going to face the guy the next time."

Carew's baseball mind was always on overdrive. Nothing was taken for granted—not even the weather. He knew a pitcher's curveball would not be as effective in colder weather, as it would make it tougher for the pitcher to get the necessary grip on the ball for maximum spin. He used such knowledge to his advantage. To this day, Carew maintains that he hit better at night or in cold weather.

When each game was over, Carew's careful, thoughtful ways left him with yet another unique approach. Before leaving the clubhouse, he would fastidiously clean his bats using alcohol to remove any extra weight caused from dirt or pine tar, and then place them near the sauna to keep them dry.

His all-business attitude and intense preparation once almost landed him on his butt, courtesy of Thurman Munson. The Yankee catcher was famous for trying to get into hitters' heads, messing with their concentration by tapping their bat with his catcher's mask or throwing dirt on their shoes. Knowing that Carew didn't like anyone talking to him in the batter's box, Munson made it a point to harass him whenever he could.

"What are you gonna do today, big boy?" Munson asked as Carew walked to the plate one day.

"I think I'll get a hit this time up," replied Carew coolly. "In fact, I'll tell you what I'll do. I'll call every pitch Catfish is gonna throw me."

"Yeah, right!" snorted Munson.

"No, I will. Just before he releases the pitch, I'm going to yell out what it is."

On the mound, Catfish Hunter went into his stretch and fired away.

"Fastball, inside!" called out Carew as soon as the ball left Hunter's hand, guessing correctly.

"You got lucky," Munson muttered as he tossed the ball back to Hunter.

Catfish readied for the next pitch, and as he launched it Carew predicted a slider, down and in. It was, and now the agitated Munson accused him of peeking at his signs and called a time out to go out to the mound and warn Hunter.

When he returned from the mound, Munson told Carew, "Catfish told me to tell you if you're peeking, your gonna get knocked on your ass!"

Carew smiled, "That's all right. I'll take my chances."

"Fastball away, base hit, left field line!" announced Carew as he swung into the next pitch. He knocked the fastball down the line for a double, and an upset Munson again called time to visit the mound. "You SOB!" the catcher yelled out to Carew on second. "Next time I'm gonna drill your ass. I know you're peeking!"

Carew wasn't peaking, though. The consummate student of hitting had merely memorized the sequence of pitches Hunter always threw him.

His superiority at the plate was never more apparent than in 1977, when he nearly became the first player in a quarter-century to hit .400. The press had a feeding frenzy, and "The Enigma," as Carew was called, could no longer hide from the spotlight he had always taken pains to avoid. It took Carew the first ten games of the season to get his average over .300, but once he did he never looked back. By the end of April he was hitting .356, and he continued a steady climb, breaking .400 on June 26 before settling at .394 at the All-Star break. By the beginning of September, his average had dipped all the way down to .375. But a 15-game hit streak brought his average back up ten points to .385. Despite going 12-for-22 over the season's final week, his average ended up at .388.

"It was a Cinderella year," Carew recalls. "It was as if the baseball just slowed down. I was in such a groove that a guy could be throwing 95 miles per hour, and to me it looked like a beach ball. I was so dialed in that nobody could get me out. No matter what I did, it was right."

Considered by many the greatest hitter of all time, Ted Williams—who hit .406 in 1941—was a big fan of Carew and marveled at what a physical specimen he was. "A picture book athlete," Williams told *Sports Illustrated* in 1977. "His swing is a thing of beauty. So smooth, he seems to be doing everything without trying."

The media circus finally forced manager Gene Mauch to limit Carew's availability for interviews to allow the new superstar to fully concentrate on the task at hand. *Time* magazine came out with a cover story on Carew that coincided with the Twins' visit to Anaheim. The visiting club's batboy purchased the magazine and placed it in front of Carew's locker. Fifteen years before, Carew had been a new immigrant to the United States. Now he was on the cover of a major news magazine and one of the most celebrated athletes in the world.

The celebration continued in the offseason, as Carew was named A.L. MVP, and was also selected as the recipient of the Roberto Clemente Award and the Major League Player of the Year Award. His 1977 season will go down as one of the most impressive in the modern era of baseball. In addition to his lofty average, he collected 239 hits, 100 RBI, and scored 128 runs.

Thrilled as he was about Carew's season, Twins owner Clark Griffith knew that with free agency looming it would be difficult to keep him in small-market Minnesota. After Carew hit .333 the following year to win his seventh batting crown, Griffith traded him to the Angels. At the time Griffith had made some unfortunate remarks regarding race, but Carew maintains the remarks had nothing to do with his decision to leave the Twin cities. He left because Griffith didn't have the money to keep him when he became a free agent after the following year. Carew had ten years' seniority in the league, and so he was able to choose where he wanted to go. He told Griffith he would only accept a trade to a handful of teams. Among those were the Giants, Yankees, and Angels.

Carew preferred the Angels because he liked the location and the laid-back atmosphere of Anaheim, but mostly because he just wanted to win. He thought he could play a big role in getting the team to the World Series.

"He was what we needed to win," says Buzzie Bavasi, who signed Carew to a multiyear pact worth $4.4 million upon acquiring him from the Twins.

Carew's impact on the community and in the clubhouse was immediate. Except for Ryan, the Angels had never had a player of his caliber. Season ticket sales tripled, and his new teammates rejoiced to have him on board.

"He was a stabilizing and quieting force and was instrumental in the success of that team in that he carried a lot of the media load," recalls Bobby Grich. "There was a huge amount of excitement about him coming over, and the writers paid a lot of attention to him. It was great because we just kicked back and let Carew take the brunt of it, and Baylor and I had great years."

Playing on a contender in '79 was a welcome change for Carew, who had spent the entire decade of the Seventies playing for a mediocre Twins franchise. "People just went berserk the way we just kept coming back game after game," Carew recalls. "It was unbelievable the role the fans played that year!"

Rod Carew's impact on ticket sales—and the Angels clubhouse—was felt immediately upon his arrival in Anaheim.
Courtesy of Bob Case

The highlight of the Angels' season came during Game 3 in the playoffs against
the Orioles. With the Angels down two games to none, Carew played a pivotal role
in what proved to be their lone victory of the best-of-five series. The Angels came up
to bat in the bottom of the ninth inning trailing 3-2. Baylor began the inning by flying out to left for the first out. But then Carew doubled and Brian Downing walked,
putting the go-ahead run on first. Grich hit a sinking line drive to center, which
Orioles centerfielder Al Bumbry couldn't make a clean play on. The play was ruled
an error on Bumbry, but more importantly it allowed Carew to score from second.

"I read the spin right away," says Carew, "and when I saw the ball sinking I
knew Al Bumbry wasn't gonna catch it. I just took off and, sure enough, it deflected off his glove."

Carew slid home—just beating the throw—to tie the game. Downing advanced
to second on the play, and then easily scored the winning run when left fielder
Larry Harlow doubled to center. The Angels were on the board in the series, but
the next day Scotty McGregor shut them down 8-0, ending the series.

Making the playoffs was a big positive, but the season left a sour taste in Carew's mouth. He missed on his third-straight batting crown when injuries cost him over 50 games, and the Angels' quick exit in the playoffs was disappointing. In addition, Carew's relationship with manager Jim Fregosi was rocky. Ever since Fregosi had accused Carew of spiking Bobby Knoop in 1967, the two had never seen eye to eye. Part of the problem was that Fregosi chose to bat Carew in the third spot in the lineup to start the season. Fregosi was frustrated by Carew's decision to continually bunt runners over instead of driving them in. He had envisioned Carew as more of an RBI threat and was disappointed to have to move Carew to the leadoff slot in the order.

But Carew got along well with the other superstars on the team. He and Nolan Ryan were even neighbors for a while, and would often carpool to the park together. Carew learned quickly that Ryan was a far cry from the image he had of him prior to joining the team.

"I used to wonder about Nolan, because after he'd punch you out he would always get the ball back and kind of strut around the mound, and I'd think, 'I wonder what this guy is like? Is he cocky, or what?'" recalls Carew. "But when I came over here and got to know him, I realized he's the ultimate professional and one of the nicest people I've ever met in the game."

In 1979 the two were actually neighbors. Carew likes to tell the story of how the search for his furnace gave him the scare of his life.

"I'm looking all over tying to find the furnace in my house, and I finally called Nolan. 'Man, Nolan,' I said, 'where's the furnace?' He comes over, opens the closet and [there it is]. I went downstairs while he was lighting it, and the whole time I'm saying, 'Nolan, don't blow up, please don't blow up!' I didn't want to have to explain to Mr. Autry that he was upstairs lighting my furnace, something went wrong, and he exploded."

In all the excitement of '79, Carew got a taste of the passion of Southern California fans. But in 1981, after two years of losing, he saw the flip-side. Bobby Grich recalls one night in August when the fans' indifference overshadowed an amazing performance. Cleveland's Len Barker was one of baseball's hottest pitchers at that time, having thrown a perfect game earlier in the '81 season. So most Angels batters dreaded the idea of facing him. But not Carew.

"Rod Carew got four hits off Barker [that night] and another off of [reliever Bob] Lacey," recalls Grich. "He smacked all of Barker's pitchers—fastball, slider, curveball, splitty, and change—to all parts of the field for solid hits. Barker was shaking his head on the mound going, 'How do I get this guy out?'"

When Carew got his final hit that night, Grich went to the top of the dugout steps anticipating that the crowd would be on its feet in appreciation. Instead, the customers just sat there as bored as a convention of accountants.

"I always regretted not waving a towel to get those fans to give him a standing ovation," says Grich. "It was an amazing performance. That gives you an idea what you had to contend with if you didn't win in Southern California."

As affable as Carew was most of the time, he could be temperamental if he felt he was treated unfairly. Sportswriters came to understand that once they got on the bad side of Rod Carew, he would likely never speak to them again.

"I thought Rod could be sensitive and overreact to certain things," recalls Ross Newhan of the *Los Angeles Times*. "Part of it may have been his problem, or the media didn't work hard enough trying to really understand who he was and where he was coming from."

Carew says his reputation for aloofness was overblown.

"Sure, there were times I didn't want to talk to anybody," admits Carew. "But does that make me moody? When I'm in my zone and didn't want people to disturb me, I gave them a look. Because I gave them that look I'm moody? No. It means that I'm concentrating on something and I don't want to be bothered. If you're sitting in your office doing something that's important to you, do you want me to come in and bother you? No!"

Before he got to know him as a member of the Angels, Don Baylor figured Carew was guilty as charged. "When I played first base against him, the most he ever said to me was 'Hi.' He never talked," remembers Baylor. "I would look at him with his big chew in his cheek and figured he was distant and mysterious. Later when we became teammates, I soon realized he was as genuine as they come and there was nothing phony about him. People really didn't understand him because he was so quiet, but he's a deep thinker and very committed to the game."

Reggie Jackson played with Carew for four seasons and maintains that while Carew was one of the premier hitters of his era, because he was so quiet and played in Minnesota he was always under the radar.

"I always thought Rod felt unappreciated," says Jackson. "He got rapped about not knocking in runs, which was unfair because he wasn't that type of hitter. For four or five years in a row he hit .355 or so, and in an off year he'd hit .330. What can you say? He was a great hitter, period."

With the acquisition of Jackson in 1982, the Angels drew closer to the top than ever before. The four team MVPs—Jackson, Baylor, Lynn, and Carew—proved a diverse and potent mix. While they were putting up big numbers in the box score, their equally big egos had to share space in the clubhouse. Carew says the clubhouse banter could get vicious at times. Carew wasn't intimidated by Jackson, and vice versa. They respected one another, but that didn't keep them from, in Carew's words, "circling around each other like two lions in the same den."

But even big personalities could be tamed when the team was winning, and the '82 Angels did plenty of that. Carew considers the Angels' failure to close out the Brewers in the 1982 A.L. playoffs one of the two biggest let-downs of his career. After the team won the first two games of the series in Anaheim, Carew says he left the clubhouse quickly after seeing his teammates acting as if they had it all wrapped up.

The most dramatic moment of the series came in the fifth and final game in Milwaukee. With a trip to the World Series on the line and the Angels trailing by a run heading into the ninth inning, Carew came up to bat with two outs and the

tying run at second. Brewers manager Harvey Kuenn had hard-throwing right-hander Pete Ladd in the game to get the final out.

Kuenn's first pitch was a fastball. Carew swung late and fouled it down the left
field line. Carew figured that Brewers shortstop Robin Yount, having seen him
swing late, would move to his right, opening a bigger hole toward centerfield; but
for some reason Yount didn't move. The next pitch was an outside fastball just
where Carew liked it. He hit it well, but right at Yount.

"It was a hard, one-hop groundball," Carew recalls, "and if Yount had moved
like I thought he would, it would have gone through for a hit and we would have
tied it."

Some disappointed Angels fans have never forgiven Carew for not getting the
job done in that situation, but he says, "All I can do is hit the ball hard, and I did.
If Yount had been over another foot or so, it would have been a different story."

The bus ride to the Milwaukee airport was grim and also messy, thanks to
Brewers fans who pelted the vehicle with fruit and beer as it headed out of the
County Stadium parking lot. That postseason collapse—coupled with the loss of
Baylor to free agency in the offseason put a damper on the club, and according to
Carew, the rest of his stay in Anaheim was mostly a haze. In 1983, at the age of 37,
Carew posted his last truly great season, hitting .339 to finish second in the bat-
ting race to Boston's Wade Boggs. The following season Carew saw his average dip
below .300 for the first time since 1968.

Carew was on the last year of his contract in 1985, and with rookie first baseman Wally Joyner waiting in the wings and Buzzie Bavasi set to retire from the
front office, Carew figured his days as an Angel were numbered. But one major
goal remained: 3,000 hits. Heading into the '85 season, Carew was only 71 hits shy
of that milestone, and by August he was closing in on that magic number.

"He won't dare come in on me," Carew thought to himself as he got down in
his flex stance to face Frank Viola. "If it's a breaking ball outside, I'll take it the
other way, aim for the gap."

Viola ran the count to 1-and-2, and Carew knew he'd be seeing more breaking
balls. Viola didn't have his best stuff this inning. He had already surrendered a
home run to shortstop Dick Schofield, walked Downing, and thrown a wild pitch.
He was going to come right after Carew. Sure enough, the next pitch was an outside curve and, tracking it well, Carew got just enough wood on the ball to punch
it over the shortstop. It wasn't a pretty stroke, and the awkward motion of his
swing almost knocked the helmet off his head, but his 3,000 hit was in the books.
On August 4, 1985, Rod Carew had joined one of baseball's most elite clubs.

As the crowd stood and cheered, Carew doffed his helmet. One by one, his
teammates joined him at first base. Manager Gene Mauch, who had given Carew

the nickname "Pro" in Minnesota on account of his strictly professional attitude, gave the 39-year-old first baseman a warm embrace.

"You don't start the game thinking you're going to get 3,000 hits, but when you're around long enough and get close, you can't help but get excited," Carew says. "I was joining a select group of players. You can imagine all the thousands of players that have played this game that didn't come close."

A sore wrist hampered him for most of the 1985 season, and his final average of .280 marked the second time in two years in which he failed to hit .300. To new general manager Mike Port, that wasn't good enough, and he notified Carew that his services were no longer needed. An offer came from the San Francisco Giants to spell first baseman Will Clark, but Carew had had enough. The aches and pains of another season weren't worth it. With a lifetime .328 batting average, 3,053 hits, 18 consecutive All-Star appearances, and seven batting titles, Carew quietly bowed out.

In hindsight, it would have been to the Angels' advantage to have Carew stick around for one more season. He was certainly open to being platooned with Joyner, and would have even taken a pay cut to do so. As it turned out, Joyner pulled up lame in the 1986 ALCS and refused to play, leaving the Angels without a first baseman. Meanwhile, Carew was at home in Villa Park, coaching his girls' softball teams and running a batting school. He had always enjoyed teaching the art of hitting, and his years operating the school were enjoyable.

When Buck Rodgers was hired as Angels manager in 1992, he offered his old friend a job as team batting coach, which Carew accepted. The players were initially stunned by Carew's discipline. With his penetrating whistle, Carew constantly reminded his hitters during both games and batting practice that hitting was no longer a casual event. Players were instructed to meet with him every day to review video of the previous game's at-bats and to discuss opposing pitchers. If a struggling hitter didn't show up for extra batting practice, look out! Rookies in particular needed to stay on their toes. If they failed to live up to Carew's expectations of a Major Leaguer, he would dress them down and fine them golf balls.

One season, when some players were having a difficult time executing the hit-and-run, Carew recommended to manager Terry Collins that they be brought in early the next day for extra practice with him. The skipper agreed, and when the early practices commenced Carew made it competitive by having hitters go the opposite way. If they failed they would have to run to the outfield and retrieve the balls. The players enjoyed the challenge, and Carew thought everything was going smoothly until, at a team dinner in Toronto, pitching coach Joe Coleman started ragging him about all the extra work. Coleman had a few drinks under his belt, and told Carew, "You know that 'High School Harry' shit you did, that's a bunch of BS."

Stunned and stung, Carew responded, "Do I ever tell you about your pitchers? I'm trying to get more runs for your pitching staff, and you're sitting here bad-mouthing me. Why don't you just take your drunk ass up to bed?"

Coach Larry Bowa took Carew's side and told Coleman he didn't know what he was talking about. But Collins said nothing. Carew left the dining room, got as far as the escalator, and decided the matter was far from finished. Returning to the dining room, he told Coleman, "You know, I feel like knocking you on your butt. Here you are talking trash, telling me stuff about my hitters. Who the hell are you? Do you know anything about hitting? Do you even watch what the offense is doing? Or are you just paying attention to your pitching? Do I ever rip your pitching staff?"

Finally Collins piped up. But instead of backing Carew, he told him to drop it. Disgusted, Carew walked away. Later, Carew told Collins: "I work my fanny off for you, and all I ask in return is that you respect me. The day you lose respect for me, I will not respect you anymore. I came to you and said this is what I am doing and you said it's a great idea because we were not executing, and then you didn't back me when this loudmouth was popping off."

Collins was one of several managers Carew outlasted during his tenure as batting coach. For eight seasons he sharpened the batting skills of hundreds of players, including Garret Anderson, Darin Erstad, Jim Edmonds, and Troy Glaus. His prize pupil was Anderson, who was eager to learn about hitting from the master.

"Each spring we would work on something new," Carew says of Anderson. "One year it might be elevating the ball into the gaps, another it might be going the other way. Because I was honest and shot straight with him, he trusted me and took to heart the things I was trying to teach him. Garret plays the game identical to the way I did, so it made my job a lot easier."

The memory of those sessions is treasured by Anderson, too. "In our profession, it has a lot to do with what the pupils are asking that allows a teacher to become good or great," Anderson says. "I bombarded him with questions and he was willing to listen. We talked about the hitting approach, what to do with pitchers, and hitting the ball where it's pitched. He loved hitting and loved to talk about it, and that was the whole key."

Pitchers also benefited from Carew's knowledge.

"I would be in the bullpen, and if there was a guy I didn't know I would call Rod on the bench and ask him what the batter's strengths and weakness were," says Troy Percival. "He might say, 'If his hands are low, he's not gonna be able to get to a high fastball,' or, 'If he has his hands high he won't get the drop on a low fastball.' He was incredible! I've never met anybody that could read hitters better than he could."

"Rodney had a thought on every pitcher he faced, and as a hitting coach on every pitcher we faced," says Joe Maddon, who got to know Carew when both were coaches with the Angels. "To me, he's kind of like Pete Rose in regard to being the first singles hitter to become a superstar based purely on the ability to consistently recognize pitches and hit them accordingly. His ability to use his fingertips to his elbows was about as good as anybody."

Away from the field, Carew's life was very satisfying until something happened in 1996 so catastrophic that it tested the faith and resiliency that had carried him through his youth growing up in an abusive household and his transition to life as a big leaguer.

His daughter, Michelle Carew, was a vivacious teenager who always seemed most concerned about making others happy. A good athlete herself, Michelle was beginning her first year at Cyprus College and writing a paper on "Athletes as Role Models" when, on a Sunday morning in September, the unthinkable happened.

Recalls her father: "We had a game that day, and when I got back she complained about a headache and being dizzy. Since it was a hot day, we thought maybe she had allergies. We gave her some aspirins and she went to sleep, but when she got up the next day and was still feeling bad, we took her to the doctor. They took some tests and within a few days she was diagnosed with leukemia."

It was an aggressive type of cancer known as acute nonlymphocytic leukemia. Chemotherapy forced the cancer into remission, but doctors said that Michelle would need a bone marrow transplant to keep the disease at bay. Neither of her parents were compatible matches, and of the 1.8 million persons in the National Marrow Donor Registry, only five percent were African-American. Michelle was the product of an interracial marriage, and her genetic makeup made finding a bone marrow match more difficult. Time was of the essence, and if a transplant wasn't done before the cancer reappeared, Michelle's chances of surviving were slim.

Although it went against his reclusive, private nature, Carew had no choice but to go public with his daughter's dilemma in an effort to register as many potential African-American donors as possible to help his daughter and other people with her form of cancer.

"Michelle told me, 'Whatever happens, whether I live or die, I want you to help other kids,'" says Carew. "That's why I came out. I wanted to keep it private, but she said no. She said, 'By you coming out and getting publicity, other people will join the marrow program, donate blood, and get tested.'"

Carew began a series of TV appearances urging African-Americans to sign up for the donor registry. He got his teammates to raise money for the cause through signings and memorabilia auctions. He even approached strangers out in public and handed out cards with the phone number of the National Blood Marrow Donors Foundation.

Michelle's plight became front-page news. Carew's call to action resulted in the addition of thousands of names to the donor registry, and over four million dollars in donations. Michelle's courage touched the nation. Twice she almost succumbed to septic shock, and as her condition deteriorated she suffered temporary blindness and kidney failure. But she never complained, and nurses at Children's Hospital in Orange County nicknamed her "The Comeback Kid."

"She could have cried and complained, but she never did," says Carew. "She didn't want us crying or coming into her room being sad, or any of that. She just kept a positive attitude even when she realized she probably wasn't going to make it."

Rod with his daughter, Michelle. Courtesy of the Angels

A bone marrow match was eventually found, but by then Michelle's health was too compromised. In March of 1996, doctors performed a last-resort umbilical cord transplant. Her condition continued to deteriorate, and on April 15, 1996, Carew went to the hospital chapel and asked God to end his daughter's suffering. The following day the family huddled at Michelle's bedside. Charryse urged her sister to hang on. "Go Michelle, go!" She pleaded. But as her pulse weakened and as she took her final breaths her father caressed her arm for the final time.

"Have a safe journey," Carew whispered softly. Then she was gone.

Among the millions touched by Michelle's plight was the U.S. congress, who in 1997 approved legislation—at Carew's urging—that appropriated millions for bone marrow research. President Clinton made a special effort to acknowledge Carew's efforts, presenting the Hall of Famer with an award to observe his courage.

Since Michelle's death, Carew has dedicated his life to helping children with life-threatening illnesses. He is permanently "on call" at several hospitals, and will drive at a moment's notice to meet with a family in need.

"People have different ways of going through a healing process, and this is my way," he says. "My way of healing is trying to help other people, even if it's just trying to put a smile on a kid's face."

Carew has maintained his Panamanian citizenship. Whenever he visits his homeland—where he is considered a national hero—he is given a military guard. Carew says that it is important to remain connected with his heritage to set a good example for the kids of Panama.

"Every time I go back and walk the streets, the kids know who I am," he says. "They know what I've done and can recite all my accomplishments for all the years I played in the big leagues. I kept my citizenship there because I wanted kids to have someone to look up to and say, 'If Rod Carew can make it, any of us can.'"

Leave it to a kid from Panama who was once in great need himself to embrace his desire as an adult to provide today's children a glimpse of hope.

13

"JAX"

REGGIE JACKSON

"**W**hen I went to the plate I looked for a ball I could hit *hard!*" says Reggie Jackson. "I didn't go to the plate to hit a line drive to left field and stop at f---ing first! When I was in the batter's box there was a man in scoring position and that motherf---er was me! I went to the plate looking for a ball out over the plate, belt high that I could drive fence distance. I didn't go up and try and hit a ball to left field for a single. If that's what the team needed I would, but even if I got a single I still wanted to hit the ball hard!

"I was a home run hitter; I wanted to drive the ball fence distance. That's what I wanted to f---ing do! I wanted to hit the ball out of the ball park! I wanted to put the ball into play so it would go out of play!"

Nolan Ryan stood on the mound glaring in hard at the pinstriped slugger digging in at home plate.

"Hey, Reggie!" Ryan called out. "All fastballs!"

Reggie Jackson touched the brim of his helmet and said to himself, "Bring it, Tex. Bring on that flaming dead red! Show me what you got."

It was the ultimate power pitcher versus the ultimate power hitter, and nobody loved these shootouts more than the principals themselves.

"He did it to me twice," Jackson says of Ryan calling out his pitches. "Both times in Yankee Stadium. I think one time I may have struck out. Another time I flew out, but it was a bullet to left."

Ryan has a different recollection of that particular 1977 exchange. If you ask Reggie, he hit a vicious line drive to left field, but if you ask Nolan Ryan he hit a lazy fly ball to left field. The truth may lie somewhere in between.

"Reggie was not well liked by the opposition because he was a self-promoter," says Ryan. "Reggie promoted Reggie, and he has done real well with it. There is nothing wrong with that, because Reggie backed it up."

For 20-plus seasons, Jackson backed it up. And in those two decades, legions of fans and press debated the merits of Jackson's audacious style versus his equally menacing swing. Love him or hate him, Reggie Jackson was one of the game's most deadly home run hitters—and one of its most polarizing figures. Jackson's fondness for the limelight was a double-edged sword, however. He loved the adoration but abhorred the baggage that came along with it.

Steve Vucinich, the Oakland A's equipment man, has known Jackson personally since he was a rookie in 1967, and has seen both sides.

"There were times in Oakland—and they could be 10 minutes apart—when Reggie could be the nicest guy in the world, and the next thing you know he would be bitching about something or complaining about somebody," recalls Vucinich. "Reggie came with great fanfare out of Pennsylvania to Arizona State, where he was a two-sport athlete. He was king of that campus, and all of that probably contributed to Reggie's ego. Love-hate is a great way to explain Reggie. He wasn't afraid to give people shit or be on somebody's bad side."

Friend and teammate Rod Carew says Jackson's cocky attitude was warranted, even essential to his success. "He wasn't afraid to speak out because he knew what his standard of the game was," says Carew. He always had that cocky confidence and it's great. I think every player should have that feeling about himself."

Los Angeles Times writer Ross Newhan agrees, saying that Jackson's intent was often misconstrued. "Reggie was bigger than the game itself," says Newhan. "And because he wore his emotions on his sleeve, he rubbed some people wrong. I think he was misunderstood because of what was printed in the press. A lot of people think Reggie is a blowhard. But an egomaniac he's not."

Jackson's flair for controversy often overshadowed his excellent work ethic. Ever since his father, Martinez, showed how him to sew on pockets at their home-tailoring business in Wyncote, Pennsylvania, "Jax" was determined to get the job done. Jackson credits his father for setting him on the right path. His father witnessed the difficulties his children faced in a segregated America and made sure they possessed a strong work ethic and a good education—both things that were under his control.

"When I grew up, blacks weren't supposed to talk back," says Jackson. "We were supposed to be glad to be here and to be thankful to have the opportunity. But I was educated and I spoke well. My father always told me, 'Don't slur your words. And if you can't think of something [to say], pause. It will make someone pay attention.'"

They paid attention, all right; in high school Jackson's bat as well as his prowess as a running back earned him national notoriety. When college coaches came calling in his senior year, Martinez was all ears. For Reggie, the decision to leave home for Arizona State wasn't very hard.

"I wasn't leaving much behind, and I had nowhere to go," Jackson says. "I didn't have much of a house and there wasn't a job for me. My dad told me, 'Go away and get your education at college. They'll never be able to take it from you. You'll lose your skills as an athlete, son, but you won't lose your education.'"

Martinez's "get it done" attitude was driven into Reggie at a very young age, forcing him to become a self-sufficient youngster who didn't look for excuses.

"I remember him sending me to the store one day to get a pint of Neopolitan ice cream," recalls Jackson. "I went down to Fleischer's Drug Store and they didn't have any. So I went across the street to Kelso's Market, where we shopped, and borrowed 25 cents and told them to put it on Skippy's bill. "Skippy" was my dad's nickname. And then I went to the Atlantic Station and borrowed 25 cents and put it on my dad's bill.

"I went back across the street to Fleischer's and bought a pint of vanilla, a pint of chocolate, and a pint of strawberry, and ran back home and told my dad the story of [what I did]. He patted me on the head and said, 'Good job, son.' There wasn't a rant and rave about how much thinking and much creativity I had—it was expected. His philosophy was 'Do what you're supposed to. *Get it done.*' And I took that to the game of playing baseball."

There were times later when his drive was severely put to the test. No more so than after his spectacular 1969 season, when he electrified baseball with 47 home-runs for the A's. Unprepared for sudden stardom, Jackson floundered the following season, hitting just 23 home runs with a .237 average. Jackson searched for answers that offseason while playing winter league ball for the Santurce Crabbers in Puerto Rico. There, his manager, Frank Robinson, got him back on track.

Don Baylor, who was present that winter as well, remembers Jackson as a young man seemingly at odds with his place in the world.

"You had a great player managing in Frank, and Reggie, being a superstar on the verge, wanted to test him," remembers Baylor. "Robinson had one rule: he wanted everybody to run the ball out. One night in San Juan, Reggie popped the ball up and just stood there like he did sometimes and just looked at it. Sure enough, the ball fell in and Reggie, who wasn't even halfway down the line, got thrown out at first. Frank said, 'If you do that again, it's gonna cost you $500 bucks.'

"A week or two later Jax committed the same offense and just like last time he was thrown out. Frank said, 'That's going to cost you $500!' Reggie replied, 'I'm going home, then!' So Frank said, 'After this inning, I'm going to come up and help you pack!'"

Jackson moved, all right. Every time he popped the ball up after that he moved hard down the line to first base. "Frank let him know this is how we play the game," says Baylor, "and Jax took it to heart."

Reggie remembers the incident, and the lesson it taught him. "I love Frank Robinson. He's special. At a very crucial moment in my career he built my confidence and showed me who I was," says Jackson. "He taught me discipline and how to manage my personality and control myself to be more professional. He was very important in helping me develop into a great pro."

Jackson took the lessons learned from Robinson—in addition to those learned from Arizona State football coach Frank Kush and baseball coach Bobby Winkles—to become one of the hardest workers in baseball. He was a key cog in the A's three consecutive world championships in 1972, '73, and '74. Over those three seasons, Jackson combined to hit 86 home runs and drive in 285 runs. Although his detractors focused on his ego, what he produced on the field was beyond reproach.

"You're supposed to play hard!" Jackson says. "You have an obligation to play; it's your responsibility to the game. It doesn't take any ability to play hard. It takes care. It takes respecting the game, your teammates, the paycheck, the fans, the boss, owner, manager, and yourself. That's why you play hard."

Jackson played nine seasons for the A's and would probably have stayed longer had it not been for owner Charlie Finley's distaste for free agency. Refusing to go with the flow when baseball adopted free agency, Finely traded or sold off his stable of All-Stars. In the winter of 1975, Jackson and Ken Holtzman were dealt to the Orioles for Baylor and Mike Torrez. After spending the '76 season with Baltimore, Jackson became a free agent and signed with the Yankees. It was in New York that Jackson found a stage big enough for both his talent and his ego.

In the saturated New York sports market, Jackson became a phenomenon of sorts. The combination of his quick tongue and an even quicker bat made him a big story in the sports pages. His infamous squabbles with Billy Martin, Thurman Munson, and George Steinbrenner became national news, often overshadowing his success on the diamond. Jackson transformed himself into a lightning rod who dazzled the press with his bravado. Possessing a reported IQ of 160, he was a human quote machine whose memorable one-liners rolled off his tongue with the ease of a great stand-up comic. Scribes flocked to his locker before and after games, and he rarely disappointed.

Whenever Jackson butted heads in New York, it was Martinez who'd remind his son to focus on the big picture and not worry about the ongoing bickering with teammates and management.

"If I had a problem with Billy Martin, my father would say, 'That's nonsense. Do what you're supposed to do, and the manager's just a bystander. Get it done! Work your way through it—no excuses! You can't make the money you're making outside of baseball, so respect it! Honor the God-given skills and don't worry about the sidebars or the little things that clutter your life,'" Jackson says.

Legendary owner Bill Veeck once said of Jackson, 'You put him up there with two out and two on in the ninth inning, and it's like giving Popeye a can of spinach."

Jackson was uncanny in big-money games. The "Missiles of October" that exploded off Jackson's bat every fall brought the Yanks two world championships and three pennants. It was there in the Bronx Zoo where "Mr. October" was born.

In spring training in 1977, a reporter for *Sport* magazine quoted Jackson as calling himself "the straw that stirs the drink" on the Yankee team. Jackson, who was brand new to the team, renounced the accuracy of the statement. But when the article was published all hell broke loose, and an already divisive Yankee clubhouse came unglued.

The constant bickering was draining, and despite the Yankees' pair of World Series titles in 1977 and '78, the team began to wear down. After finishing fourth in the division in 1979—the year that Munson tragically lost his life in a plane crash—the Yankees rebounded in 1980 under new manager Dick Howser to win 103 games and capture the division title. However, the team faded badly in the second half of the strike-shortened 1981 season, and in that offseason Jackson again became a free agent. He decided to test the waters and eventually signed with the Angels in January of 1982. Steinbrenner has always lamented losing Jackson, calling it one of his biggest mistakes. With five world championships already under his belt, Jackson packed up his bags and took his act West.

"I really wanted to be near home," Jackson says. "I was living in Oakland, and I wanted to come to California. I thought the Autrys were fabulous people. I liked Gene, I liked his wife, and I had known Buzzie [Bavasi] and his family for years. I liked the people, and that's why I came to the Angels."

What Bavasi liked was the idea of having the biggest stick in the game in his batting lineup. A shrewd judge of talent, Bavasi knew a "boy of summer" when he saw one. In Jackson he detected the same fire he'd seen in Jackie Robinson, Duke Snider, and Roy Campanella of his legendary Dodger teams of the 1950s.

When word got out that Jackson was seeking free agency, Bavasi put in a call to the boss. It didn't take a lot of arm-twisting to convince Autry to go after Jackson. A meeting was set up at Autry's compound in Palm Springs, and Jackson didn't take long to make a decision.

"I want to bring this man [Autry] a world championship," Jackson said at the press conference announcing his signing.

Jackson's four-year contract netted him approximately $900,000 a year. It also included a clause giving the slugger 50 cents for every fan over the 2.4 million attendance mark. The signing was costly, but it brought immediate dividends. Season ticket sales jumped from 12,000 to 18,000, and in 1982 stadium attendance would double to a club-record 2.8 million, pocketing Jackson an extra $200,000.

It took a while for Jackson's new teammates to get accustomed to him. The superstar athlete was intimidating, and most people didn't know how to act

"I want to bring a championship to Anaheim," Reggie Jackson told the press in 1982—and he very near-ly did. Courtesy of the Angels

around him. A notable exception was Carew, who wasn't bowled over by Reggie's stats and regal presence.

"We had a bunch of guys who could get on each other relentlessly," Baylor recalls.

One day Reggie was getting on Carew for being "only a singles hitter." Rod took it for a while and then quietly said, "Hey, Jax. How about the s-o column you're a member of?"

"What s-o column are you talking about?" Jackson wondered.

"Strikeouts!" shot back Carew, breaking everybody up.

"It's hard to shut Jax up," Baylor recalls, "but I think that quieted him down a little bit."

Jackson's bat wasn't quiet, though. He hit a solid .275 in 1982, with 101 RBI and a league-best 39 homers. But while Jackson found success on the field, some fans were still less than impressed. His love-hate relationship with the fans in New York followed him to Anaheim. Bavasi thinks it was due to the diversity of Southern California fans as much as anything else.

"Anaheim, like Los Angeles, was made up from fans from all over the country," Bavasi points out. "There were people there from the midwest who didn't like the Yankees or the Angels. To them, Reggie represented both teams, and they hated him. Their attitude was, 'If you don't like the Yankees, you don't like Reggie.' For the most part, Reggie was popular with the fans, but I admit I did have four fans who wanted four box seats in right field—not to cheer for him, but to boo him!"

Jackson gave the Angels what they wanted in 1982—a division championship. But during the playoffs, the big Angel guns, with the exception of Fred Lynn and Baylor, were strangely ineffective. After falling behind two games to none, the Brewers ran over the Angels like a loose beer truck upon returning to Milwaukee, winning three in a row to take the series.

On their flight home from Milwaukee, Jackson wore a bandage on his eyes, and the press had a field day speculating about the reason for it. It was rumored he had been in a bar fight or had fisticuffs with Baylor, which both players denied. In fact, the injury was an infection caused from dust particles that got into Jackson's eye when he slid into third in the final game of the series. The black eye Jackson suffered served as a metaphor for the whole sorry series.

"We were more concerned on the way to Milwaukee about wives and tickets and where people were going to sit, and not focused on closing out the Brewers," Jackson says. "There was too much chit chat on the bus. ... The bottom line was that we were a better team but had lost our focus. By the time we had it figured out it was the fifth game, and by then it was too late."

Jackson is adamant that the blame for the team's collapse doesn't belong to manager Gene Mauch, who became a scapegoat for the team's failure and resigned that offseason.

"Gene Mauch didn't have anything to do with it," says Jackson. "What we did was more important than what Gene Mauch did, and we didn't do the job. We had three games to do it right. We have no one to blame but ourselves."

Jackson piled up some impressive numbers in 1982, but the following year he only hit .194, with 14 homers in 116 games. His weak numbers and slowing reflexes coincided with the team's overall lackluster season. The offense struggled to replace Baylor's production, and the aging team had clearly lost a step, finishing 22 games under .500.

John McNamara, Jackson's old manager in Oakland, took over the reins in 1983. "Mac," as the skipper was known, and Jackson first met during Jackson's minor league days in Birmingham, Alabama. There, Jackson remembers, Mac stood up to racial prejudice.

"You were colored, and that's what you were," Jackson says of his time spent in Birmingham in the mid-Sixties. "You were second-class and there wasn't anything you could do about it but just play hard and do the best you could. But Johnny McNamara was someone who saw the injustice and did what he could to right it. If we went somewhere and I couldn't eat, the team wouldn't eat. If I couldn't stay in the hotel, the team didn't stay in the hotel, and we moved on until we found another one in town."

With McNamara at the helm, Jackson bounced back in 1984. His 25 homers and 81 RBI—along with substantial contributions from third baseman Doug DeCinces and outfielders Fred Lynn and Brian Downing—helped to lead the Angels back to a respectable record. That season was memorable for Jackson on an individual level, as he neared 500 homers, a milestone that would virtually guarantee him entry into baseball's Hall of Fame.

On September 17, 1984, a half-game separated three teams—the Royals, Twins, and Angels—from first place in the American League West. The league-leading Royals were in town and had taken a commanding 7-0 lead into the seventh inning when Jackson stepped to the plate. Pitcher Buddy Black was behind 3-1 in the count when he threw a high inside fastball that Jackson deposited deep into the right field bleachers for his 500th dinger. The 28,862 fans in attendance gave Jackson a 10-minute standing ovation, which he acknowledged with several curtain calls.

"It was fastball, up, and the type of ball that Reggie would murder," says Black, who has been the Angels pitching coach since 1999. "As he rounded third base he kind of gave me a quick glance. It wasn't like he was saying, 'Thank you for giving me the 500th.' It was more of an acknowledgment. Like 'Hey, I went after him and he got me.'"

A perfect game by Mike Witt on the final day of the season put the Angels at the .500 mark for the year, just three games behind the division-winning Royals. That positive momentum remained with the club the next year as they cruised to a 90-72 record. During 1984, 90 wins would have easily been enough to win the division, but just as the Angels had improved, so had the Royals, who once again outpaced the Angels to capture the division by a single game. Jackson's 85 RBI and 27 homers paced the team on offense, while Witt and closer Donnie Moore anchored the pitching staff.

After the season, the Autrys hinted strongly to Jackson that his contract wouldn't be renewed beyond his option year, so he knew that 1986 would be his last shot at a pennant with the Angels.

In 1986, Jackson became the full-time designated hitter at age 40. He primarily batted clean up in a lineup dominated by veterans that included Brian Downing in left field, Gary Pettis in center field, Rupert Jones in right field, Doug DeCinces at third base, Dick Scofield at shortstop, and Bobby Grich and Rob Wilfong at second base. Veteran catcher Bob Boone was the anchor behind the plate, and a pair of valuable vets—George Hendrick and Rick Burleson—contributed from the bench.

But it was Carew's replacement at first, 24-year-old Wally Joyner, who won the fans' hearts. Nicknamed "Wally World," the boyish-looking rookie hit .290, with 22 home runs and 100 RBI. Joyner made his first—and only—All-Star team and was a close runner-up to Jose Canseco for Rookie of the Year honors.

The pitching staff was anchored by the ageless Don Sutton, who at 41 years of age put together a 15-11 campaign. But a youth movement was on the way. Mike Witt, still only 25 years old despite pitching in his sixth Major League season, finished third in the league's Cy Young voting after winning 18 games and posting a 2.84 ERA. Another 25-year-old, Kirk McCaskill, won 17 games, while 23-year-old rookie Chuck Finley posted a 3.30 ERA from the pen.

It took a while for things to click in '86, however. The team struggled out of the gate, but despite being one game under .500 heading into June, they were just a half-game out of first in the standings. However, they began to catch fire in mid-June, and by the All-Star break they were 48-39 and atop the A.L. West. The Angels cruised through the months of August and September, going 36-20, to clinch the divisional title.

This eclectic mix of players won 92 games, good enough to take the division by five games over the Texas Rangers. But getting into the Series wasn't going to be easy. They had to first get past the Boston Red Sox, a tough veteran team led by sluggers Jim Rice and Dwight Evans, batting champion Wade Boggs, the soon-to-be infamous Bill Buckner, 23-year-old pitching phenom Roger Clemens, and a designated hitter named Don Baylor. At their helm was John McNamara, the same Johnny Mac that Mauch had replaced in 1985 when McNamara suddenly quit to manage the Red Sox. McNamara was feeling the heat when Mauch was brought in as an advisor in 1984. When Buzzie Bavasi stepped down after the '84 season, Mac, feeling uncertain with new general manager Mike Port at the helm, jumped ship when Boston offered a job.

The Angels came out of the chute fast, pouncing early on Cy Young and MVP Award-winner Roger Clemens in Game 1. Witt threw a complete game for the Halos, who won 8-1. Boston rallied in Game 2 thanks to some sloppy Angels defense to take win 9-2. The Red Sox tacked on three runs in the seventh inning to blow open the game on a single, a walk, and a playoff-record three errors—one each by DeCinces, Grich, and Schofield.

The momentum swung back in the Angels' favor in Game 3 with a 5-3 victory. John Candelaria, who had went 10-2 with a 2.55 ERA during the regular season—pitched brilliantly for seven innings, and Donnie Moore saved the game despite allowing two runs to score. Homers by Schofield and Pettis were the difference on offense. But the postgame celebration was derailed when Joyner was suddenly struck by a mysterious bacterial infection in his leg. Some claimed it was a spider bite, but no one knew for certain what caused it. The only thing that was certain was that Joyner, the Angels' hottest stick through the first three games with a .455 average and three extra-base hits, was out indefinitely.

The Angels showed resiliency and guts in Game 4 when they pulled through for three runs in the bottom of the ninth to take the game to extra innings. Down 3-0 heading into the final frame with a dominant Clemens on the mound, the Angels were in need of a minor miracle. They got it as DeCinces stepped to the plate to lead off the inning and promptly hit a home run to get the Halos on the board. Schofield and Boone followed with one-out singles, sending Pettis to the plate. Mauch decided to pinch run youngster Devon White for Boone, making White the tying run at first. McNamara went to his bench, too, lifting Clemens for

Like Nolan Ryan and Rod Carew before him, Jackson gave the Angels a national media presence—as well as plenty of home runs.
Lou Sauritch/Sauritch Sports Photography

reliever Calvin Schiraldi. Pettis greeted Schiraldi with a double to left, scoring Schofield and getting himself in scoring position in the process. Rupert Jones was walked intentionally to load the bases with just one out for Grich, who struck out.

Schiraldi was one out away from finishing off the Angels—all he had to do was get Downing out. Instead, he hit Downing with a pitch, forcing in White from third to tie the game. With the bases still loaded and the winning run 90 feet away, Jax came up empty by grounding out to second to end the inning. But his teammates picked him up in the bottom of the 11th as Grich singled home Jerry Narron to win the game.

For the second time in five years, the Angels stood on the brink of winning the A.L. pennant. Witt, who had pitched so well in Game 1, was on the Anaheim

Stadium mound for Game 5. Everything seemed in order for the Angels to make it to their first World Series in 26 years.

Prior to the Angels World Series title in 2002, Game 5 of the 1986 American League Championship Series had long been considered the most memorable game in Angels history. The result of the game forced the team—and its fans—into plenty of soul searching. For a generation of diehard Angels fans, it was the last straw for a team that had already supplied enough heartache to last a lifetime. For Reggie Jackson and Gene Autry, 1986 was their last shot at a World Series. For relief pitcher Donnie Moore, it signaled the beginning of a downward spiral that would eventually end in tragedy. For Gene Mauch, it began a lifetime of second-guessing. And for Boston's Dave Henderson, it marked the beginning of a wondrous and productive career.

Henderson's turnaround actually started the night before with, of all things, an injury. In his only at-bat in Game 4, Henderson fouled a Doug Corbett fastball off his left knee and tore the cartilage so badly that he was ordered to sit down for the rest of the Series. But that order changed midway through Game 5 when Sox centerfielder Tony Armas injured himself making a play against the wall. With Armas out, McNamara realized he had no more outfielders and was forced to call on Henderson. Henderson threw on his jock, found a heat pack for his knee, gulped down a couple of aspirins, and ran out to center in the fifth inning. His real act of heroism wouldn't come for another five innings, however.

Boston struck first when Rich Gedman slammed a two-run homer off of Witt to give the visitors a 2-0 lead. Red Sox starter Bruce Hurst gave a run back in the third on a Boone homer, but then kept the Angels at bay until the sixth, when the Angels struck for two more runs. With DeCinces on second, Grich hit a towering fly ball to Henderson in center. As he leaped against the fence, Henderson's bad knee gave way and the ball deflected off his glove and plopped over the fence for a two-run homer and 3-2 Angel lead. As Grich rounded second, he did a victory jig. The Angels were just nine outs away from a trip to the World Series, and the 64,000 fans in attendance were delirious with joy.

The Angels tacked on two more runs in the seventh to make it 5-2. Witt made quick work of the Sox in the eighth inning, and down in the Angel clubhouse champagne bottles were iced and lockers wrapped in protective plastic in preparation for the celebration that was already taking shape. Gene Autry himself began making his way to the elevator so he could be there when his conquering heroes arrived.

Meanwhile, a contingent of policemen had moved over by Boston's dugout, and Don Baylor couldn't help smiling at the sight of his rugged Red Sox teammates all bunched up in a corner like Little Leaguers. As the team's elder statesman, it was his responsibility to rally his troops. Bat in hand, he made his way over and addressed his team.

"Guys, this is the deal," he said tersely. "If we're going down, make sure your last at-bat is a good one. Because you've got to live with it till next April."

Witt remained in the game to start the ninth, and Buckner singled off of him to start the frame. Rice followed and struck out, raising the crowd noise another decibel level. That brought up Baylor with the season on the line for Boston. He worked Witt to a 3-2 count. Knowing Witt could ill afford to walk him, Baylor looked for something over the plate. Sure enough, Witt fired an outside breaking ball that hung. Baylor deposited the pitch over the centerfield wall 440 feet away for a two-run home run. Angels 5, Red Sox 4.

Baylor's shot quieted the crowd, but they soon were roaring again in approval as Witt induced Evans to pop up to DeCinces for Boston's second out. On the mound, Witt appeared cool and under control. He needed to get just one more out—Rich Gedman, who already singled, doubled, and homered off of Witt in the game. In the Angels' bullpen, Gary Lucas and Donnie Moore were doing their best to warm up in the midst of mounted police and security personnel who had overrun the area. The noise in the stadium was so deafening that bullpen coach Bob Clear could barely hear the phone ringing. It was Mauch on the other end with a one-word message for Clear: "Lucas." The Angels skipper wanted the lefty on the mound to face the lefty batter.

As Mauch marched out to take the baseball from Witt, first baseman Bobby Grich pondered the move.

"As he's walking out I can hear everyone booing, and I say to myself, 'If you're the manager, what do you do right now?' I'd take him out," says Grich. "Gedman was 0-4 during the course of the season off Lucas. He'd never hit the ball out of the infield. You go with the percentages."

But percentages meant little on this night. Lucas's first pitch drilled Gedman in the back. Once again, Mauch picked up the phone to the bullpen. He told Clear to send Moore to the mound. In the on-deck circle, Dave Henderson was concerned. He knew Moore could be tough on right-handers, and he would have much preferred to face Lucas.

Grich again felt Mauch was making the right decision. "Donnie had been struggling and was given a cortisone shot that morning or the night before," Grich recalls. "He was hurting and wasn't at the top of his game, but Gene had no choice. I'm thinking he's got to bring in Moore now. That's the move you've got to make."

Moore blew the first pitch by Henderson, and Mauch looked like a genius. Henderson fouled off the next pitch, and just like that he was behind in the count 0-2. One more strike and the Angels were headed to the World Series.

Moore wasted a pitch, then threw another fastball that Henderson fouled off. Henderson was battling, no doubt recalling a similar situation the previous June when Moore had thrown him a slider away and he nailed it to tie the game. He figured Moore would also be thinking of that time and guessed that the pitcher would now come in with another fastball.

Wrong. It was a hanging forkball. The momentarily flummoxed Henderson swung late, but got enough of his bat on the ball to send it over the fence. Red Sox 6, Angels 5. As the crowd in the stadium sat in stunned silence, Henderson forgot all about his bum knee and jumped up and down. He had given his team new life.

But the Angels weren't ready to give up on the game. Boone singled to left to lead off the inning. Jones replaced him as a pinch runner and moved over to second on a sacrifice bunt from Pettis. Wilfong then singled home Jones to tie the game, but failed to advance to second when the throw came to the plate. That mistake ended up costing the Angels a precious run, as Wilfong wasn't in scoring position when Schofield followed with a single. Downing was then intentionally walked to load the bases with one out. The Angels missed their opportunity to end the game, however, as DeCinces popped up on the first pitch and Grich lined back to the pitcher.

In the top of the 11th, the Red Sox loaded the bases with no outs, setting the stage for Henderson's sacrifice fly to put the Red Sox in the lead for good.

Much has been made of Mauch's decision to pull Witt with two outs in the ninth. Grich still thinks it was the right move, but Ross Newhan considers the decision to go to the pen a crucial mistake.

"When Gene went to the mound to bring in Lucas, it just seemed like everything changed," says Newhan. "It brought that emotional tide to a close, and I think more than anything that was a mistake. In June or July, percentage-wise the move might have made sense. But with the stadium rocking and people on their feet waiting to crash the field, it put excessive pressure on Lucas. But no matter what Gene did, they had plenty of chances to win. Better base running by Rob Wilfong in the ninth, and more patience by Doug DeCinces would have made the difference."

The series moved back to Boston, where the Angels acted as if they were already beaten. Behind poor starting pitching from Kirk McKaskill and John Candelaria, the Halos lost 10-4 and then 8-1 in the finale. In both games the Angels fell behind early and couldn't recover.

Jackson batted .192 in six series games, with no homers and two RBI. He has always maintained that the Angels lacked the necessary ingredients to be champions. Although both the 1982 and '86 playoff losses were similar, he recalls the latter as uglier and harder to swallow.

"We had a chance to win the game here, and Doug popped the ball up on the first pitch with a man on third base and one out," Jackson says. "After that, we went back to Boston and we never had a chance. We should have won the second time around, but we just didn't have the killer instinct that was necessary to win. We lost, but we didn't get beat. We were not ready to play—players, management, and staff, everyone."

Fans never forgave Moore for allowing Henderson's home run, and for the next two years he was the target of incessant booing and taunts. In 1987, he suffered a debilitating back injury, but the press and management insinuated that he was just malingering. Moore's woes continued in 1988, when he was largely ineffective in 27 appearances.

Following a brief stint with Atlanta in '89, he went back home to Anaheim where he became despondent, started drinking, and began beating his wife. On

July 18, 1989, he shot his wife in the neck. Thinking he had killed her, he turned the gun on himself and, with his children watching, fired a single fatal shot into his own head. According to some press accounts, Dave Henderson's home run killed Donnie Moore. Although it undoubtedly contributed to his state of mind, it is more likely that Moore's chronic depression and dependency on alcohol were the true culprits.

Jackson battled a different foe following the 1986 playoffs: age. For the man known as "Mr. October," his poor performance in the playoffs was a rude awakening. At age 40, it was obvious his once lightning-like reflexes were diminishing, and by early in the 1986 season, there were signs that the end was in sight.

"There was a game early on in the season when I got a ball that normally I would have taken out of the park, but instead just fouled it off," Jackson recalls. "It was the first time I couldn't turn the water on when I wanted. The opportunity presented itself with a ball that was out over the plate, and I left it on the screen behind me. I said to myself, 'Damn boy! You can't hit that ball?' I knew then that my career was close to being over."

Following the playoff defeat to Boston, Jackie Autry confirmed that she had no intention of renewing Jackson's contract, officially bidding adieu to Jax.

"It wasn't anything personal, and I don't hold it against the Angels," Jackson says. "I was disappointed because we had a chance to get in the World Series twice and didn't get there but should have. It was painful, but it got to a point where I realized it was time for me to get out."

Newhan, who covered Jackson throughout his five years in Anaheim, says the Angels were not shortchanged at all by Jackson.

"He, like Carew and Ryan before him, gave the Angels a national presence. He embellished that identity, and I thought he was great for us," says Newhan. "He was a tremendous quote; win or lose you could always count on Reggie. He was in the twilight of his career but still he tied for the home run title that one year. I thought he was sensational."

In 1987, Jackson returned to Oakland. It was his way of ending a long and distinguished career on his own terms. In his final year, Jackson hit .220 with 15 home runs in 115 games. He finished his career with 563 long balls, good for sixth on the all-time list at that time. But Jackson paid a high price for a career spent swinging for the fences: his 2,597 career strikeouts were also a major league record that still stands today.

First and foremost, Jackson brought the stadium alive with each and every at-bat. To compare him to a modern player, his effect on a crowd was like that of Barry Bonds. The Giants' slugger generates the same love-hate emotions among fans and the press as well.

"Like Barry, I was unaffected on the field. I played hard every day and didn't show my emotions," Jackson says. "I was an intense player, and it's easy to see Bonds is intense as well. If you watch him, he's not happy or sad, he's even-keeled. He plows through his emotions all the time, and there's our similarity—not wearing your heart on your sleeve makes people dislike you. He knows he's great and he continues to move forward because he understands that if he stays the course he's going to win out in the end."

Jackson agrees with some historians that his impact on baseball was actually revolutionary.

"Without sounding egotistical or self-ingratiating, I guess I did revolutionize the game by speaking out, and I had more showmanship in my home run trot. I was the first player to stand and admire a home run. I was a great TV player," he says. "I said what I felt and tried not to embarrass people, and everything I did on the field was done from pure enthusiasm. I enjoyed playing well. I loved the game! I spoke what was on my mind and that wasn't very acceptable as a young player, and especially a black player."

Baylor calls Jackson the "Muhammad Ali of baseball." "During our times in the '70s," Baylor remembers, "he'd talk the talk, and he could walk the walk, too. He might strike out, but I'm gonna tell you one thing: he was gonna get his three swings."

Steve Vucinich, the Oakland A's equipment manager, has a slightly different take on the issue.

"I don't know if he was the first outspoken black, but he was certainly one of the earliest ones," Vucinich said. "How can you say Curt Flood wasn't an outspoken black player?"

Angel coach Joe Maddon has his take on Jackson as well. "He just didn't break an African-American barrier, he broke a barrier for everybody," says Maddon. "I think Ali, Joe Namath, and Jackson kind of said it was okay to be good and say what you think."

It was in the "Me Decade," the post-Martin Luther King era, that black America finally stepped from the shadows and insisted on being heard. Ali, with his in-your-face antics and sense of humor, was a courageous example. Jim Brown, Bill Russell, and Curt Flood all stepped up and were heard. Suddenly, African-American players were speaking out on a myriad of issues and the world was listening.

Reggie Jackson was perfect for the times. Brash, smart, self-assured, and talented, Jackson's posture fairly screamed, "Look! I'm a ball player who happens to be black—take me on my terms!" For all his dialogue with the press, though, Jackson was rarely political like Ali. But by being himself and standing up to management and the league office, he helped break longstanding psychological barriers in regard to race. And despite all of the home runs, that may be Jackson's greatest legacy.

But Jackson paid a price for his supreme confidence and outspoken nature, as he was often ridiculed and chastised by fans and the press. Jackson says today that had his skin color been white, nothing would have been made of his outspoken nature. His image as a self-promoter, unfortunately, has overshadowed much of what he accomplished on and off the field.

"No one chooses to recognize it!" Jackson says of his legacy in baseball. "If I was white, I would have been considered a great leader. I would have been a 'very bright, high-intellect individual.' As a black, I was 'boisterous,' 'loud,' 'braggadocio,' 'self-centered,' 'ornery,' and 'arrogant.' It's very similar to Magic Johnson and Michael Jordan, who were both known as fantastic athletes in contrast to Larry Bird, who had similar skills but was known as a coach on the floor. They said when a white athlete spoke out, he was bright and he should be a general manager some day. 'Reggie Jackson,' they'd say, 'he's like a Philadelphia lawyer—he talks too much.'"

Jackson claims that racism and injustice still exist in the upper echelons of Major League Baseball and corporate America. He also believes that former stars of African-American descent choose to stay relatively quiet on the subject for fear of being labeled malcontents. Jackson has no such qualms.

"I remember in '69, in Mesa, Arizona, in spring training, going to the Cubs' camp to visit with Ernie Banks, Fergie Jenkins, and Billy Williams," says Jackson. "Those guys would tell me, 'Reggie, be careful what you say—it might hurt you in the future.' Nowadays, I know the Ernie Banks's, Henry Aarons and the Willie Mays's appreciate my forthrightness. They appreciate my command of the language and are proud that I'm able to speak out."

Jackson says the price he's paid for being outspoken can't be measured in mere dollars and cents.

"What has happened to me continually as a black man is sad and sick, and I don't like to really talk about it that much. No blacks do. Hank Aaron doesn't, Ernie Banks doesn't, Willie Mays doesn't, Bob Gibson doesn't, and Frank Robinson doesn't. We don't mention it, because if we do, people will say we're bitter. They will say we're angry," explains Jackson. "Well, sometimes if you want the truth, it's sad and uncomfortable."

Jackson says that his race—and his outspoken nature—have hurt his standing in the conservative world of baseball and prevented him from moving up the ranks of baseball management.

"If I weren't a Hall of Famer, I wouldn't even be in the game [still]. If I didn't have a renegade as an owner in George Steinbrenner, I wouldn't be around baseball at all. I wouldn't be in the game like a Ted Simmons or a Pete Vuckovich, a Bill Stoneman, a Jim Beattie, or Mike Flanagan," says Jackson. "Black players? Where are they? Frank Robinson: In order to keep him quiet, they give him a managing job. He should have a cake job like Sandy Alderson has. A one-to-two-million-dollar-a-year job to do whatever you want."

But Jackson admits that things have improved somewhat for blacks seeking management roles in baseball, even if they still have a long way to go.

"As I climb the ladder economically to try to get into a different level business-wise, I fight the same battles. I am pursuing a Major League Baseball franchise and

I've had a tough time. I offered more money than [Lewis] Wolff in Oakland, but I didn't get the club. I don't know what the reasons were. They're inexplicable," says Jackson. "How can you not let me own a team, and especially in Oakland? It's a perfect fit. The only way I'm going to get a team is I'm going to have to go public and ask for one. We're not going to get one from the commissioner. I've tried twice. … I offered $25 million more than the guy who bought the A's, and would have paid $50 million more. We could have paid $100 million more, but I didn't even get a chance to bid! What's that about?"

This much is for certain: Reggie Jackson's stature as a great ballplayer is one thing he'll never have to go public about—it's common knowledge. He has five World Series rings, 14 All-Star appearances, and a plaque in the Hall of Fame to back him up. But the man himself doesn't rely on statistics and rings to measure his or any other man's worth.

"Baseball's a great game, but what is more important is what do you stand for?" asks Jackson. "What did you accomplish? What was your history? What was your impact and your handprint? In the end, it doesn't matter what you think about yourself or what they say about you. It only matters how you act and how you affected others."

Easy for Mr. October to say—he's been affecting others for 35 years and counting.

PART THREE

14

—— **MIRACLE ANGEL** ——

JIM ABBOTT

*R*ex Hudler wasn't his usual gregarious self in the gym the day after he became the father of a brand-new baby boy in November of 1995. His teammates were concerned. No cigars, no smiles, no bragging, no nothing. Chuck Finley, JT Snow, and Jim Abbott had all been prepared to shower him with congratulations, but his quiet behavior stopped the celebration in its tracks.

It had taken Hudler a long time to gather the courage to come back to the gym and face his teammates. How do you tell your friends that your newborn son has Down Syndrome? It wasn't supposed to be this way. Hudler had told himself that a million times. His son, Cade, was the son of a professional athlete, after all. Wasn't he naturally supposed to be strong and vital? For the always upbeat and positive Hudler, it was a blow that sent him spiraling into depression.

When he finally told his teammates the news, he became so overwhelmed that he collapsed on the bench press and burst into tears. His teammates did their best to console him, but what could they say? Jim Abbott watched all this with a keen and compassionate eye. More than anyone else in that room, he knew what Hudler was going through. "Abby" bided his time, and when Hudler started warming up on the treadmill he sauntered over and took a place on the machine next to him.

"Hud," Abbott said with a smile, "you and your wife are great parents. You stay with that kid because *miracles can happen*. And with you and Jennifer as Cade's parents, something great is gonna happen. I just know it!"

Hudler was taken aback. It was the first time since Cade was born that anyone had spoken to him in a positive tone. What struck him, too, was the way Abbott spoke. He wasn't patronizing; he was speaking straight from the heart. Abby's message sunk in and, like magic, Hudler's optimism and positive energy came flooding back.

"You're right, Abby. Look at you. Look at what you did," Hudler thought to himself.

Hudler ended his workout early, got in his car, and drove home. His wife, Jennifer, was shocked when her husband exploded through the door and proclaimed, "Honey, Cade came to the right home and we're gonna embrace him! And, starting right now, we're gonna help him reach his full potential. Let me tell you what Abby shared with me today. He said, 'Hud, miracles can happen!'"

Jennifer looked at him, noticed the conviction in his eyes, and started to cry. On the spot they made a silent pact: come hell or high water, they would love Cade with all their hearts and make sure they did everything in their power to make his life a special one.

Hudler raised his palm. "Put it here," he said, and as Jennifer returned the high-five their fingers entwined and she said, "Let's go with it!"

"All right, then," Rex replied. "Go, team!"

Hudler had discovered what legions of people already knew—that Jim Abbott could inspire.

"Hey Stumpy!" screamed the voice from the opposing dugout. "Your hand looks like a foot!"

Jimmy Abbott flinched. It wasn't the first time a cruel remark like that had come from the opposing bench. As always, his first reaction was anger; but then he quickly suppressed the emotion and reminded himself: "There are other ways to get even."

Smart kid, this 11-year-old. Abbott's next pitch was inside for ball four, and as Jimmy deftly switched the glove back on his right hand the tormenting voice bellowed anew: "Hey claw, nice pitch!"

Jimmy turned in the direction of the bullhorn and glared. That nobody else on the other team joined in the mindless taunting was of some consolation, but it only took one loudmouthed slob to bring on the hurt.

Jimmy knew they were testing him, and he could almost sense what was going to happen next. On the next pitch the batter bunted. In a flash, Abbott switched his glove back to his right hand and snatched up the ball. Then, balancing the glove on his right arm, he turned gracefully and fired a perfect strike to the first baseman. The batter was out by two feet.

For the rest of the game the other dugout was silent. By keeping his cool and staying above the fray, Jimmy had single-handedly silenced their bats and their mouths. That in itself was an empowering feeling, but the slow acceptance of him from the other side was more satisfying than anything.

That need for acceptance drove Jim Abbott. For the next 20 years, that desire to be respected along with a natural competitive streak would be the major motivations in his athletic life. They would help him defeat the outside demons and eventually push Abbott to dizzying heights—and, later, to devastating lows. How he handled those polar opposites became an ongoing struggle and the key to his character.

For Jim Abbott, living with one hand was as normal as wearing glasses. Born with only one hand, he never accepted the notion that he was handicapped. For the most part, as a youngster he was treated normally. On occasions when his abnormality was pointed out, it was nothing he and his family couldn't handle.

"Maybe I blocked it out in my own mind, but I seldom remember anybody being cruel," Abbott says. "Maybe there was something here and there, but it was more like calling someone wearing glasses 'Four Eyes.' Everyone is dealt a problem in life, and mine is missing four fingers."

Fearing he would become an outcast, Jim's folks encouraged him at an early age to be outgoing and to participate in sports.

"My dad wanted to get me into sports and get involved, but he wanted me to do it with sportsmanship and hard work. He wanted me to do it the way other kids were doing it," recalls Abbott. "There was no special pat on the back for 'Great job just for trying.' He definitely had expectations of doing things the right way, but he was always more concerned with the lessons the sports held, and I'll always be thankful for that."

Jim loved baseball, and by age six he had taught himself to switch his glove back and forth between his hand and stump. He would start by balancing the glove on the stump of his right arm, then while completing his follow through he rapidly switched the glove to his left hand so he could handle any balls hit back to him. The speed at which he did it was almost discernable to the human eye, but once accomplished he became as efficient as anyone else on the field.

He and his dad worked for hours perfecting the "catch and switch." When alone, Jim would head to the brick wall across from their apartment and practice by himself, throwing a ball against the wall repetitively. Eventually, catch and switch became as natural to him as breathing.

When he told his parents he wanted to join the Little League in his hometown of Flint, Michigan, they supported him wholeheartedly. They liked the idea of him being a part of a team and cultivating friendships. But even the Abbotts were amazed when within a few weeks Jim had established himself as not only a pitcher—but his team's best. As far as Jim himself was concerned, his performance was just a welcome bonus. The acceptance he received from his teammates was what mattered most.

"I grew up among the same group of friends for a long period of time," he says. "Within that group I was accepted pretty quickly, and sports was a big help in that transition. I didn't know it at the time, but that's why I was drawn to team sports. It's where I felt I belonged and fit in."

The success he achieved in baseball gave him the confidence to try other sports. At Flint Central High School he was also the quarterback of the football team and the star forward on the basketball team. But his passion was baseball. As a senior he played first base, left field, and shortstop, and batted .427.

His talent caught the attention of the Toronto Blue Jays, who selected him in the 36th round of the 1985 amateur draft. But Abbott decided to pass up the Jays' offer in favor of college. He had several scholarship offers from all over the country and ended up choosing the University of Michigan because of its academic reputation and his passion for Wolverine football. As a freshman, Abbott exceeded everyone's expectations, going 6-2, with a 4.11 ERA. As a sophomore he threw 31 consecutive scoreless innings, and had a record of 11-3 with an ERA of 2.08. His performance earned him the "Golden Spikes" award as outstanding amateur baseball player, and the Sullivan Award as the best amateur athlete in the country.

Abbott earned a berth on the 1988 Olympic team and was on the mound in Seoul, South Korea, when Team USA defeated Japan in the gold medal game. The exposure put him squarely in the national spotlight, and major-league scouts again came calling, including Angels chief scout Bob Fontaine. On Fontaine's recommendation, Abbott was selected by the Angels with their first-round selection in the 1988 draft.

Bill Bavasi was the Angels' farm director then, and says that Abbott was the only player he ever drafted whose character was evident at first meeting.

"He had gone through things most other kids never had to go through," Bavasi says. "I did have one concern, however, and that was his glove. Because he wanted to get in the glove as quick as he could, he never really threw a true curveball. To throw a curve, you've got to follow through with your wrist, and that takes more time.

"I asked coach Marcel Lachemann if we could outfit him with a special glove that would work on the right arm. Marcel looked at me and said, 'He wouldn't know what to do with it. This is the way he grew up. It's all he ever knew.'"

The boy searched the four-diamond complex feverishly. He had already been to the main field, and figured the adjacent practice fields were his last hope. As he scanned the vast complex he noticed a couple players doing wind sprints, and someone throwing off the pitcher's mound. The man throwing pitches was tall, and between pitches the boy noticed a blur of flashing arms and leather.

It was Abbott, the boy thought to himself. Had to be.

The boy started toward the field, and when he could make out that it was indeed Jim Abbott there, he began to sprint. When he arrived at the chain-link fence on the sideline, he leaned against it, stuck his face right into the holes and stared.

Anyone watching might've taken the boy for just another fan at first glance, until he noticed that he, like his hero, had only one hand. The athlete before him

With a devastating cut fastball and relentless desire, Jim Abbott captivated the hearts and minds of Angels fans.
Courtesy of the Angels/Photo by John Cordes

was not just a bubble-gum fantasy, but rather someone to identify with and measure his own life by. To him, Jim Abbott was a living, breathing reassurance that he, too, could someday lead a useful and fulfilling life.

Abbott noticed the youth, and when he finished his workout came over and chatted with him for several minutes. Whatever they talked about wasn't as important as the fact that Abbott made the effort to reach out. Even as a rookie at his first spring training, Abbott was well aware of the weight and expectations people placed on him.

But fame always rested uneasily on Abbott. He wanted desperately to be known solely for his ability to pitch, not for surmounting a perceived handicap. He appreciated the attention, but knew in his heart that in order to be true to himself, the adulation could only be validated by performance.

"I know the way I played and the differences I had growing up were bound to attract attention," says Abbott. "If there was a different path for me to take to the major leagues because of that, then it's just the way it was supposed to be. I do know that my playing was different, and for a lot of people that means a lot, and it's something I don't take lightly."

When Abbott finally broke away to do wind sprints, the boy took the ball the pitcher had given to him and returned to the car in which his mother was patiently waiting. She noticed right away that her son was different now, and as they drove off he talked for the first time about reaching for his own dreams. Jim Abbott proved it could be done.

In his initial spring outing against the San Diego Padres, Abbott struck out the first two batters he faced, earning the win after five innings of work. For his effort, manager Doug Rader rewarded him with a lemon drop and hinted to the press of things to come.

"It might be a tad more expensive for general manager Mike Port down the line," Rader suggested, insinuating that Port would have to fork over money—not candy—if he wanted to keep Abbott an Angel.

Throughout the spring, Abbott continued to impress. At the end of March, Rader had to make a big decision—send the 21-year-old Abbott to the minors for more seasoning, or start the season with him on the big league roster. Rader was impressed by Abbott's 94-mile-per-hour fastball, but most of all he admired his character and attitude. "He's the most mature, resilient 21-year-old I've ever seen," Rader told *Sports Illustrated.* "He's well-rounded, stable, well-traveled, and educated. He's been prepared for this. He's certainly one of the 10 best pitchers in our organization. And if he's one of the 10 best we have, how can he not make our pitching staff?"

Rader's decision was made for him when, a few days before the season started, veteran Dan Petry, projected to be a part of the rotation, went down with an arm injury. On March 29, Rader told the press Abbott had made the team. But not everyone welcomed the news. Some in the press thought Abbott needed more seasoning and felt that the Angels were rushing him to capitalize on his uniqueness and popularity.

Abbott himself thought his performance justified Rader's decision.

"I felt comfortable with the decision at the time," he says. "With hindsight you can look at it a number of ways, but I think, all things considered, I was pitching well enough to stay there and probably deserved to make the team."

On April 8, 1989, in front of the world's press and a packed house at Anaheim Stadium, Abbott got his first major league start. Nolan Ryan sent him a congratulatory telegram and Japanese camera crews accompanied him everywhere he went. Overwhelmed by all the attention, Abbott surrendered six runs in five innings, struck out zero batters, and lost the game, 7-0. When he lost his second outing as well—receiving no run support yet again—the second-guessers came out in full force. One writer made the mistake of calling his presence on the team a publicity stunt, which drew immediate fire from Rader.

"Do you have the guts to sit there and tell me he has a handicap?" the manager asked the writer. "Well, he doesn't. He's the least handicapped person I know. To me, all this talk about a publicity stunt is distasteful. He could have pitched a perfect game and it wouldn't have been different. He'll still have to prove himself."

In his third start, Abbott defused the critics by defeating the Baltimore Orioles, 3-2, for his first major league win. The game was significant not just for Abbott, who proved to himself that he now belonged, but to the game of baseball as well.

"Getting that first win against the Orioles and Cal Ripken was a big relief," Abbott says. "Things had happened so fast, and just figuring what it took to get these guys out, it was a difficult transition. So to get that first win was just a tremendous feeling, and a big boost to my confidence."

The victory only intensified the media attention, and Abbott began hearing from disabled children and their families seeking encouragement and wanting to meet with him.

"Jim has received more attention than any Angel I can remember," said Tim Mead, Angels director of publicity. "More than Wally Joyner when he was a rookie, more than Reggie Jackson, more than Rod Carew."

Mead had a charitable heart and tried to have Abbott meet with as many of the disabled children and their families as possible. The meetings were often consuming and emotional, but became as important to Abbott as they were to the youngsters.

"Some of the greatest highlights of my career were with Tim Mead and the times we spent at the stadium with the kids," he says. "It wasn't always easy to take the time off from my conditioning to meet with them, but now that my career's over I'm so thankful. To this day I still get some of the most gratifying cards and letters from kids who are growing up and playing baseball, doing things and seeking opportunities. Really, those things go further beyond anything you can do on the field."

One of the letters Abbott received came from five-year-old Erin Bower of Indianapolis. She described how she had been shopping with her mother in a drugstore when she spotted a tube of toothpaste that had been left on a counter. But it was no ordinary toothpaste tube. The madman who'd placed it there had a grudge against the store, and when Erin picked up the tube it exploded, blowing off her hand.

Jim's response to Erin's letter was printed in Jim Murray's column in the July 18, 1989 issue of the *Los Angeles Times*:

Dear Erin:

Perhaps somewhere later in your lifetime you will probably understand this letter and the feelings that go behind it. Regardless, I wanted to send something along now after being made aware of your terrible accident.

As your parents have probably told you, I was born without a right hand. That automatically made me different from the other kids I was around. But you know what? It made me different only in their eyes. You see, I figured that's what the Good Lord wanted me to work with. So it was my responsibility to become as good as I could at whatever I chose to do, regardless of my handicap.

I just won my first major league game. When the final out was made, a lot of things went through my mind. I thought of my parents and all the help they provided; my brother and his support; and all of my friends along the way. The only thing, Erin, that I didn't pay attention to was my handicap. You see, it had nothing to do with anything.

You're a young lady now with a tremendous life ahead of you. Whether you want to be an athlete, a doctor, lawyer, or anything else, it will be up to you, and only you, how far you go. Certainly there will be some tough times ahead, but with dedication and love of life, you'll be successful in any field you choose. I'll look forward to reading about you in the future.

Your friend,
Jim Abbott

As the season progressed and the wins kept mounting, the idea that Abbott was on the team as some kind of publicity stunt faded away. By the All-Star break, Abbott was 8-5 with a 3.56 ERA. When veterans convened for an old-timers event prior to the All-Star Game at Anaheim Stadium in July, the one player everyone wanted to meet was Jim Abbott. Hall of Famers like Warren Spahn and Bobby Doerr came in a day early to have Abbott autograph baseballs for them, and Ernie Banks requested a photo with the Angels ace.

Abbott finished the season with 12 wins, four complete games, and two shutouts in 1989, helping the Angels finish third in their division with 91 wins, eight games behind the Oakland A's. To no one's surprise, equally satisfying to Abbott was the acceptance and respect shown by his teammates.

"I always felt the need to be accepted, so succeeding with the Angels that first season was important," says Abbott. "I validated to myself that I had a right to be there and was not someone who was only there as a publicity stunt."

Publicity was something that the Angels welcomed after two sub-par seasons, but Abbott's talent was of more importance to the Angels' improvement in the standings. After falling a game short of the World Series in 1986, the Angels took a huge step backward the following year when they finished in a tie for last place in the mediocre American League West. That season, Wally Joyner enjoyed the best season of his career when he hit .285 with 34 home runs and 117 RBI. Devon White made his rookie debut in the outfield, hitting 24 home runs, stealing 32 bases, and driving in 87 runs. But the bulk of the offense and pitching staff slumped, causing the team's slide.

The following offseason, the Angels failed to make a splashy move, opting to re-sign free agent pitchers Mike Witt, Donnie Moore, and Greg Minton, and trading Gary Pettis to the Tigers for pitcher Dan Petry. The only significant upgrade to the team was the acquisition of free agent outfielder Chili Davis. Chuck Finley was moved into the rotation, but struggled en route to a 9-15 record. The pitching staff was relatively young, but ineffective, posting the next-to-worst ERA in the league. The offense was led by Davis's 21 homers and 93 RBI, but despite the midseason signing of Tony Armas, was not potent enough to compensate for the team's lackluster pitching.

The Angels rebounded in Abbott's rookie season, however, thanks to a reconstructed pitching staff. A trade with the Twins brought 38-year-old Bert Blyleven to the Angels. The Dutch veteran anchored the rotation, going 17-5 with a 2.73 ERA. Reliever Bob McClure was signed as well, and his addition bolstered a strong Angels pen. But it was the rotation that showed the most improvement. In addition to Abbott's solid rookie campaign, Finley put together his first great season, going 16-9 with nine complete games and 2.57 ERA. Kirk McCaskill enjoyed a career year, winning 15 games and posting a 2.93 ERA. The team's ERA of 3.28 was good for second in the league and made up for the struggles of an offense led by a cast of usual suspects—including Joyner, Davis, White, Johnny Ray, Dick Schofield, Jack Howell, Brian Downing—and newcomers Claudell Washington and Lance Parrish.

In 1990, the Angels—and Abbott—slipped a bit. Abbott suffered from a sophomore slump, going 10-14 with a 4.51 ERA, and the Angels fell to 80-82 and a distant fourth place. That offseason, Abbott worked often with pitching coach Marcel Lachemann, who encouraged Abbott to work inside and stop nibbling away with off-speed pitches. The results were not immediate, but today Abbott says Lachemann was his biggest influence and a large reason for his emergence as an All-Star caliber pitcher the following year.

"The greatest thing I felt from 'Lach' was loyalty," says Abbott. "He took a real responsibility for all of his pitchers. I'll never forget, in my third year, I started off 0-4, and there was talk of me being sent down to the minor leagues. He said, 'I'll go to the minor leagues with him if he gets sent down.' I'll never forget that kind of generosity."

Another factor in Abbott's burgeoning success was his relationship with conditioning coach Jimmie Reese. During his rookie season they developed an intense workout regimen that included wind sprints and fielding thousands of sharp grounders. Abbott took pride in his fielding and credits Reese's program for helping him overcome his fear of balls hit sharply up the middle.

"I fielded well during my years with the Angels, and a lot of it had to do with working with Jimmie," Abbott says. "The way he treated people and the kindness he showed to everybody he met serves as an inspiration to this day. I only have a few pictures up on my office wall, and several of them are of Jimmie."

Another one of Reese's favorites was Chuck Finley, whose 165 wins with the Angels is still a club record. Like Abbott, "Fin" often engaged in good-natured banter with the grizzled coach before games. Reese had several custom-made fungo bats of his own he used to exercise the pitchers. One was used so long that Reese's

Abbott found kinship with the wise Jimmie Reese, the "grandest gentleman in the game."
Courtesy of the Angels

handprint was literally embedded in the handle. Before one game, trainer Rick Smith recalls, Finley's exuberance and joshing got a little out of hand.

"Chuck was messing around with Jimmie like he usually did, when for some reason he grabbed his fungo and whirly-birdied it over the rightfield fence," recalls Smith. "It bounced off one of the light standards and got a big old crack right in the handle. We worked furiously to nail, glue and sand it back, but the bat was just never the same. Fin was heartbroken because that bat was Jimmie's favorite and hitting fungos was the way Reese made his living.

"If Jimmie was mad at you he wouldn't talk, and if he stayed silent over two or three days, you were in trouble. This time he didn't speak to Fin for over a week before he forgave him. But Chuck was always one of Reese's favorites, and the man could never stay mad for long."

Abbott enjoyed a banner season in 1991. The team didn't share his success, though; despite winning 81 games, the Angels finished last in the highly competitive West. Still, Abbott finished among the league leaders in wins (18), ERA (2.89), and innings pitched (243). For his efforts, he finished third in Cy Young Award voting. Finley also won 18 games that season, and Mark Langston paced the staff with 19 victories. Bryan Harvey's 46 saves led the league. But again the offense and the pitching staff couldn't get on the same page. The offense sputtered despite a return to form from Joyner, and solid contributions from newer Angels Luis Polonia and Dave Winfield. Rader was replaced mid-season by Buck Rodgers, who was let go by Montreal earlier in the year.

The arrival of Rodgers, the former Angels catcher, couldn't steer the ship right in 1992. The Halos won just 72 games, and again a league-worst offense was the culprit. Abbott's 7-15 record that season was deceiving. His 2.77 ERA was fifth-best in the American League, but the run support was not there to reflect his effectiveness on the mound. All five Angels starters posted sub-.500 records.

"We tied for last and didn't score a lot of runs, and I had my share of losing one-run games," Abbott recalls. "I take responsibility for losing the games that I lost, but I really felt the difference between '91 and '92, pitching-wise, was minimal. In fact, I probably pitched better in '92."

Part of the reason for the '92 Angels' dismal record may have been the devastating bus accident that nearly killed Rodgers in May of that year. The team was traveling in two buses near Deptford County, New Jersey, when one of the buses careened off the New Jersey Turnpike, crashed through a guardrail, and ended up lying on its side in a desolate wooded area. Sitting in the manager's traditional seat on the right front side, Rodgers was the most seriously injured of all the passengers. He had to be replaced for a majority of the remainder of the season by coach John Wathan, and the emotional impact his departure had on the team was devastating.

Rod Carew served as bench coach during much of Abbott's tenure, and remembers him as primarily a one-pitch pitcher who relied mainly on a hard cutter that would sail straight into a right-handed batter's hands.

"He broke more bats than any pitcher I've ever seen," Carew says. "If you wanted firewood, go to an Angels game when Abby pitched, because afterwards you could just scoop up the broken bats."

Gentle and soft-spoken off the field, on the diamond the bulldog-tough Abbott sported an intense game face.

"Some guys were vocal and talked a mean game, but you could tell it was a lot of fluff," says teammate Rex Hudler. "But there were also guys like Jim who were quiet and could back [up] their shit. He had a sweet disposition, but behind that was a ferocious lion. He was the kind of guy who, in a macho locker room with a lot of tough guys, was someone nobody would mess with.

"There were times when teams would bunt on Abby and our guys would say, 'That's chicken shit!' But he would say, 'That's okay, man, let 'em bring it!' Guys wanted to protect him, they wanted to step up for him, but he didn't need them to because he was a stud.

"He was a strong man with strong legs, and when it came to backing up another player he was always the first guy to drill somebody or step up if there was a brawl. He worked harder then anybody I've ever seen. I'd have to say there was a respect level higher with Abby than any other player I've ever played with."

Longtime trainer Rick Smith says Abbott was an impressive snapper. "When he would lose a tough game, he was known to take it out on immovable objects, including bat racks, Gatorade coolers, and things of that nature," recalls Smith. "Some of his snaps were pretty legendary only because of the quality of the person and the intensity of his competitive nature."

Buck Showalter, who managed Abbott when he was with the Yankees in the mid-Nineties, believes Abbott's intensity was a big factor in his success. "We were out on the road once and I took him out of the game early, and he just ran around the stadium the rest of the game," says Showalter. "He was a competitor, and whenever he had a bad outing it was frustrating, but he knew how to deal with it."

Abbott used exercise as a way of coping with the pressure and was a fanatic when it came to conditioning. In addition to his running regimen, he was a regular in the weight room. For pull-ups he had a little strap he would attach to the bar, and for the bench press he had a device that supported his arm and stub and balanced the bar.

In many ways, Abbott's tenure with the Angels mirrored the times. The 1990s represented one of the most chaotic periods in Angels history. From 1989 to 1996, the team had two owners, three managers, two presidents, and three general managers (including two at one time). In that same time period, Abbott won 18 games one season and lost 15 the next. He was then traded and brought back to the club.

In Ross Newhan's excellent book *Anaheim Angels: A Complete History,* Buck Rodgers aptly nicknamed this period in the team's history "circus at the top." Indeed, it seemed at times what the team needed most was a ringmaster. It started in 1987, when Gene Autry elevated business manager Mike Port to general manager. Port's appointment was rescinded when Richard Brown, the Autrys' personal counsel, was hired as club president. Brown's first order of business was firing Port and bringing in Mike O'Brien in 1992.

As a personal favor to her husband, Jackie Autry then hired former coach Whitey Herzog as an advisor. Gene had always lamented the loss of Herzog, who went on to glorious successes as the architect of the Kansas City Royals' and the St. Louis Cardinals' baseball dynasties. Gene wanted Herzog back, and in '92 his wife acceded to his wishes.

Herzog briefly shared the GM role with O'Brien, who found out soon enough that he was no match for Herzog's experience and savvy and was phased out. Whereupon Herzog himself abruptly quit, leaving Bill Bavasi in charge of player personnel.

Jackie Autry has called Herzog's actions detrimental to the club and a major disappointment to her husband. But according to Joe Maddon and Bavasi, it was Herzog who ultimately set the Angels on a course that would one day make them one of the elite franchises in baseball. For years the front office had been routinely dealing away their young players to the highest bidders and signing free agents and acquiring players well past their prime. Herzog believed strongly in sticking with the youngsters. His policy of building from within remains a cornerstone of the club's philosophy.

"Those of us in the organization were left with the understanding that Whitey was brought in because ownership really didn't have faith in our scouting or player development," says Bavasi. "After a year looking at the minor league system with Bob Fontaine Jr., Herzog came away with the opinion that the way we were going to fix this thing is to do nothing. Whitey had the guts and the stature to come in and say, 'Here's how I'm gonna fix it: I'm just gonna leave it alone. We're just not trading these kids!'"

According to Bavasi, Herzog abruptly took a powder from the Angels when he reckoned that his job was done. If Herzog had one drawback, it was his distaste for the politics of modern baseball. He had come up the old way and had no patience when it came to negotiating through third parties. As Jim Abbott soon discovered, Herzog did not like dealing with agents.

When Abbott's contract came up in the 1992 offseason, his agent demanded $19 million over four years. Herzog and the Angels countered with an offer of $16 million, which was deemed too poor. When Abbott's agent then nixed a compromise offer of $17.5 million, Herzog promptly traded Abbott to the Yankees for J.T. Snow and Russ Springer.

The take of some in the press box was that Abbott had gotten greedy and finagled the trade on his own. Not so, according to the man himself. Abbott says he wanted to remain an Angel and was unaware of any deadline from Herzog. Figuring his contract was still being negotiated, he went on vacation. Upon his return, his mother-in-law told him the shocking news that he was now a New York Yankee.

"I certainly didn't want to leave a bad impression with the fans that I was money hungry or I was seeking out the last dollar," Abbott says. "It certainly didn't seem it was that way to me at the time. There wasn't a lot of great communication between anybody, and it just came to a point that I was traded. I can't really make sense of it to this day."

Abbott pitched two fairly productive seasons in New York, tossing a no-hitter against the Indians in 1993. The gem ranks with his first big league win and his Olympic victory among his greatest on-field achievements.

With Abbott's abrupt departure in 1992, many in the Angels organization privately mourned the loss of their most popular and recognizable player. Meanwhile, the Angels continued to struggle as a team, winning just 71 games in 1993. The team looked different on paper but played the same on the field. After signing Chili Davis for a second tour of duty, the Angels added outfielder Stan Javier, pitchers Scott Sanderson, Ken Patterson, and Gene Nelson, and traded first baseman Lee Stevens to the Expos and Luis Sojo to the Blue Jays. Several young players stepped into regular roles, including Rookie of the Year right fielder Tim Salmon, who at the age of 24 hit .283 with 31 home runs and 95 RBI. But the offense was inconsistent and again struggled to score runs, leaving one-two punch Chuck Finley and Mark Langston to win just 32 games despite making 70 starts between them and finishing with the sixth- and seventh-best ERAs in the league.

The strike-shortened 1994 season wasn't any better. The expansion of the National League caused the American League to reconfigure its divisions into a three-division system. The A.L. West shrunk from seven teams to four, with Chicago, Kansas City, and Minnesota moving to the newly created Central division. The Angels finished fourth in the division, their best standing in four seasons—except for the fact that fourth now meant last. At 21 games below .500, it was another discouraging season for the Angels, who finished dead last in the league in offense, and near the bottom in pitching as well. Veterans like second baseman Harold Reynolds and shortstop Spike Owen were on their last leg; youngsters like infielder Damion Easley, first baseman J.T. Snow, and outfielders Jim Edmonds and Chad Curtis were going through growing pains; and Salmon, Bo Jackson, and Chili Davis weren't able to overcompensate for their teammates' flaws. The pitching staff featured no bright spots whatsoever.

Meanwhile, Abbott gobbled up headlines in New York as the '94 Yankees headed into the strike in first place. Several within Angels management hoped to reacquire him in the offseason. But late that offseason, Abbott signed with the Chicago White Sox, for whom he went 6-4 with a 3.36 ERA in 17 starts. The Sox were struggling that year and made it known that Abbott was expendable. When Tim Mead and others learned of this, they pushed hard for his return.

Rex Hudler remembers the atmosphere on the team heading toward the trade deadline in July of 1995. "We already had two lefties, Langston and Finley, and we were hoping Bavasi would pull the string on David Cone," remembers Hudler. "When they said it was Jim Abbott, we looked at each other and said, 'Shit! We don't need Abby.' It was nothing against Jim, but we needed a right-hander. We already had two great lefties in Chuck Finley and Mark Langston. When we got Abby, the first response was, 'Oh man, he's left-handed.' It had nothing to do with his competitiveness; he was a good pitcher then. And once he joined us we loved him and embraced him and forgot all about David Cone."

When Abbott rejoined the team on July 27, 1995, the Angels were in first place and dominating their division. The youngsters were finally beginning to bloom. Snow found a power stroke and was hitting for average, too. Edmonds, Salmon, and 23-year-old rookie Garrett Anderson formed the league's best young outfield. And new additions like third baseman Tony Phillips, closer Lee Smith, and rookie reliever Troy Percival were all making huge contributions.

But after finishing July with a 20-7 record, the team began a horrid free fall. On August 9, the Angels were leading the Mariners and Rangers by 11 games. One month and a nine-game losing streak later, the lead was down to just six games. Two weeks and another nine-game losing streak after that, the lead was gone. They had finished their season on an 18-31 dive, and not even a five-game winning streak in the final week of the season could preserve the division lead.

The Halos finished 78-66, in a tie with the Mariners. The two squared off in a tiebreaker game to decide who would earn a berth to the playoffs. On the mound for Seattle was Randy Johnson, who was 17-2 at that point in the season. The Mariners won easily, 9-1, as Johnson pitched a three-hit complete game in defeating Langston. The Angels' season was over. The team's finish that year ranks as one of the five worst collapses in baseball history. Neither the finish of the 1964 Phillies, the 1969 Cubs, nor the 1951 Dodgers—all legendary free falls—had accounted for a lead that significant lost in so short a time.

Hudler, who was in his second of three seasons with the Angels that year, prefers to look at 1995 with rose-colored glasses. "I don't think about '95 as a collapse," he says. "We did lose a huge lead, but the last week of the season we had to win almost every game, and we did. We took two out of three from Texas, and four straight from Oakland. We didn't like our chances, but we played our butts off and we swept them. We caught Seattle, who had lost three games, and forced a one-game playoff. We had to face Randy Johnson, who had seven days' rest, and he beat us."

Abbott went 5-4 down the stretch, halting a couple losing streaks in the process. He believes the problem that led to the team's poor play was that they had become the front-runner early in the season and didn't know how to handle their comfortable lead.

"I think our fast start caught a lot of players by surprise," says Abbott. "It took us a while to grow into the idea of being a contender, and by the time we had it figured out it was too late."

Rex Hudler is correct in the sense that 1995 was not a total failure. Often overlooked in the postmortems was the emergence of Percival, Edmonds, Salmon, and Anderson. Together they would take the lessons learned from '95 and store them away for future reference. A sense of identity was also established that season, and for the first time the Angels *were* Angels, going about business the "right way."

The following season began with high expectations for Abbott individually, and for the Angels as a team. Unfortunately, 1996 was the beginning of a torturous collapse for both player and team. By the end of the '96 season, the Angels were back in the A.L. West cellar, and by April of 1997, Abbott's tenure as an Angel would end in his release. Abbott believes the reason for his implosion was a breakdown of confidence, and the inability to adapt to a new pitching approach.

"I was moving away from power pitching to using off-speed pitches, and I lost that trust and confidence that it takes to throw," Abbott says. "When I started losing it became a downward spiral that I couldn't stop. I felt I was letting the team down and it was devastating. It was my biggest regret in my career and one of the most difficult periods of my life."

"He lost confidence," Hudler explains. "When you go out there against the world's greatest players you take that extra man with you, and that's confidence. If you get beaten down and you don't have that confidence you might leave a little off your pitch. He lost some velocity that year. He wasn't throwing 90 [miles per hour] anymore. He was throwing mid- to upper 80s. All he really had was a cutter and a curve, and when he couldn't get the cutter over, they were sitting on his curveball, and it wasn't pretty. It wasn't like he was having hard-luck losses; he just didn't have good stuff. But it didn't matter, we still fought for him."

Abbott's 2-18 record and 7.48 ERA that season was among the lowest lows of any Angel pitcher in history. His teammates felt awful playing behind him, knowing that there was nothing they could do to help him.

"We wanted to win so badly for Jim Abbott, and it just wouldn't happen," says Hudler. "But in my mind that year is greater than when he had his greatest season. When you're down, your peers watch how you carry yourself and how you handle failure. That year Jim carried himself with total class. In front of his teammates he never hung his head or blamed anybody else. He had already experienced greatness, but he was taking his lumps now. Much to his credit, he never let it show."

Abbott not only impressed his teammates during this challenging period, but seasoned reporters as well.

"Not only was Abbott there to face us after every game," recalls Bill Shaikin of the *Los Angeles Times*, "but he insisted we first talk to the players who were making more of a contribution, and he would answer all our questions when we returned. We would ask him, 'What do you think about going to the minor leagues? Is this the end?' Those are questions no one wants to face, but he was doing them every five days and answering them with class and honesty. He wasn't throwing up clichés just to get it over with. He had thought these things through and was honest enough to share his thoughts, and that to me was one of the most courageous things I've ever seen."

Abbott reported to camp the following spring determined to reverse his fortunes, but when it became obvious his troubles could not be remedied, management decided to make a change.

"Billy Bavasi called me into the into the manager's office and told me, 'This is unacceptable. We just can't have you pitching like this,'" recalls Abbott. "He said I was going to have to make a decision: 'Either go to the minor leagues or take a release.'"

When the disconsolate pitcher returned to his locker, he threw his gear into his duffel bag with tears in his eyes. A couple players said goodbye, but Abbott didn't wait for the bulk of his teammates to return from the field. He simply packed his bags and left before most knew what had happened. What irked him most was that his exodus from the game was not on his own terms. "Keep your salary, but your services are no longer needed," Bavasi had told him.

Abbott's mind was swimming. He knew he had given 100 percent of himself in trying to discover a solution. As he started to drive, his mind turned to his wife and month-old baby girl and the new house they had just purchased. As he drove into the setting sun, he decided he would not hang around the minors and be a distraction. He knew that wherever he went the Angels would be second-guessed, and that wasn't what he wanted, either. Better to just quit outright, he told himself. Just get away from Arizona as fast as humanly possible.

The decision wasn't as easy or as cold-blooded as it sounds for Bill Bavasi, either. Sure, the Angels had to pay off the remaining $5.6 million left on Abbott's contract, but that wasn't the worst of it.

"I didn't care that he was a legend, that didn't matter to me," Bavasi says. "It just seems we're always releasing the good guys, and he was one of them. From his point of view, someone was saying that temporarily you're not going to compete, and that had to fry him. It was difficult for me, because of the money involved but also because of the person involved."

In the first few weeks after his dismissal, Abbott fell into a funk. The routine of everyday life was monotonous and unfulfilling. With nothing to fill the void he became restless and questioned whether he had made the right decision. He realized that the restlessness and drive that had sustained his career and dreams were still alive. He couldn't quit. Not yet, anyway.

Encouraged by Buck Rodgers and Mark Langston, among others, Abbott eventually got back on the horse and began the long road back to the majors. He resumed his workouts, and prepared to showcase himself for Major League teams. When the Chicago White Sox indicated an interest in reacquiring him, Abbott jumped at the chance.

His first stop was with the Hickory Crawdads of the Class-A South Atlantic League. It was his first exposure to the minors, but Abbott was willing to pay his dues to get back to the bigs. It took a full year, but in 1998 Abbott was back in Chicago and wowed everybody by winning all five of his starts.

"His comeback with the Sox showed more about his character than any of his wins," says Hudler. "That one year showed me more about Jim Abbott than anything else. He needed to start from scratch, and he persevered and he made it back!"

When the season ended, Abbott signed on as a free agent with the Milwaukee Brewers. He struggled from the start in 1999, and then chafed at his diminished role. Finally, in July, he realized that he had finally reached the end of the line. On July 23, 1999, the Brewers came to the same conclusion and released Abbott. His record was 2-8, and his ERA stood at 6.91.

Jim Abbott's lifetime record of 87-108 seems insignificant when compared to the enormous contributions he has made to the game and society. To the multitudes of people with special needs, Jim Abbott continues to be an inspiration. He characteristically downplays his influence and instead considers the attention he generated as just part of his overall baseball-playing experience.

"I look at my career in terms of living up to ability," Abbott says. "Regardless of how I was born, I was blessed. I was given a lot and had an obligation to live up to those talents. I know that my playing has touched people, and I'm incredibly thankful for that, too. I am extremely grateful to baseball for allowing me to have touched so many lives."

Joe Maddon believes that if Abbott had two hands to work with he might have pitched a lot longer, and that all the extra motion required to switch his glove back and forth probably took a toll on his endurance. Yet what impressed Maddon most about Abbott was that despite incredible odds, the pitcher always rose to the highest level.

"You look at him and you just assume, okay, he's pitching in the big leagues; but try and put yourself in the position to do what he did and on the stage that he did it on, and you begin to realize what an incredible athlete he was," says Maddon. "As a kid he goes out and competes with people that have an added advantage of an appendage he doesn't have, but he keeps going up the ladder and suddenly he's at Michigan. He hears all the crap being said to him behind his back but he doesn't pay any attention. Then he goes on and pitches against the Cubans in the Olympics and he sticks it up their butt. Then he goes professionally and he ends up throwing a no-hitter in New York! Come on!

"For all of us who don't have that kind of disadvantage, we don't have any idea what that means. I couldn't be a big league ball player with both my appendages, and he's doing it minus one! He proved to kids that have problems, 'Listen, you can still do it.'

"Jimmy personified sticking to what you believe in, don't take no for an answer, and don't worry what other people say. If you really want to do what's in your heart, go ahead and do it, because you can."

Today Abbott is busier than ever giving inspirational speeches to corporations and private groups. In a way, it is just a continuation of what he did when he was playing, without having to worry about the runner at first.

"I speak about the things that were very helpful to me in my best years and some of the things that escaped me when I struggled," Abbott says. "It's been very enjoyable in that it has allowed me to keep in touch with families, kids, and others who have questions about playing baseball and have had different ways of growing up. I talk about adjustability and the challenges of learning to do things in a new and different way. I talk about conviction and doing things with belief and trust."

In the end it can be accurately stated that Abbott got the acceptance for which he always strove. In many ways, his goal of being known simply as a good pitcher—to be treated the same as everyone else—was achieved. More than anything, his release by the Angels proved just that. Yet Bavasi was with him every step of the way, and he wasn't surprised that Abbott achieved his dreams.

"To get to where he did, he had to go through different things than the rest of the players out there," concludes Bavasi. "Was it a hardship for him? I don't think

Rex Hudler considers Abbott's base hit against the Dodgers in 1996 "as fine a moment as you'll ever see on a ball field."
Courtesy of the Angels/Photo by John Cordes

so, and that is what makes him unique. When he first came up he was known as 'the guy with one hand.' But from then on, he was a left-hander. When I picture Jim, I just see this strapping, good-looking young guy with a great attitude. I see a guy with a beautiful wife and a great family—that's all I see."

Among Rex Hudler's fondest memories of Abbott is one that occurred in an exhibition game in 1996 against the Los Angeles Dodgers. Abbott was pitching, and, acting on a whim, manager Marcel Lachemann decided to let him bat. Because of the DH rule, few Angels had ever seen Abbott with a bat in his hand. What they didn't know was that he had hit .400 in high school and had a mean golf swing.

When he came to the plate early in the game, Abbott held the bat with his left hand and placed his stump on the bottom of the lumber. The Dodger pitcher threw a couple fastballs for strikes, but then Abbott punched a shot into right field for a base hit. No one in the stadium, including the on-deck hitter, Hudler, could believe it.

For a moment the crowd sat in stunned silence. Then, one by one, people began to stand and cheer. By the time Hudler arrived at home plate, the entire crowd was on its feet applauding and shouting. Hudler's eyes welled up, and he was forced to call time before taking his batting stance. When he looked at Dodger catcher Mike Piazza and umpire Tim McClelland, Hudler saw that they were affected as well.

"Can you believe that?" Hudler said, shaking his head.

"Unbelievable!" Piazza agreed.

Years later, Hudler still can't forget that scene.

"That was as about as fine a moment as you'll ever see on a ball field," he says. "I only cried a couple times in my 21 years of playing, but when Abby lashed that single to right, that's all I could do.

"Jim Abbott—what a battler! What a gamer! He had everything—and he could hit, too!"

15

ROAD TO THE
PROMISED LAND

*W*hen the Angels launched an aggressive build-from-within policy in the early Nineties, they placed themselves—at long last—on a winning course that forever transformed the franchise. The sea change actually began around the time Buzzie Bavasi retired in 1984, and Mike Port took over as general manager. It was Port who took on the Herculean task of rebuilding the club by phasing out the aging, past-their-prime veterans and easing the organization's young, hungry prospects into major roles with the team.

"Every year Mike was letting go of a significant player," recalls Buzzie's son, Bill Bavasi, who was a minor-league administer at the time. "Whether it was releasing Brian Downing, Doug DeCinces, or Rod Carew, he had a real tough, tough period here. But that was the very beginning."

While Mike Port initiated the policy, Whitey Herzog took it to the next level. Hired by the Autrys in 1992 to "fix the problem" with the team, Herzog saw immediately that the most prudent way to accomplish that task was by concentrating on the talent the Angels already possessed.

"Whitey came in and, almost like the Pope, blessed our prospects and said, 'These guys can play,'" says Joe Maddon, who was a minor-league instructor at time. "I don't know what Whitey's master plan was. All I know is that we had a really good thing going in the minor leagues that was not being recognized, and Whitey came in and recognized it."

Although Jackie Autry and Herzog never quite saw eye to eye—particularly when it came to his insistence on working from his home in St. Louis, and Whitey's habit of "forgetting" to return Gene's phone calls—Jackie gamely went along with the program. With the franchise going bankrupt, she recognized Herzog's baseball acumen and supported his measures wholeheartedly.

One of Herzog's best moves was promoting Bob Fontaine from director of scouting to director of player personnel and scouting. It was Fontaine's keen eye for talent that was responsible for the acquisition and nurturing of many of the players who would become key cogs in the Angels' world championship run. Among the players scouted and signed during Fontaine's 20-year tenure were Tim Salmon, Gary DiSarcina, Jim Edmonds, Troy Percival, Garret Anderson, Troy Glaus, Jarrod Washburn, Bengie Molina, and Darin Erstad.

Although things were coming together on the baseball end, the economics of modern baseball were making it impossible for the Autrys to operate at a profit. For years they had run the Angels as a family, mom-and-pop organization, but by the mid-Nineties the times were changing. A restrictive stadium lease, industry inflation, collusion fines, and soaring salaries made it infeasible for the Autrys to make money. No longer able to absorb the losses and faced with mounting debt, they decided to sell the franchise.

The Disney Corporation, with its rising presence in Anaheim with the newly acquired NHL's Mighty Ducks, had an interest in purchasing the club right from the start. CEO Michael Eisner believed the synergy the Angels and Ducks brought to the area could help boost attendance at Disneyland. A competition for the team began, with a group headed by former Major League Baseball commissioner Peter Ueberroth serving as the frontrunner. A last-minute bid by Disney won out, however, when they agreed to not only match Ueberroth's offer of 130 million but to take on Autry's debt of 10 million for baseball operating losses as well.

Disney's reign was a rocky one. New Angels president Tony Tavaras spent little on new players, had one of the lowest paid front offices in baseball, and was not known to be player friendly. To his credit he did manage to keep the core of the team intact and kept with the philosophy of building from within started by Port and Herzog.

Not unlike the Autrys, Disney found baseball to be a losing proposition—and even their pockets were not deep enough to overcome the high costs associated with running the Angels. Disgruntled shareowners who had no tolerance for corporate losses made it plain to Eisner that they felt the Angels were a liability. Eisner agreed, and in 1999 decided he would eventually sell the team for the right price.

Part of the process of grooming the franchise for sale was the adaptation of Anaheim Stadium into a baseball-only facility. With the Rams' commitment to come to Anaheim in 1980, Anaheim Stadium began a transition from being one of the coziest and most popular ballparks in the league into a 60,000-seat, enclosed, multiuse monolith. Once the crown jewel of the American League, the "Big A" had lost much of its luster.

With the Rams' departure in 1994, the city began the slow process of dismantling and downsizing the stadium. By 1998, Anaheim Stadium had morphed again, this time into Edison Field, a state-of-the-art baseball-only facility capable of seating 40,000-plus. The new park included fake rock canyons in the outfield, a waterfall, dugout luxury boxes, bleachers, and an area designed with kids in mind. The familiar vistas of the Saddleback Mountains returned to view, and the Angels now had a stage equal to any in baseball. The changes seemed to parallel the team's new

As of the end of the 2005 season, Tim Salmon is the Angels' all-time home run leader with 290. Courtesy of the Angels

ideology and vision, which had been ready for a facelift for some time. More importantly, though, the new Edison Field was considered an attractive bonus to potential buyers.

Although the Angels struggled throughout the 1990s, beneath the surface they were building a strong foundation. That became evident in 1996. The club finished in fourth place that year, 19 1/2 games out of first place. However, the young players—Salmon, Anderson, Edmonds, Erstad, and Percival—were forming a striking core. The following year—under new skipper Terry Collins—they improved to second in the division, with Erstad stepping into the everyday role at first base and 24-year-old Jason Dickson leading the staff with 13 wins. The Halos finished in second again in 1998, but this time were just three games out. Management added a wrinkle to the youth movement by signing 34-year-old Cecil Fielder to play first.

But to counter the addition of a veteran, the 21-year-old Glaus began to be eased into action.

The forward progress was interrupted in 1999, as the team took a huge step backward, finishing in last place, 25 games behind division-champion Texas. Free agent Mo Vaughn was signed to a huge contract—one that would eventually prove to be a bust. Despite falling in the visitors dugout and spraining his knee on opening night and missing several games, he proved to add a significant punch to the middle of the batting order. He led the team with 33 home runs and 108 RBI, and Glaus won the third-base job and contributed 29 home runs. But injuries struck Salmon and Edmonds, and the pitching staff failed to make up for the offense's struggles. Chuck Finley, in his last season with the Angels, won 12 games to lead the rotation, but the remainder of the starters were less than impressive.

In the offseason, Bill Bavasi stepped down, and Bill Stoneman, former general manager of the Montreal Expos, came aboard.

"To his credit Bill did not blow the team up," says Maddon. "He came in and evaluated first before he started to do certain things, which was very impressive. He recognized the talent we had, built around it, and stayed the course of building from within established by Herzog and Bavasi."

Stoneman's first move was firing Terry Collins and bringing in Mike Scioscia, a former Dodger catcher and protégé of Dodger manager Tommy Lasorda. According to Maddon, Scioscia was the "the final brick" in the foundation.

"The manager is the most crucial position in an organization," says Maddon. "He can bring a stability and consistency to an organization that others cannot. Over the years we were subject to so many changeovers as far as managers went, and the philosophy was constantly changing. We were constantly telling players what we said last year is not really how we want to do it this year. One of the reasons the Angels are still successful is that Scioscia has remained in the skipper's chair. When you have that same guy in that seat for a period of time, you have some stability."

Stoneman addressed gaps in the rotation and infield in 2000 with a key trade that sent Jim Edmonds to the Cardinals for second-base prospect Adam Kennedy and starting pitcher Kent Bottenfield. Stoneman agreed to leave the rest of the core of the team unchanged, and in doing so ensured a chemistry and cohesiveness to develop that would eventually enable the Angels to come together in spectacular fashion.

In 2000, the team improved by 12 victories from the previous year as more youngsters flourished in their new starting roles. Bengie Molina hit .281 and drove in 71 runs as the starting catcher, and newcomer Kennedy drove in 72 runs and scored 82 as the starting second baseman. Glaus earned his first All-Star appearance by putting up massive numbers, including 47 home runs, a team record. Anderson's transformation into a power hitter was complete as well: his 40 doubles, 35 home runs, and 117 RBI solidified a potent outfield that combined to hit 94 homers. The team probably should have boasted a better record, but the pitch-

Mike Scioscia set the Angels on a new course with his arrival in 2000. Courtesy of the Angels

ing staff posted a poor 5.00 ERA. The only bright spot was Washburn, who went 7-2 with a 3.74 ERA in limited action.

The Mariners ran away with the division in 2001, and the Angels regressed to 75 wins, losing 19 of their final 21 games. Mo Vaughn missed the entire season due to his arthritic knee, but there were reasons to be optimistic. Glaus achieved a rare franchise feat with back-to-back 40-homer seasons, and Anderson continued to pummel the ball, driving in 123 runs and collecting 194 hits. Rookie shortstop David Eckstein, grabbed off of waivers from the Red Sox in August of the previous year, was a pesky sparkplug at the top of the order.

In the offseason Vaughn was dealt to the Mets for pitcher Kevin Appier. After the New Year, the Angels signed free agent pitcher Aaron Sele and acquired Brad Fullmer in a deal with the Blue Jays. Soon thereafter interim president Paul Pressler initiated "Red Dawn," a public relations brainstorm to present the Angels with a new look and hopefully a new attitude. The players' new red uniforms soon came to symbolize the team and would add significantly to fan participation later in the season.

That spring, sporting their new red garb, Scioscia focused on fundamentals, drilling them into his players relentlessly. The discipline transformed the team into a genuine contender.

"After 2001, we really made an effort to say that we're not going to be where we want to be unless we can implement a style of baseball that is going to be aggressive with good situational hitting," says Scioscia.

"Ersty and Eckstein personified the theory of playing situational baseball better then anybody in '02," says Joe Maddon. "Those two guys at the top of the batting order set this tone for the rest. Now Fish [Salmon] does it, GA really buys into it, Glaus and Spiezio, too. It was a simple concept that's been around 80 years, but how you get it apart to the group makes all the difference. And I guess we did a good job that spring as it carried through the whole year."

At first the 2002 version looked strikingly close to the '01 version that lost 87 games. The Angels fell on their face out of the gate, losing 14 of their first 20 games. But once the team found its stride, it broke into a mad sprint for the finish line, going 93-49 over the balance of the season to finish four games in back of division-winner Oakland. But the team's 99 wins were six better than the Red Sox and good enough to clinch the wild card. For the first time in 16 years, the Angels were headed to the playoffs.

In the divisional series, the Angels were underdogs to the vaunted New York Yankees, winners of 103 games that season and enjoying their eighth-straight play-off berth. These Yankees featured a usual cast of All-Star heroes, including Derek Jeter, Jason Giambi, Bernie Williams and Roger Clemens—and a rookie second baseman, Alfonso Soriano, who clubbed 39 homers in the regular season. But the Angels could hold their own in the batter's box, thanks to the continued success of Glaus and Anderson, who combined for 59 homers and 234 RBI; the steady presence of Salmon; the on-base abilities of table setters like Eckstein, Kennedy, and Scott Spiezio; and the contributions of key platoon players Fullmer and Orlando Palmeiro. And the pitching staff—led by 18-game winner Washburn—finished just a decimal point behind the A's for the best ERA, at 3.69.

In the opening game of the series, the Yankees grabbed the upper hand with an 8-5 victory. Glaus homered twice, and the top of the order got on base often, but Washburn couldn't keep the Yankees in check, allowing three home runs before the bullpen was touched up for another four runs. But the Yankees' formidable pitching staff was hardly perfect in the opener, and if the series was going to come down to whom could outscore whom, the Angels had a shot. The Yankees had averaged 5.57 runs per game in the 2002 season, but the Angels were only a few slots behind them at 5.25 runs. In Game 2, the Angels racked up 17 hits, knocking Pettitte out of the game after just three innings en route to an 8-6 slugfest victory.

Heading back to Edison International Field, the Angels had made their point.

"The biggest thing they had going for them was that they weren't scared of us," says Yankees manager Joe Torre.

Indeed, they were not. In Game 3, the Angels fell behind 6-3, but then battled back, tacking on runs in the sixth, seventh, and eighth innings. John Lackey, just a 23-year-old rookie, pitched three innings of scoreless relief, while another rookie, 20-year-old Francisco Rodriguez, worked two scoreless frames. Percival finished off the Yanks in the ninth, and the Angels completed the come-from-behind 9-6 victory.

With the mighty Yankees on the ropes, the Halos' bats took on the burden of lifting the team to victory in Game 4 with an eight-run fifth inning. Angels hitters struck for ten hits off of three Yankees hurlers in the frame. With a comfortable margin of error to work under, Rodriguez and Percival worked the game's final innings to seal the 9-5 victory.

The Halos set records for highest team batting average in a postseason series at .376, and for most runs scored in one inning in a division series game. Not only did they defeat the Yankees—they beat them at their own game. And for the first time in franchise history, the Angels were walking away from a postseason series as victors.

In the best-of-seven A.L. Championship Series, the Twins were waiting. The Twins had not been in the playoffs for over a decade themselves. But under new manager Ron Gardenhire, they cruised to the Central Division title. The Twins were the antithesis of the Yankees. Their roster featured few All-Stars and little in the way of big-name celebrities. Instead, they were led by a pair of potent outfield bats, Jacque Jones and Torii Hunter, All-Star catcher A.J. Pierzynski, a robust designated hitter by the name of David Ortiz, a steady rotation, and a deadly bullpen anchored by closer Eddie Guardado.

After dropping a tight 2-1 game at the opener in Minnesota, the Angels swept the next four games to clinch their first-ever pennant. They won in all ways imaginable. Their relief pitching picked up the slack in a 6-3 win in Game 2. Then in Game 3, Washburn gave the team seven strong innings, and Glaus provided the go-ahead run in a 2-1 decision on an eighth-inning homer. In a 7-1 victory in Game 4, the offense came around late in the game for seven runs while Lackey, making the first postseason start of his career, threw seven scoreless innings for the win. And in the finale, a 13-5 win, Kennedy, voted the series MVP, became only the sixth player in postseason history to connect for three home runs in a single game.

As a reward for earning their first trip to the World Series, the Angels would have to figure out a way to get Barry Bonds out. Following up a year in which he broke the single-season mark for home runs with 73, Bonds had gone yard 46 times, hit .370, and walked an astonishing 198 times—68 of those of the intentional variety. In the first two rounds of the playoffs, Bonds had already clubbed four home runs, walked 14 times, and driven in 10 runs. Help in the Giants batting order came in the form of All-Star second baseman Jeff Kent, veteran outfielder Reggie Sanders, and catcher Benito Santiago. But the Giants' true strength was in their pitching, where they melded a balanced rotation featuring Jason Schmidt, Kirk Rueter, Russ Ortiz, and Livan Hernandez with one of the game's best closers in Robb Nen.

The Series seesawed back and forth in dramatic fashion. As expected, Bonds ravaged Angels pitching from the start, homering in his first at-bat of Game 1. Despite two solo home runs from their own slugger, Glaus, the Angels fell 4-3. The Halos collected 16 hits in Game 2 and won, 11-10. After jumping ahead 7-4 after just two innings, the Angels relinquished the lead quickly and were trailing 9-7 after the top of the fifth. By the bottom of the sixth, though, they had tied the game up, and Salmon gave them the win with a two-run homer in the eighth. The Angels had escaped with an ugly win, but not before Bonds reminded them of what lurked ahead by crushing a solo home run in the top of the ninth.

The Angels overcame Bonds's third homer of the series to win Game 3 by a 10-4 margin at Pac Bell Park. The Giants struck back, winning 4-3 and then 16-4 to give them a three-games-to-two edge in the series. But in the Angels' favor, Games 6 and 7 would be played in the confines of Edison International Field, and their fans would be ready.

In what proved to be a classic, a dramatic Game 6 came to symbolize the Angels' incredible season. At one point, the fate of the franchise literally hung on the tilt of one ball.

16

A MONKEY ON
OUR BACK

"If we ever needed a comeback," thought Mike Scioscia, standing at his usual perch in the Angels dugout, "now's the time." The team was behind 5-0 heading into the bottom of the seventh inning of Game 6. If the Angels dropped this game, their first trip to the World Series would go for naught. For all that, anyone looking at Scioscia's face at that moment would not have picked up the slightest hint of desperation. For the fact was, all season long he had seen the Angels demonstrate an uncanny knack for coming from behind in the later innings of games. Really, why should tonight be any different?

Standing in the dugout behind him—in various stages of preparation—were the team's big guns: Garret Anderson, Greg Fullmer, Troy Glaus, and Scott Spiezio, who had morphed into an RBI machine during the playoffs. Appearing from the press box was Jackie Autry, who was at the game that night, waving a stuffed "Rally Monkey" in the air. As if on cue, a gyrating Angels "Rally Monkey" appeared next on the stadium scoreboard, and the hometown crowd of 44,000 whipped itself into a frenzy.

Spiezio grabbed his batting helmet, stood near the dugout steps, and nodded approvingly at the scene. In the San Francisco Giants' dugout, manager Dusty Baker had no intention of monkeying around with what was working for his team. His starting ace, Russ Ortiz, had pitched a gem up to that point, allowing only four baserunners in six innings. In the Giants bullpen were several strong relievers who could patch up any leaks should Ortiz get into trouble. But for now the ball remained in his hands.

Baker's optimism was buoyed when Anderson grounded out to start the inning, quieting down the crowd. But then Glaus and Fullmer followed with a pair of singles, and as the Rally Monkeys danced anew, Baker decided to make a pitching change. He marched to the mound and gave the signal for right-hander Felix Rodriguez. As they waited for Rodriguez to arrive at the mound, Baker presented Ortiz with the baseball as a reward for his impressive shutout performance. Later, the press would play the incident up as an in-your-face gesture by Baker; but in truth, the home team barely noticed.

As he waited for Rodriguez to complete his warmup tosses, Spiezio was surprisingly calm in the on-deck circle as he visualized his next at-bat. He had been in a similar situation several times before, albeit under drastically different circumstances. When Spiezio was a boy playing ball with his father in their backyard in Illinois, he created his own World Series situation night after night.

"It's Game 7, bottom of the ninth, and the bases are loaded!" his dad would say before tossing a pitch to Spiezio. "There's a full count, and you're down by one run. Here you go!"

As Giants catcher Benito Santiago threw to second base to signal that Rodriguez was ready, Spiezio tapped his bat for good luck and headed for the plate. He reminded himself to wait on the pitch as long as he could, and to try to drive the ball into the gap. He knew Rodriguez was a hard thrower, but figured if he could get the bat head out there, the ball would jump.

Rodriguez's first two pitches—both fastballs—were low and outside. Spiezio figured a strike was coming next, and sure enough, Rodriguez fired a fastball into the strike zone. Spiezio fouled it off. "He's throwing corners," Spiezio told himself. "Nothing but the black of the plate."

The fourth pitch was yet another fastball, and Spiezio fouled it off. Now, with two strikes, his primary objective was to protect the plate, sit on the change-up, and if anything came close to the strike zone to just react to it. Look for a good pitch to drive, and whatever happens don't get called out on a pitch an inch outside. After fouling off pitch five—more heat—Spiezio glared at Rodriguez. His message was clear: Just mess up and get something over the plate!

Another fastball, another foul. On second base, Glaus had a front-row seat for the duel and had a feeling that Spiezio had the upper hand. "He was getting closer and closer each time he fouled the ball off," Glaus recalled later. "You could almost see that if Rodriguez ever got the ball down, Spiezio was going to be on it."

From his vantage point shading the gap in right field, the Giants' Reggie Sanders saw things unfolding differently. To him Spiezio couldn't get around on Rodriguez's fastball, and it was only a matter of time before Spiezio struck out. But to Sanders's right, veteran centerfielder Kenny Lofton was uneasy. "If he keeps throwing the same pitch," Lofton thought, "eventually the guy's gonna hit it."

Rodriguez looked in at his catcher, who was straddling the outside corner. After checking on Glaus at second, he turned and fired his seventh straight fastball. Ball three—full count. Now the crowd was really booming, but Spiezio, totally zoned in, was oblivious to the pandemonium surrounding him. He needed to be on guard for a change-up or something off-speed from Rodriguez.

Up in the press box, Fox television commentator Tim McCarver, more focused on location than pitch selection, made a prescient comment: "You could see Santiago wanted that fastball in. That's a dangerous area right now; if you make a mistake away, it's a single. If you make a mistake inside, it's 5-3."

Although Reggie Sanders was still confident that Rodriguez would get his man, he also knew that with a full count, Spiezio would be swinging at anything close to the plate. His worst fear was that he would hit a double to the gap. Taking a deep breath, Sanders got into a crouch and waited.

In the video room adjacent to the Angels dugout, Salmon had one eye on a video replay of his strikeout from his last at-bat, and the other on the live broadcast of the game. He noticed that after Santiago signaled for a pitch, he shifted toward the inside of the plate.

Rodriguez glanced at Glaus behind him and went into his windup. It was—yet again—a fastball. But instead of painting the outside corner as the other pitches had, this pitch was down and in, right in Spiezio's wheelhouse. He might as well have engraved an invitation on it: "You are hereby invited to …"

Crack!

Sanders knew right off that it was hit well, but figured he could haul the ball in at the warning track. "But it just kept carrying," Sanders recalled later. "I kept going back, kept going back, kept going back, kept going back. I was lining up to jump for the ball. I was about to jump when I nudged myself on that pad on the bottom wall, then I ran out of room. I just couldn't believe it."

Neither could Spiezio. "I was going back and forth watching the ball, watching Sanders," he would recall. "I saw him get closer and closer to the wall, but the ball was so high I didn't know if the wind was gonna knock it down. I knew it had good carry on it because I had the right spin on it, but I just didn't know.

"Then there was this sonic boom: *Psssssst! Kaboom!* Just this incredibly loud eruption. That's when I heard the fans for the first time. When you suddenly hear 45,000 people screaming at the top of their lungs, it just about knocks you down.

"Adrenaline was rushing through my body, more than I've ever felt. I don't usually celebrate, but somewhere I did a little pump with my fist. When I started running to second the fans were going crazy, and I was, too, and I had to remind myself it was only 5-3 and we had to settle down. I jogged in, and Darin Erstad was the first guy I saw. He was absolutely going crazy, shouting, *'Let's go! Let's go!'* I could see the fire in everybody's eyes and knew this was the spark we needed. I just had this great feeling that this was the first step for us coming back."

5-3, Giants.

Deep in the bowels of Edison Field, in a room next to the Angels clubhouse, visiting equipment manager Brian Harkins and his four-man crew were frantically icing down 150 bottles of Mumms champagne with "World Champion Giants" stickers affixed to the sides of the bottles. When Spiezio hit it out of the park, everybody paused. After a brief discussion, they decided to continue—needless to say, with far less conviction—icing down the champagne.

In Harkins's small office, former Giants greats Bobby Bonds and Willie Mays—the father and godfather, respectively, of Barry Bonds—watched Spiezio's homer on TV, then asked for more drinks. Something told them it could be a long night.

In the Giants clubhouse, dozens of technicians—busy putting the finishing touches on the victory platform where the postgame TV interviews and trophy presentation would take place—stopped their hammering. In the hallway leading to the dugout, MLB officials who were preparing "World Champion Giants" hats and shirts for distribution to the San Francisco players momentarily set them aside. One of the electricians working on the TV platform finally broke the silence. "Looks like we got a ballgame now!" he blurted out. The team's traveling secretary averted an instant lynching by yelling, "Everybody clear the f---ing clubhouse now!"

Only one Giants player was unfazed by Spiezio's heroics. Unable to stand the tension, Jason Schmidt had gone to the weight room before the fateful pitch and sat there listening to music on his Walkman.

"I didn't want to hear anything else," Schmidt later explained. "I wanted to see the looks on the guys' faces when it was over and I came in the clubhouse."

If Mike Scioscia's mug had been the first face he saw, Schmidt would've still been clueless. Clearly, Spiezio's dinger had caused a huge momentum shift in the game, but the Angels manager never broke from his poker face. "Just play the game," he told his troops. "Let's just keep this going."

There was still work to do. Scioscia called on Brendan Donnelley to pitch in the top of the eighth. He walked Santiago to start the inning, but then retired the next three batters. Erstad led off the bottom of the inning for the Halos and promptly slammed a home run into the rightfield pavilion. 5-4, Giants.

"Ersty's homer was huge," recalls Troy Percival. "After that, there was no doubt we were well on our way. Suddenly it's 5-4, and we got the meat of the order coming up. I felt strongly we were gonna tie this game up."

Salmon, who'd spent the previous inning reviewing his hitting stroke in the video room, put what he learned to good use by lashing a line drive to left for a base hit. The tying run was on first. Earlier in the evening, Scioscia had informed Chone Figgins that if he got in the game as a pinch runner, he was expected to be aggressive and take chances. Figgins remembered those instructions now, when the manager sent him in to run for Salmon. Anderson hit a little flare to left that fell in front of Bonds. Figgins motored around second base and headed for third. His boldness caused the surprised Bonds to bobble the ball, and consequently not only was Figgins safe at third, but Anderson made it safely into second.

"I figured if I take the extra base, even if I get thrown out, Garret's still gonna be at second," Figgins said.

With Glaus due up and the winning run on second, Baker called for his closer, Robb Nen, to take the mound. The Giants bullpen was depleted by this point in the playoffs, and Nen himself wasn't in the best shape of his career. An arm injury suffered late in the season had taken the edge off his fastball, and he was still hurting. But desperate times called for desperate measures. And Baker had no other options.

Troy Glaus's game-winning double in the eighth inning of Game 6 of the 2002 World Series was the death blow in one of the most memorable games in Angels history. Courtesy of the Angels

With runners on second and third and their season on the line, the Angels couldn't have asked for a more reliable man at the plate than Glaus. Throughout his career, the tall slugger had been unflappable in pressure situations. He seemed as relaxed and confident stepping to the plate in the World Series as he did in a meaningless spring training game.

Nen's plan was to feed Glaus nothing but fastballs and keep him from getting his hands fully extended to drive one into the gap. The first pitch missed 18 inches off the plate, but Glaus, who was more anxious than he looked, started his swing as soon as the ball was released and missed the pitch by two feet. Nen's second pitch was a ball, and his third offering sailed high and inside. Glaus could tell upon impact that he had hit it at least hard enough for a sacrifice fly. Nobody was more shocked than he was when Barry Bonds gave a wave of frustration as the ball sailed over his head. By the time Bonds chased down the ball, Figgins and Anderson had crossed the plate, and Glaus was standing at second. 6-5, Angels.

"I was just hoping Anderson could get to third," Glaus said later of his crucial hit. "You couldn't imagine my surprise when it went over [Bonds's] head and everybody was able to score."

Percival set down the Giants in order in the ninth, and the Angels celebrated their most remarkable game in the team's 41-year history. In the clubhouse following the game, reporters mobbed Spiezio and Glaus. Standing out of the postgame limelight was John Lackey, who had turned 24 just four days prior, on the same day as his first World Series start. Scioscia pulled Lackey aside and gave him a bit of news: He was starting Game 7. Tomorrow.

There appeared to be no tomorrow in the visitors' clubhouse, however, where the setting was grim. Rodriguez sat by his locker, his head in his hands. Nen looked like he had been steamrollered. Ortiz sat in silence, completely dejected. The ball Dusty Baker had given to him in the seventh inning as a memento of his great outing rested in his glove.

That night, after celebrating with his family, Spiezio went back to the team's hotel and read passages from his Bible. Most of the other Angels had restful nights, but not Troy Percival. And it wasn't just excitement about Game 7 that kept him awake.

"I didn't sleep because I had death threats," Percival said later, referring to calls that started after he hit Alfonso Soriano with a pitch and then struck out Derek Jeter to beat the Yankees. "The FBI called and said there was some guy who had flown out and was a real threat. It had them concerned enough to tell me I had to look out. One of my best friends was a police sergeant out in Riverside, and he made sure two units were sitting in front of my house all night."

That wasn't the only precaution Percival took. "I carried a gun with me to the park," he said. "It was not a very comforting time, but I had a job to do."

As the combatants attempted to rest, visiting equipment man Harkins and his four-man crew returned to the stadium's laundry room where they carefully put the Giants' bottles of Mumms back into their cartons. Like the disappearing ice in the horse trough before them, the Giants' best chance of winning seemed to have melted away. Also in the laundry room lay several cartons of Piper Heidsieck, the Angels' champagne of choice. Like looming sentinels, their presence could not be ignored. It was if they were waiting in the wings, anxious for their own turn in an icy trough in the Angels' locker room.

Outside in the stadium parking lot, the flashing halo on the Big A signified victory. On the face of the old scoreboard-turned-marquee—which for so long was the bearer of lousy batting averages and losing scores—flashed words once thought unimaginable:

ANAHEIM ANGELS
2002 AMERICAN LEAGUE CHAMPIONS
TONIGHT: ANGELS VS. GIANTS
WORLD SERIES GAME 7

To many the words were still difficult to fathom, yet there they were in big bright block lettering as tall as Troy Glaus. Inside Edison Field, as workers cleaned the stands to the rhythm of field sprinklers, the cursed phantoms that had ruled the Angels universe for so long seemed to be scampering for cover. Tonight an entire baseball nation had gone to sleep with that same sense of wonderment that was in essence Gene Autry. Tonight they had learned just as he did, that optimism, faith, and perseverance can sometimes produce magic.

Scioscia didn't have any blood-and-guts speech prepared for the game the following day. In fact, the only thing even resembling a team meeting was a chapel service, where the topic, fittingly enough, was the story of David and Goliath. The Angels knew which role they wanted to play. "We were pretty pumped up," recalls shortstop David Eckstein. "We felt we couldn't be beaten."

Anderson, though, was cautious. As long as Bonds was playing, he knew the Angels would have their hands full. "The only thing to our advantage the night before was that we had the last at-bat," he said.

The Giants had reason to be optimistic in their own right: Throwing for them was Livan Hernandez, a veteran of the world-champion Florida Marlins.

"We knew we gave up a big opportunity to win the series in Game 6," said Giants shortstop Rich Aurilia. "Everybody in the clubhouse believed we could still win this thing. We had a guy going for us who had several postseason wins against a rookie who we had hit pretty good earlier in the Series. We felt confident that we could come out and win Game 7."

But John Lackey was no ordinary rookie. The 24-year-old had pitched several crucial games that year, including the wild-card clincher against the Texas Rangers and Game 4 of the A.L. Championship Series against the Twins. Still, it was Lackey's third Series appearance, and Lackey himself wasn't sure how much he had left.

"Stamina-wise, I knew I probably wouldn't be able to go as long as usual," he recalled later. "I was hoping to get five or six innings and hand over to the bullpen and let them run with it. I knew if we could get to those guys with a lead, it was pretty much over."

Like everybody else, Lackey was worried most about Bonds, who'd already hit four homers in the Series. "The strategy going into the game," says Lackey, "was that if there was nobody on base to go at him and try to pitch him down and away, like a typical power lefty. But he was the guy we definitely wouldn't let beat us; if guys were on base, we were gonna be more careful."

If Game 6 was a classic crescendo, its sequel was a slow burn that was actually over before anyone really realized it. The Giants drew first blood in the second inning when Sanders hit a sacrifice fly to drive in Santiago and put San Francisco in front, 1-0. But in the second, the Angels tied the game when Bengie Molina's clutch RBI double drove in Spiezio from first.

Garret Anderson's clutch third-inning double in Game 7 of the 2002 World Series put the Angels ahead for good. Courtesy of the Angels

Then Hernandez opened the third by giving up singles to Eckstein and Erstad. With two on and nobody out, he then drilled Salmon on the hand to load the bases, bringing Anderson to the plate with a chance to blow open the game. This was precisely the sort of situation in which Anderson had thrived all season long. His .317 average with runners in scoring position was second-best on the team that season amongst starters. But so far in the Series he had come up 10 times with runners in scoring position, and had collected just two hits and three RBI.

But as he approached the plate now, there was a sense of inevitability. "[Hernandez] didn't want to walk me because he didn't have anywhere to put me," Anderson recalls. "It was still early in the game, and he needed to throw strikes."

Anderson worked Hernandez to a 1-1 count, and was thinking fastball on the next pitch. Then came an inside heater that Anderson was able to turn on. J.T. Snow at first had no chance as the ball rocketed by him and sped into right field. As Sanders chased it into the corner, a fan reached over the fence and started pounding him on the back with a thunder stick. Seeing this, Aurilia was outraged.

"God, how could that not be an interference call to at least save us a run, or something?" he says. "He was getting the crap beat out of him!"

But no call was made—even though the fan was ejected—and by the time the beleaguered Sanders retrieved the ball, Anderson was on second base and three runs were across the plate.

"Given the time frame of when it occurred in the game, I don't think it had the magnitude it would have had had it happened in the eighth or ninth inning," Anderson recalls. "It would have been a little more dramatic. As it was, they had a lot more outs so you leave that behind and just go on."

Glaus was walked intentionally to continue the inning, and that was all she wrote for Hernandez. Baker brought reliever Chad Zerbe into the game, and combined with a stellar defensive effort, the Giants made it through the rest of the inning unscathed.

The Angels got the outs they needed in the fourth and fifth innings thanks to Lackey pitching the game of his life. In the sixth inning, another rookie pitcher, 30-year-old Brendan Donnelley, relieved him. After two more scoreless innings, Donnelley gave way to yet a third rookie, Francisco Rodriguez. Known as "K-Rod," Rodriguez had pitched brilliantly throughout the Series, and his slider and fastball were on the mark now. In the eighth, the 21-year-old struck out the side, allowing just one baserunner—Bonds—on a walk. His cut fastball was so wicked, with so much movement, that even the catcher Bengie Molina had trouble differentiating his pitches. At one point he was so confused he called time and ran to the mound.

"Are you crossing me?" Molina asked. "Are you throwing a slider when I call fastball?

"No, No! That's my fastball," was the rookie's retort. "Look at the scoreboard—it's 97 miles per hour."

Molina glanced out at the radar gun indicator on the scoreboard. Sure enough, it read 97. The veteran catcher sighed; no one could throw a breaking ball that hard. Shaking his head, Molina returned to the plate thinking, "If I can't pick the ball up, just imagine what the Giant hitters are going through."

In the ninth, with just three outs to get, Scioscia turned to his closer. Percival had taken a two-hour nap in the clubhouse before the game to make up for his sleepless night, but it wasn't tiredness or even the death threats that threw him off when he took the mound. It was horse piss. As the game had wound on, the Anaheim mounted police had taken up positions inside the Angels bullpen.

"The horses had been pissing all over the mounds," recalls Percival, and "the stench was awful. I thought I was going to gag."

Percival gave up a single to Snow to start the inning. Snow was then forced out at second by Tom Goodwin, and Goodwin took second base on defensive indifference. A walk to David Bell brought the tying run to the plate in Tsuyoshi Shinjo, who was pinch-hitting for Pedro Feliz. After two quick strikes, Shinjo hunkered close to the plate, and Percival knew that he was thinking home run. So he wisely kept the next pitch away. "Sure enough, I threw it eight inches off the plate, and he swung through it for strike three," he recalls.

Just one out separated the Angels from their first world championship: the dangerous Kenny Lofton. Percival stepped off the mound and went over in his mind what he needed to do. He knew the left-handed Lofton had limited power, and for him to hit a home run the opposite way he would have to hit it perfectly. With Jeff Kent just two batters away—and Bonds after him—Percival could ill afford to walk anybody. Therefore, he would have to challenge Lofton.

Molina was on the same wavelength and called for the pitch outside. Percy rocked and fired. Lofton swung and hit a fly ball to Erstad in centerfield, and Percival knew by the sound of the bat striking the ball that it was over. He raised his fists in victory as he turned to watch Erstad make the historic game-winning catch.

Percival turned back just in time to see the wide-eyed Molina running full bore at him to start the victory pile-on.

"There's no better feeling in a team sport than piling on in the middle of the field," says Glaus, whose three home runs and eight RBI earned him Series MVP honors. "It's kind of a juvenile act, but it's real, not fake, and that's the greatest part about it."

Before the game had even started, Maddon—completely confident in his team—had placed a hat that had been worn by his late father in the dugout. He wanted to share the win with his old man. Now, as all hell broke loose, Maddon grabbed his father's hat and stuffed it inside his jacket and headed out into the scrum.

"You ask yourself, 'How am I supposed to act? What am I supposed to do?' And then you just say, 'Screw it!' and jump in there," Maddon recalls. "My mind started racing to all the close people who were involved. My dad symbolically being in the middle of the whole thing was a powerful thing for me.

"I know it's just a game, but it's a game on a pretty big stage. You wanted to do it since you were six, and all of a sudden you do it. It was pretty amazing, almost spiritual. … Hugging Bengie Molina, seeing my granddaughter, looking up and seeing all the people, the confetti—all this stuff is happening simultaneously, and it's indescribable."

Scott Spiezio was thinking about his own dad. Ed Spiezio had won two World Series with the Cardinals in the Sixties and had warned his son about fans running on the field and stealing hats right off players' heads during the celebration. With this in mind, Scott removed his lid before charging into the pile. A picture on the front page of the *L.A. Times* sports section the next day showed a grinning Spiezio clutching his precious hat in his hands. The photographer would've gotten a better picture a moment later, when Spiezio told himself, "To hell with it!" and tossed the cap into the stands.

Right before Erstad hauled in the final out, equipment man Kenny Higdon and an assistant stood in the laundry room next to a gigantic horse trough filled with ice, champagne, and beer. "The trough was as big as a couch, and the son of a bitch weighed more then I could handle," Higdon recalls. "I said to my friend, 'We've got to get this thing in the clubhouse by the next out, or this is gonna be embarrassing as hell.'"

They muscled the monster trough in just in time, and as the Angels celebrated in the clubhouse more than a few players ended up getting dumped into the trough—without complaint. In the Giants clubhouse it was shoes that got dumped, as several players tossed their footwear into trash bins to underscore their disgust at blowing the Series that could've been theirs. Outside, nobody wanted to leave the stadium.

"What stands out more than anything about the whole playoffs and World Series was that I saw the fans and the game from a whole different perspective than I'd ever seen in Anaheim before," recalls Salmon. "The fans were electric, the color, the excitement, the true sense of home-field advantage in every sense was evident. You'd feel it at times in Anaheim before, but there was never a time like during the postseason when you had a sense that you had a true home-field advantage."

Salmon took the championship trophy around the field for a victory lap to share his joy with the fans. Then, at a podium set up in the middle of the field, Jackie Autry brought her husband back for a last, joyful ride into the sunset. "Gene is with us tonight," she told the crowd. "He just had a better seat." In her hand was one of Gene's prized Stetsons, which she eventually placed atop Salmon's and Eckstein's heads.

As the wild celebration spilled out into the parking lot and throughout the neighborhood and city, Angels radio announcer Rory Markus also invoked the name and spirit of the late owner whose dream had finally come true.

"Gene Autry, I know you're up there, and I know Jimmie Reese is there with you!" he said over the airwaves. "Your beloved Angels have done it! Your Angels are the champions of all of baseball! They defeat the San Francisco Giants 4-1 in Game 7 of the World Series at Edison Field! There are streamers coming down from the sky, fireworks going off in centerfield, a mob of media surrounding the Angels on the field! Yes, the Angels, the 'Yes We Can' Angels, the heartbreak Angels, the team that could never quite get there—they made it!"

At Forest Lawn Cemetery in the Hollywood Hills, it was quiet as always. The marble stone on Gene Autry's grave was undisturbed, but what was going on six feet underneath might have been another story. "In the movies, I never lost a fight," Autry had once said. "In baseball, I hardly ever won one." But anyone seeking to commune with his spirit would probably have had more luck going 40 miles south to Edison Field. In Autry's time it had been known simply as the "Big A," and there his resilient spirit had been tested over and over. Always, Autry responded to the heartbreak with a winner's attitude: "We'll get 'em next year."

Finally, it was "next year."

17

VISIONS OF
MORENO

*D*isney had no more success turning a profit with a baseball franchise than the Autrys had achieved over parts of four decades. But thanks to the Angels' World Series championship, a long line of suitors formed when news got out that the team was up for sale. Fastest out of the gate was Arizona billboard magnate Arte Moreno. A self-made billionaire, Moreno had been a minority shareholder with the Arizona Diamondbacks when they won the World Series in 2001. When his attempt to buy the D-backs outright failed, he set his sights on the Angels.

In May 2003, the former Vietnam vet and father of three purchased the team for $184 million. His first action as team owner was launching a major marketing blitz throughout Southern California, blanketing buses and billboards with the red Angels logo—even in areas of Los Angeles that were considered Dodgers' turf. Moreno's boldness, enthusiasm, and commitment endeared him to the community—especially when he slashed ticket and concession prices and rechristened Edison Field "Angel Stadium."

"Moreno's vision of the club is what most baseball officials always thought it should be—a major market team in a major market," says Bill Shaikin of the *Los Angeles Times*. "Both the Autrys and Disney seemed to think of the Angels as an Orange County team first, and to that Arte's saying, 'No, we're part of the L.A. market and we're going to try and increase our payroll and revenues accordingly. We're going to try and win every year and not luck into it if we have a window every two or three years, which is what happened before.' Jackie Autry's point always was that since the major television stations and the *L.A. Times* are all based in Los Angeles, an Orange County team would never be able to tap into the media revenues that the Dodgers did. The difference between her and Arte is that he is betting he can get the media interest, attendance, and revenue up to a level where he can be a Los Angeles market team with a Los Angeles market payroll year in and year out. So far, he's been right."

Under Moreno's reign the Angels had come full circle. After years of a cold corporate relationship with Disney, Moreno's attitude was refreshing. His accessibility was a welcome revelation to both players and coaches.

"Mr. Moreno comes down before batting practice, shakes our hands, and asks us how we're doing," says former coach Joe Maddon. "That leaves us really believing he cares. Whereas [Disney], you'd never see them unless something good was happening or maybe something really bad was happening. From an employee perspective, you'd much rather see the family touch as opposed to the corporate touch."

Shaikin agrees: "Disney was content to have their people running the team and really didn't bother with the club until something major happened. Otherwise there was a hands-off attitude that said, 'We're in Burbank, you're in Anaheim, go have fun.'"

With the pennant drive in October 2002, all that changed. Until then, sightings of Disney CEO Michael Eisner at the ballpark were practically nil. But with the Angels victory over the Yankees in the American League Divisional Series, he was suddenly as omnipresent as a peanut vendor. Shaikin recalls Eisner's appearance in the clubhouse during the pennant celebration against the Twins:

"Players were going nuts, but none of them appeared to know who [Eisner] was. Now, here's one of the most powerful men on earth, ostensibly—certainly one of the most powerful men in the entertainment industry—but no one went up to him and talked to him. Some of the media did, but it wasn't as if the players were embracing this guy, saying, 'Hey boss, way to go!' I didn't see anybody who seemed to recognize who he was. With Gene that never happened, because he was always around. Arte isn't there at all the games because he still lives in Phoenix. But he certainly comes to a lot of them and is available on the field and in the clubhouse for anybody who wants to talk to him."

Moreno is baseball's first Hispanic owner, which certainly doesn't hurt when it comes to recruiting Latino players, who now make up 44 percent of all players in the majors. His presence certainly helped to bring Vladimir Guerrero, Orlando Cabrera, and 2005 Cy Young winner Bartolo Colon to Anaheim. Moreno has wisely tapped into the huge Hispanic market in the Southland, and has his eye on eventually having a Spanish-language TV station broadcast Angels games.

A few of Moreno's ideas, however, have raised some eyebrows and caused resentment. In 2005, much to the chagrin of the Anaheim City Council and thousands of Orange County fans, Moreno changed the name of the club from Anaheim Angels to the rather cumbersome "Los Angeles Angels of Anaheim."

In 1996, the city fathers agreed to contribute $20 million to Disney for stadium renovations, in return for having the California Angels renamed the Anaheim Angels. When Moreno went with "Los Angeles Angels of Anaheim," the City Council said it was a violation of the spirit of the lease, and could cost the City of Anaheim prominent media exposure and millions of dollars. Now the lawmakers are suing for $100 million. Moreno says that as long as Anaheim is contained in the formal name of the team, he has kept his part of the bargain. The case is currently in litigation.

Arte Moreno is the first owner to view the Angels for what they actually are: a demographically diverse gold mine waiting to be tapped. Courtesy of the Angels

Critics quick to jump on the anti-name change bandwagon are overlooking that Moreno and the Angels have already done wonders for the financial viability of the area. The team is required to pay the city two dollars for every ticket sold during the season over 2.6 million threshold. Since 2003, the Angels have sold over three million tickets every year, putting an extra $5 million in the city coffers. And, since Moreno took over the team in 2003, he has put $34 million of his own money into repairs and maintenance for the city-owned Angel Stadium, plus $2 million to upgrade the team's spring training site. Annual revenue is on a steep increase over the past three seasons, corresponding directly with an increase in season ticket sales and now, a long-coveted agreement with the Fox Sports Network that puts them on a par with the Dodgers.

Although much has been made of the name change, the modern economics of baseball indicate it could benefit the club in the long run. Today, network and cable TV contracts play a huge factor in clubs' profitability. For maximum media exposure and bigger cable contracts, a Los Angeles Angels brand is a much more effective marketing tool than Anaheim Angels.

In a 2005 interview with MLB.com, Moreno told reporter Doug Miller that for a team to be competitive long term, it has to be able to earn the dollars. "For us, all of our media comes from the L.A. metro area—all the papers, all the TV, all the radio. ... In the total market, from the media perspective, and to represent the whole metro area, it will give us a good, solid economic balance. Anaheim is 300,000-plus people, Orange County is three million, and the metro area is 16.5 million people. For us to get an opportunity to market the entire metro area, long term, you have to do the right things. [The name change] will give us more viability in the long run."

How would Gene Autry have felt about the name change? Given the Cowboy's respect for the power of the marquee, he might well have gone along. Gene nixed an offer to move the team to Long Beach in 1964 when city officials there wanted it to be called the Long Beach Angels. Autry knew that name would be a public relations disaster, and quickly set his sights on Anaheim because city officials there had no problem with California Angels as the team name.

On the other hand, Autry was a gentleman and always did his best not to offend. It was not his style to make waves, nor to incur the legal costs that a name change would entail. But it's important to remember, too, that Autry never had to deal with the modern mechanisms of today's game that make cable TV revenue and national branding so important to a franchise's viability.

Unless a court decides otherwise, the team will be officially known as the Los Angeles Angels of Anaheim, and as of today they are firing on all cylinders. Although they finished a disappointing third in 2003, the team rebounded strongly in 2004, winning their fourth divisional title by a mere game over the Oakland A's. The season ended promptly, however, when they were overpowered by the Boston Red Sox in the first round of the divisional playoffs. However, the foundation was laid in 2004 for another run in 2005 with the signings of free agents Bartolo Colon and Vladimir Guerrero. Colon won 18 games in 2004, and Guerrero was awarded the MVP trophy after hitting .337 with 39 homers, 126 RBI, 124 runs scored, and 206 hits—quite possibly the best offensive season in franchise history.

In 2005, the Halos maintained course and won the division again, marking the first time in franchise history the team had won back-to-back titles. The team was led in part by exceptional utility player Chone Figgins—who scored 113 runs and swiped 62 bases—and the outstanding starting pitching of 21-game winner Colon, John Lackey, Paul Byrd, Jarrod Washburn, and rookie Ervin Santana.

After beating the Yankees three games to two in a hard-fought American League Divisional Series, the Angels faced the Chicago White Sox for the pennant. The Angels won Game 1 at Comiskey Park, 3-2, on the strength of Byrd and the bullpen. But the White Sox rebounded to win a nail-biter in Game 2. With the score tied 1-1 heading into the bottom of the ninth, it appeared as if the game was destined for extra innings. But then a bizarre play drastically altered the outcome—not only of that game but the entire series itself.

With two outs and nobody on, Angels reliever Kelvim Escobar was savvy enough not to challenge White Sox catcher A.J. Pierzynski with a fastball. With the game tied, Escobar knew the gritty veteran, who had already collected three homers in the postseason, could easily end it with just one swing. So he wasn't about to throw anything near the plate.

When catcher Josh Paul signaled for a change-up, Escobar rocked and fired. By the time the ball reached the plate, Pierzynski was so flummoxed—he'd been thinking fastball—that he swung and missed by half a foot. As Paul plucked the ball a couple inches from the dirt, umpire Doug Eddings raised his arm to signify the third strike.

In the dugout, coach Joe Maddon watched Paul roll the ball toward the mound and head for the dugout stairs to congratulate Escobar on a job well done. He was about midway there when, out of the corner of his eye, Maddon saw Pierzynski charging for first base.

"I didn't think anything of it, because I knew [Paul] had caught the ball and didn't see any reaction from the umpires that indicated differently," Maddon said later. "So when Pierzynski started running, I immediately looked for the umpires, and when I saw no kind of demonstrative call I said to myself, 'Uh-oh, they're not sure.' And I'm thinking, 'My God! They're not getting this right!'"

As Mike Scioscia headed out to argue the call, several Angels players ran upstairs to the clubhouse to check the replay monitors. But not Maddon.

"I didn't have to see the video, because two things happened," he said. "Number one: If [the ball] had bounced, Paul would have tagged him. Number two: If it had bounced, the home plate umpire normally says something in the catcher's ear to alert him to the fact that it is not strike three and the guy's not out yet. He would yell something like, 'You've got to tag him! Ball's in the dirt!' There's gonna be some kind of indicator from the umpire that the out hadn't been made, and that didn't happen."

Scioscia's lengthy argument with the umpires went nowhere. Pierzynski was awarded first base—which he reached without a throw from the Angels—and suddenly the Sox had the winning run on and hot-hitting Joe Crede at the plate. Pablo Ozuna was sent in to pinch-run for Pierzynski, and he promptly stole second base.

Meanwhile, Escobar worked the count to 0-2 against Crede. Despite the misfortune, the Angels were one strike from getting out of the jam. But Escobar's next pitch was a split-fingered fastball that hung up too long. Crede lined it into deep left field for a double, driving in Ozuna for the winning run.

After the game, Eddings defended his decision to allow Pierzysnki to reach first. Paul maintained that he clearly caught the ball, and Pierzynski said that in the absence of a definitive out call from Eddings it would've been foolish for him not to head for first.

Maddon agrees: "The bottom line is Pierzynski is one of those kind of guys who would attempt to do something like that, and I cannot denigrate him for doing something good for his team. If one of our guys did that and it had worked, he would have been our hero."

Time will tell, but Vladimir Guerrero could be the greatest Angel of them all. Courtesy of the Angels

The Sox may have swung the momentum in their favor, but the Angels were heading home and had a fresh opportunity to regroup. But in Game 3, Lackey was roughed up for five runs early in the game, and Sox hurler Jon Garland cruised to a four-hit, complete game win. Behind two games to one, the uphill battled ensued for the Angels. The Sox starters were pitching brilliantly, however, and the Angels would collect just 11 hits and five runs over the final two games of the Series. In just five games, the White Sox had captured the pennant to advance to their first World Series since 1959. There they would sweep the Houston Astros to earn their first championship in 88 years.

Angels fans were upset and disgusted by both the controversial call and their team's poor play over the remainder of the series. But the real wonder isn't how did this team fail—it's how did this offensively inconsistent team get as far as it did in 2005.

"Pitching, defense and an overwhelming desire to win is what carried us as far as we got," says Maddon. "This team didn't have the same kind of flow offensively that it had during their championship year, and that speaks to the character of the players. Even when we were outmanned, they felt they could beat the better teams, and that's why we got as deep into the season as we did."

Thirty years in pro baseball have given Maddon a unique perspective into the kind of players a team needs to win. According to Maddon, today's players fall into one of five categories:

Category 1: "I'm happy to be here."

Category 2: "This is really cool. I want to stay here."

Category 3: "I belong here. I can do this."

Category 4: "I want to make as much money as I can."

Category 5: "I really want to win."

Maddon says the Angels today are full of Category 5 players, and that nobody typifies that type of player more than Darin Erstad.

"Ersty's actions speak so loudly," Maddon says. "If he's upset enough or thinks you're not working enough, he'll just look at you and, it's almost the equivalent of somebody putting their hand around your neck and throwing you against the wall. He leads by example, and that, to me, is the best kind of leader."

The team rock, Maddon says, is Garret Anderson.

"[Anderson] is very bright and a great teammate, but the public doesn't see that," says Maddon. "Unfortunately, some in the press choose to react to Garret based on whether he's doing really well or very poorly. If he's hitting .275 with seven home runs, then all of a sudden he's perceived as not so good. But when he's hitting .325 with 30 homers, then he's okay.

"I've talked to him about this concept for the last 10 years, and he's accepted it. But when he ends up with 3,000 hits and a ticket to the Hall of Fame, then I want to hear what his critics have to say."

Shaikin gives the nod to Tim Salmon as the Angels' heart and soul.

"Here's someone in his prime who could be counted on for 25 to 30 home runs and 100 RBI regularly, and chose to stay with the Angels through some very dark times," says Shaikin. "He had two chances to become a free agent but said no. His loyalty paid off when they won the World Series in 2002, and I'm thrilled because this is someone who in his prime should have been in the All-Star game arguably every year and has never made it. Obviously it's never going to happen now, but Salmon was very honest about saying, 'I don't care about being an All-Star. If we get to the World Series it will more than make up for it.' Happily, they got there."

The team catalyst would be Guerrero. After his phenomenal MVP season in 2004, Guerrero hit .317, with 32 homers and 108 RBI in 2005 despite playing with a shoulder injury for much of the season. He is arguably the greatest all-around player on the team, and the first bona fide superstar to play in his prime with the Angels since Nolan Ryan. He is also the envy of any organization, and at his present rate of development is sure to someday join Anderson as the first to wear Angels jerseys on their Hall of Fame plaques.

The acquisition of Guerrero in '03 is a perfect example of Moreno's commitment to bringing a winner to Anaheim.

"What people saw with Guerrero," says Shaikin, "is that the Angels era of limiting their expectations and not signing top-tier free agents was over. When Stoneman first got here, they needed a couple arms to fill out the rotation, so they signed Pat Rapp and Ismael Valdez. That's not a knock on Stoneman, but rather on the resources he had to work with. When Guerrero, Escobar, and Jose Guillen became available in 2003, Arte didn't blink—he [signed them]."

With Guerrero at their center, the Angels have put together a championship-caliber club, and their farm system is churning out some of the best young prospects in baseball. The familiar core that took the Angels to their first championship in 2002 has, for the most part, disappeared. But in its place is a new nucleus made up of an explosive group of veterans and youngsters. Today's Angels may not be your father's Angels. But they are closer than ever to the dream of team founders Gene Autry, Fred Haney, and Bob Reynolds of a championship-caliber club with legs. It's Moreno's goal to keep it that way.

From their rambunctious beginnings in the early Sixties, through the mediocrity of the Seventies, the superstar free agents and near misses of the Eighties, the corporate Nineties, to the spectacular 2002 championship campaign, the Angels have taken fans on a fascinating ride. Today, with a winning philosophy firmly ingrained, the Angels have become a staple of excellence in Southern California and beyond—proving themselves as a club that can go deep into the postseason year after year.

Thanks to the Angels, Southern California baseball fans have achieved their Cloud Nine, and will hopefully be floating there—right alongside Mr. Autry—for a long, long time.

ACKNOWLEDGMENTS

*T*hanks to Albie Pearson, Dean Chance, Jim Fregosi, Alex Johnson, Nolan Ryan, Don Baylor, Rod Carew, Reggie Jackson, and Jim Abbott for entrusting me with telling their stories. Special thanks need to be extended to my editor, Doug Hoepker at Sports Publishing, for tackling the project with a passion, providing excellent guidance and a keen eye throughout the editing process, and for keeping the facts straight. Special thanks also to Mike Pearson at Sports Publishing for taking on the project. Marshall Terrill's skills as a writer-editor were also instrumental in seeing the book through. From inception his perseverance proved invaluable. I am forever grateful for the generous contribution of his time and talents. More thanks to Jon Madian, for going all nine innings. His help with storytelling, editing, moral support, patience, and friendship is greatly appreciated. In addition, Pete Ehrmann's assistance in the writing and editing process was also a Godsend.

Angels vice president of communications, Tim Mead, provided an abundance of support and enthusiasm from start to finish. Special thanks also goes to Eric Kay, Angels communications manager, for the photos and advice. The support and friendship of Brian "Bubba" Harkins, the Angels visiting clubhouse manager, is of special merit, too. Thanks for making me part of your team. Others who are of special note for their assistance and/or willingness to be interviewed include Joe Maddon, Rex Hudler, Eli Grba, Ross Newhan, Marvin Miller, Mamie Van Doren, Elrod Hendricks, Tommie Ferguson, Stanley Spero, Rory Markas, Bill and Buzzie Bavasi, Bill Shaikin, Jose Mota, Darren Chan, Larry Babcock, Reuben Montano, and Becky Baylor.

To Scott Spiezio and the spirited Reggie Sanders, I thank you for your dramatic interpretations of Game 6 of the 2002 World Series. Thanks to others who shared their thoughts: Troy Percival, Troy Glaus, Tim Salmon, Chone Figgins, Garret Anderson, Buddy Black, Adam Kennedy, Bengie Molina, John Lackey, Mike Scioscia, David Eckstein, Darin Erstad, and Francisco Rodriguez, as well as Rich Aurilia, Robb Nen, Felix Rodriguez, Kenny Lofton, J.T. Snow, and Jason Schmidt.

I am in debt to The Ryans—Nolan, Ruth, Reid, Reese—and Sherry Clawson, for their hospitality at Round Rock. Further accolades need to go to the Yankees' Rick Cerone for getting Reggie Jackson's ear; Scotty Keene for his support and

Albie Pearson, left, and clubhouse assistant Bob Case during spring training in 1963. Courtesy of Bob Case

phone numbers; and Kenny Higdon, Zack Minasian, Steve Vucinich, Rick Smith, and Bill Ziegler for their unique take on things from the inside.

More thanks are in order for Bob Case, who shared countless stories, photos, and meals; and Alana Case, whose fabulous Bo Belinsky interview helped bring Bo back to life again.

Thanks to Bruce Bochte, Jerry Remy, Mickey Rivers, Lee Stanton, Tom Satriano, Jim Palmer, Orel Hershiser, Clyde Wright, Buck Rodgers, Doug DeCinces, Brian Downing, Bobby Grich, Bobby Knoop, Lee Thomas, Art Kusnyer, Norm Sherry, Jim Palmer, and Ed Farmer for all their contributions.

For their help acquiring photos, I thank Lou Sauritch, John Cordes, and Mel Bailey. A tip of the cap to Charlie Baker and Tom Duino for their support and critical eye, the Kendalls (Sally, Mike, Kevin, Amy, Greg and Shelly), Rick Clemens, Scott Musgrave, Dick Beverage, Dave Howells, Jesse Hoffs, Pat Kennedy, Nate Eisenman, Dan Drew, Randy Pennington, Norman Amster at All-Star Adventures, the Wallens (Bob, Betty, Bill, and Cassy), Brian Corralejo, and the Conejo Angels. To the "Clubbies"—Scott Smith, Hector Vasquez, Geoff Bennett, Aaron Castaneda, Mike Martinez, Corey Morbeck, Keith Tarter, Shane Demmitt, Dennis Franco, Dave, and Doc—I say thanks!

And finally, a big thank you to Fred Haney and Bobby Winkles, for opening the door to the Angels.

INDEX